HISTORIES OF SOCIAL STUDIES AND RACE: 1865–2000

Also by Christine Woyshner

The National PTA, Race, and Civic Engagement, 1897–1970
The Educational Work of Women's Organizations, 1890–1960. Edited with Anne Meis Knupfer
Social Education in the Twentieth Century: Curriculum and Context for Citizenship. Edited with Joseph Watras and Margaret Smith Crocco
Minding Women: Reshaping the Educational Realm. Edited with Holly Gelfond

Also by Chara Haeussler Bohan

Clinical Teacher Education: Reflections from an Urban Professional Development Network. Edited with Joyce Many
American Educational Thought: Essays from 1640–1940. Edited with A. Milson, P. Glanzer, and J. W. Null
Go to the Sources: Lucy Maynard Salmon and the Teaching of History.
Readings in American Education Thought: From Puritanism to Progressivism. Edited with A. Milson, P. Glanzer, and J. W. Null

Histories of Social Studies and Race: 1865–2000

Edited By
Christine Woyshner and
Chara Haeussler Bohan

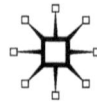

HISTORIES OF SOCIAL STUDIES AND RACE: 1865–2000
Copyright © Christine Woyshner and Chara Haeussler Bohan, 2012.

All rights reserved.

First published in 2012 by
PALGRAVE MACMILLAN®
in the United States—a division of St. Martin's Press LLC,
175 Fifth Avenue, New York, NY 10010.

Where this book is distributed in the UK, Europe and the rest of the world, this is by Palgrave Macmillan, a division of Macmillan Publishers Limited, registered in England, company number 785998, of Houndmills, Basingstoke, Hampshire RG21 6XS.

Palgrave Macmillan is the global academic imprint of the above companies and has companies and representatives throughout the world.

Palgrave® and Macmillan® are registered trademarks in the United States, the United Kingdom, Europe and other countries.

ISBN: 978–1–137–00754–4

Library of Congress Cataloging-in-Publication Data

    Histories of social studies and race : 1865–2000 /
edited by Christine Woyshner and CharaHaeusslerBohan.
      p. cm.
      ISBN 978–1–137–00754–4
      1. Social sciences—Study and teaching—United States—History.
  2. Racism—Study and teaching—United States—History.
  3. Discrimination in education—United States—History.
  4. Educational sociology—United States—History. I. Woyshner, Christine
A. II. Bohan, CharaHaeussler, 1966–

H62.5.U5H57 2012
305.896′0730071—dc23   2012010459

A catalogue record of the book is available from the British Library.

Design by Newgen Imaging Systems (P) Ltd., Chennai, India.

First edition: September 2012

10 9 8 7 6 5 4 3 2 1

Printed in the United States of America.

To my sons, Jason and Joseph
　　　　　　　　—Christine Woyshner
To Tom, Caleb, and Chloë
　　　　　　　　—Chara Haeussler Bohan

Contents

List of figures   ix

Acknowledgments   xi

Introduction
Christine Woyshner and Chara Haeussler Bohan   1

One   Race, Social Studies, and Culturally Relevant Curriculum in Social Studies' Prehistory: A Cautionary Meditation   19
Ronald E. Butchart

Two   The Racial and Cultural Assumptions of the Early Social Studies Educators, 1901–1922   37
Thomas D. Fallace

Three   The Early Years of Negro History Week, 1926–1950   57
Sarah Bair

Four   Notions of Citizenship: Discussing Race in the Shortridge High School Senate, 1900–1928   79
J. Spencer Clark

Five   Countering the Master Narrative in US Social Studies: Nannie Helen Burroughs and New Narratives in History Education   99
Alana D. Murray

Six   Race in Elementary Geography Textbooks: Examples from South Carolina, 1890–1927   115
Mindy Spearman

Seven   Atlanta's Desegregation-Era Social Studies Curriculum: An Examination of Georgia History Textbooks   135
Chara Haeussler Bohan and Patricia Randolph

Eight	Placing Social Justice at the Center of Standards-Based Reform: Race and Social Studies at McDonogh #35 Senior High, New Orleans, 1980–2000 *Erica DeCuir*	159
Nine	Black History, Multicultural Education, and Racial Desegregation in Dayton, Ohio *Joseph Watras*	179
Ten	African-Centered Education in the Detroit Public Schools, 1968–2000 *Anne-Lise Halvorsen*	195

Epilogue 213
Margaret Smith Crocco

Contributors 219

Index 223

Figures

6.1 "Your Conditions of Society." Illustration from Daniel Appleton, *Elementary Geography* (New York: D. Appleton and Company, 1880), p. 16 — 119

6.2 "Homes of the Races." Illustration from Alexis Everett Frye, *Primary Geography* (Boston: Ginn & Company, 1894), p. 73, showing the five racial groups — 120

6.3 African mother and child and Negro couple in the United States. From Jacques Wardlaw Redway and Russell Hinman, *Natural Elementary Geography* (New York: American Book Company, 1897), p. 13 — 122

6.4 a. "Among enlightened people." b. "Civilized life. A Chinese city." c. "Barbarous life. Arabs eating dinner before the tent which is their only home." d. "Savage life. Photograph by Dr. Cook in South America." From Maury, *New Elements of Geography* (New York: American Book Company, 1907), p. 22 — 124

6.5 a. "Indian, or red man." b. "White man." c. "Black man." d. "Yellow man." From Brigham and McFarlane, *Essentials of Geography* (New York: American Book Company, 1920), pp. 88–89 — 127

6.6 "Native with boomerang." Illustration from Brigham and McFarlane, *Essentials of Geography* (New York: American Book Company, 1920), p. 249 — 128

Acknowledgments

We would like to thank several people who made contributions to this edited book. First, Jennifer Ulbrich, a doctoral student and graduate research assistant at Georgia State University, helped immensely with organization, structure, and formatting. She is intelligent and thoughtful, and without her the manuscript would not have been as "clean," especially with respect to adherence to *The Chicago Manual of Style*.

We would also like to thank the many contributors who volunteered to research, write, and revise manuscripts around the concepts of social studies and race. This earnest community of historians and social studies education researchers work tireless hours in the face of ever-shrinking budgets in both higher education and K-12 schools. The current era of high-stakes standardized testing has relegated social studies teaching and learning to low status in curriculum hierarchies, but these thoughtful individuals believe in demonstrating how the field has contributed to the historical narrative of American education.

We would also like to express our gratitude to our respective institutions, Georgia State University and Temple University, for the support that enabled us to pursue our research interests at a national level.

Of course, we also must acknowledge the support of family and friends. As editors, we both have families that reflect the diversity of the human race and also inspire our interest in the intersection of race and social studies education. Our families enhance our intellectual understanding by providing emotional connections, too.

We appreciate the anonymous reviewer(s) of the manuscript who offered careful and detailed feedback for us as well as the chapter authors. Finally, we would like to thank the editor at Palgrave, Burke Gerstenschlager, and Kaylan Connally, assistant editor, for the opportunity to publish this collective volume on the intersection of race and social studies education. We hope that these contributions will advance a better understanding of the influence of racial matters on social studies education.

Chara Haeussler Bohan
Atlanta, Georgia

Christine Woyshner
Philadelphia, Pennsylvania

Introduction

Christine Woyshner and Chara Haeussler Bohan

Social studies as a field has been slow to address race and diversity. Furthermore, in the subfield of the history of social studies, race has been eclipsed by other issues, such as methods (for example, inquiry, historical thinking, controversial issues); other topics (for example, the Constitution, citizenship education); and influential leaders in the field (for example, James Harvey Robinson, Thomas Jesse Jones, Harold Rugg, Donald Oliver). One study in the 1970s declared that the field of social studies had taken a "kid-gloves approach" to race and difference and was not on the vanguard of significant change.[1] Indeed, social studies has not been known for pursuing innovative directions in research, curriculum, and teaching. Additionally, the historiography of social studies education has not employed race in its predominant lines of inquiry. To date, the social studies historiography has overwhelmingly focused on examining committee reports and the contributions its leaders, most of whom were White and male.[2]

That social studies has not highlighted race to a significant degree—in practice, in research in general, and in the historiography—is ironic, given that much of the field's origins can be traced to a course of study designed for African Americans and American Indians at the Hampton Institute in Virginia in the late nineteenth century. Although the teaching of history in schools predated educator Thomas Jesse Jones's curriculum at Hampton, the growth and development of social studies was directly affected by Jones's authorship of the 1916 Report on Social Studies.[3] Further elaborating on the genesis of social studies, Margaret Smith Crocco asserts that in the early-twentieth century "social studies...was designed to remediate cultural deficiency and create better citizens out of those some intellectuals feared were not suitable raw material for democracy."[4] Arguably, awareness of issues regarding race and diversity has always been present in the field, although these matters have not always been attended to explicitly. In this volume, we seek to investigate the interplay of the emerging social studies field, from the time of the Emancipation of enslaved peoples in the second half of the nineteenth century to multicultural and Afrocentric education initiatives of the late twentieth century. Likewise, we seek to incorporate viewpoints from various regions and local communities. With the exception of Thomas Fallace's chapter on founding social studies leaders and race, each of the authors examines how local teachers, students, and community members interpreted and implemented the teaching and learning of social studies and history, while considering racial difference and the struggle for equality.

Contributors were asked to consider the intersection of race and social studies in any time period or region of their choosing. Therefore, it is important to note that the scholars do not focus on national social studies organizations or other formal organizations, nor do most focus on national social studies leaders. This book builds instead on an emerging body of literature that examines the implementation of social studies initiatives in segregated and desegregated schools by African American and European American teachers.[5] In addition, several authors examine race and social studies in a cross-section of regions across the United States. Dayton, Ohio; Atlanta, Georgia; Detroit, Michigan; and New Orleans, Louisiana; as well as the state of South Carolina, are a few of the places represented in this collection. The authors explore a variety of education initiatives and writings, such as textbooks, curriculum plans, student government organizations, cultural celebrations, and standards-based reform efforts to situate their studies in the interstices of race and social studies education.

For the purposes of this book, we did not define social studies for the authors. The result is an expansive and flexible definition that suits each particular case history. In some chapters social studies is defined comprehensively, as contributors draw on a broad definition of social education, or what Margaret Smith Crocco defines as "teaching and learning about how individuals construct and live out their understandings of social, political, and economic relations...and the implications of these understandings for how citizens are educated in a democracy."[6] Other contributors define it as the teaching and learning of particular subject areas, such as history or civics. Finally, some chapters address the new content area developed in the 1910s called "social studies," which referred to an integration of the social sciences—civics, history, sociology, and economics—in the effort to prepare citizens for a democracy.

Likewise, we gave authors considerable leeway when it came to addressing, defining, and applying race in their contributions. Race has occupied a central role in American society since the beginning of European colonization, when enslaved people from Africa were brought to the North American continent. In this book, the authors explore the role of race in

American society with a focus on the implications for social studies education. However, we did not provide an anthropological, sociological, legal, or scientific definition of race, because of the imprecision associated with such definitions and because of the changing nature of the definition of race over the time span covered by this volume.[7] Although we did not define race for the contributors, most gravitated towards an emphasis on the dichotomy between Whites and Blacks in social studies education. As scholar Herbert W. Harris notes, "The definitions and meanings of race and ethnicity are, to a surprising degree, determined by the historical forces that shape society."[8] As Thomas Fallace posits, conceptions of race, even for prominent thinkers such as John Dewey, are context-bound and can change over time.[9] Although Dewey refused the idea of the biological inferiority of any racial group, as was believed by the nineteenth-century school of thought known as neo-Lemarckianism, he did use the terms *barbarian, savage,* and *primitive* to describe certain groups of people such as Africans, Australian aborigines, and American Indians prior to 1916.[10] Fallace argues that Dewey's employment of these words—common among linear historicists in the late nineteenth and early twentieth centuries—reveals not only Dewey's underlying assumptions about Whites and non-White groups, but demonstrates popular thought about White superiority in the time period. Rudyard Kipling's "White Man's Burden," published in 1899, is emblematic of the age of imperialism in which European racial superiority generally was accepted thinking.[11] Contemporary considerations of race reveal sharp contrasts with understandings of the late 1800s, as present-day scholars believe that race is a social construct, which nonetheless can impact human lives considerably.

Although race is socially constructed and the majority of modern researchers believe it does not exist scientifically, genetically, or biologically as originally intended, race has been and remains a powerful force in American society. Authorities such as Naomi Zack, Sonia El Janis Carlyle, and Maria P. P. Root recently have questioned the traditional categories that define race and the limitations of only considering the Black and White side of the dialogue.[12] Like Ralph Ellison's main character in *Invisible Man*, Carlyle wondered where those of mixed ancestry fit into the American story, and she pointed out that words used to define "racially impure people" such as Afroasian, mestizo, mullato, and octoroon are often negative in connotation.[13] Yet the emphasis on Black-White duality is poignant and in many ways has been shaped by the country's history.

The concept of race in American culture primarily relies on a rigid, asymmetrical kinship schema. Race was included in American legal statutes as far back as 1622, when Virginia existed as a colony.[14] Cornel West states that the "category of 'race'"—denoting primarily skin color—was first employed as a means of classifying human bodies by François Bernier, a French physician, in 1684."[15] By the mid-1800s, southern Whites developed more stringent definitions of race, such as the "one drop rule."[16] This definition of race, which identified as "Negro" a person with any African heritage, was instrumental in establishing segregationist policies.[17] American policies with regard to race contrast with definitions and more fluid understandings of race in other countries.[18] Scholars theorize that America's rigid "one drop rule" developed because of the significant interracial tension that had characterized much of America's history. This rigid understanding of race was and continues to be communicated, taught, and learned in American social studies classrooms.

A substantial Black-White tension in American society is evident, not only in history courses, but also in many other disciplines or areas, such as psychology, sociology, literature, media, and popular culture. W. E. B. Du Bois, in his classic work, *The Souls of Black Folk,* was one of the first African Americans to call attention to Black identity. He described the Black gift of "second-sight in this American world.... this double-consciousness, this sense of looking at one's self through the eyes of others, of measuring one's soul by the tape of a world that looks on in amused contempt and pity."[19] In later decades, Kenneth and Mamie Clark's psychological studies of Black children in the 1930s and 1940s influenced the Supreme Court in the *Brown v. Board of Education* decision. Yet, subsequent social science investigations questioned the validity of the Clarks' findings.[20] An irony exists with this Black-White focus, as American Indians were the first so-called racial group to reside in the Americas. In this volume, we found that overall attention to Native Americans in social studies education was minimal. One chapter on Georgia history textbooks considered American Indians and social studies education, and a few other chapters mention the indigenous peoples. Of course, the state of Georgia is notorious for its enforcement of the Indian Removal Act, so the claimed elimination of the natives occupied much of the Georgia textbook narrative. Yet, in the majority of chapters, the authors consider race through a dualist Black-White lens. Although we did not provide a specific definition of race to the chapter authors, most authors focused on issues pertaining to Black and White concerns or to the dichotomy between White and non-White peoples in their investigations of the interplay of race and social studies education.

Historiographies of Race and Social Studies[21]

The history of social studies is a recently developed branch of the broader history of education scholarship; it began sometime around the early

1970s. The turning point, from a few scattered studies over the course of the twentieth century to the idea of a more cohesive line of inquiry, is marked by Hazel Hertzberg's 1971 observation that social studies had been neglected as a field of study. In the mid-1970s, researchers generated momentum by beginning inquiries in the history of social studies, as evidenced by the increasing number of presentations at national scholarly conferences. In 1977, a special-interest group on the foundations of social studies was created as part of the National Council of Social Studies.[22] In 1980, one scholar remarked that there was "a modest surge of interest" in social studies history, yet a decade later another scholar noted that there was not a "sufficiently diverse range of writings."[23] These two comments characterize the current state of social studies historiography as of this writing in 2012. There appears to be growing interest, but the scholarship that has been produced tends to be narrow in focus and often falls into one of a handful of investigative threads.

First, social studies historiography has been preoccupied for a long time with the origins of the field during the Progressive Era (1890–1920). Numerous studies have documented the activities of the various curriculum committees of national organizations, such as the National Education Association (NEA) and American Historical Association (AHA).[24] Such investigations have typically been used to support or refute social studies' importance in the school curriculum. Research on the Progressive-Era origins typically demonstrate how the ideas and ideals of the period ended up in the new social studies curriculum and often frame it as an antidote to a narrow, elite liberal arts curriculum that focused primarily on history and geography.[25]

A second major trope in the social studies historiography is the struggle or conflict metaphor. This widely applied notion pits interest group against interest group in the clash over the social education curriculum. It generally is used by scholars researching the early years of social studies, but is applied by historians examining struggles beyond the Progressive Era.[26] In many of these studies, the focus is on antagonism between historians and educators. Broadening the examination, some historians of education look at a variety of interest groups vying for a stake in the curriculum, which includes social meliorists, social reconstructionists, and social-efficiency experts. Authors of a fair number of these studies argue that social studies courses gradually replaced history offerings, thus resulting in a watered-down curriculum for the masses, but this conclusion is not fully supported by the literature.[27] In fact, the chapters in this volume establish a different perspective; they make a case for the key role of history *in* the social studies, especially in influencing the ways that teachers, students, community members, and other stakeholders talk about race. Therefore, the either-or proposition is challenged by the reality of a both-and approach to focusing on history in social studies.

Finally, a significant degree of social studies historiography has focused on biographies of its leaders and of national social-studies-related associations. What was considered a promising approach in the early 1990s is now shopworn and in need of elaboration.[28] The central argument in biographical studies is that one social studies leader or another was important to the development of the field. Scholars attempt to uncover the contributions of well-known and less well-known leaders from the pantheon of those who influenced social studies. The majority of biographical studies have focused on White male leaders; in recent years, women's contributions to the social studies have been added.[29] In a few instances, African American social educators are considered as part of the scholarship. In order to uncover more persons of color working in leadership positions in social studies, scholars will have to employ the framework suggested by Crocco in expanding what one understands as leadership in the field; in other words, it might include those who work in schools, or practice, and not just national level organizational studies, leaders, or theoretical work.[30]

The dearth of attention to race in social studies historiography is troubling when one considers the explosion of attention to race and diversity in the wider historical scholarship. If one investigates social education and citizenship efforts within segregated schools and in African American communities, one will find an abundance of scholarship. This body of research is much too extensive to address in this introduction—just think of the voluminous titles in African American studies today—but a few categories are well worth mentioning. First, a significant number of works address Emancipation and education. These detailed studies reveal the efforts of teachers and the curriculum that was taught to the freed people and beyond.[31] Next, several historians have written books that explore Black teachers' efforts and the leadership of Black women in communities, which includes teaching and civic work.[32] Also, other authors crafted inquiries that have investigated social and civic activism around the desegregation of schools.[33] The richness of these historical investigations reveals that there is ample primary source documentation with which to explore the intersection of social studies education and race.

Likewise, this collection touches on themes in the scholarship on critical pedagogy—in particular, on what goals or purposes were believed to be the focus of teaching about race and Black history. Therefore, we believe this book raises questions about the tensions between critical pedagogy and teaching about race, which are perhaps best illustrated in Chapter One, on the notion of a culturally relevant curriculum for the freed people, and in Chapter Ten, on the Afrocentric curriculum in the Detroit Public Schools. All of the essays emphasize how teaching Black history was used to promote self-esteem and group identity, but leave open the question as to whether the various efforts addressed or intended to ameliorate broader social inequality and work toward social justice. This subtext, about the purposes and goals of teaching about race and Black history, is evident throughout the collection. Ultimately, the book is an effort to bring an understanding of the wealth of contemporary scholarship—including but not limited to African American studies and critical pedagogy—to the social studies historiography in order to round out the research by including voices that heretofore have been obscured by the attention given to committee reports, national organization leaders, and top-down investigations. Social studies was originally conceived as a curriculum field that would address issues of race and inequality, but without attending to equality and integration within the field. We turn now to how social studies was originally conceived and what its goals were.

Thomas Jesse Jones and the Early History of Social Studies and Race

In the early twentieth century at the Hampton Institute, educator Thomas Jesse Jones initiated a course of study called "social studies," which was intended to prepare African Americans and American Indians for manual labor and subservient roles in society. Jones was a Welsh immigrant who earned an AB from Marietta College in Ohio, a BD from Union Theological Seminary, and his PhD at Columbia under Franklin Giddings. He joined the staff at Hampton Institute in 1903; it had been founded in 1868 by the American Missionary Association to educate the newly freed people after Emancipation. Jones became director of Hampton's research department, taught economics, and served as the school's chaplain.[34] Hampton's founders emphasized manual training for its students, not for vocational education as much as for moral education purposes.[35]

While at Hampton, Jones developed a curriculum that integrated ideas from civics, economics, and sociology, which he wrote about in a series of articles in *The Southern Workman,* Hampton's newspaper. His vision for social studies was compiled from these and other articles and published as *Social Studies in the Hampton Curriculum*.[36] The overarching goals of the curriculum were to teach Hampton students to be more sympathetic towards those who opposed them; to help them understand that their condition was not permanent, but a step in their evolution; and to teach them to become "more intelligent in their work, more patient under oppression [and] more hopeful as to the future."[37] William H. Watkins argued that

Jones believed that the four basic essentials should be added to the three R's. Those essentials were knowledge of health and hygiene, of the physical environment, of domestic life and culture, and of recreation.[38]

Therefore, the civics curriculum focused on making change in one's local community and expecting that race prejudice would eventually disappear. The economics course focused on students' needs as future employees and on wise consumption of goods (for example, thrift and saving), while sociology was geared towards teaching Black students that their present condition was not permanent. Instead of highlighting society's responsibility for racism and prejudice, Jones's sociology course emphasized the supposed weaknesses within students' races—African Americans and American Indians—thereby applying an evolutionary approach to social issues. Students were cautioned in sociology class about impulsiveness and uncontrolled emotion. In summary, the Hampton social studies curriculum "gave scant attention to either political rights or social equality," because its overarching aim was to prepare students for their subordinate roles in society.[39] Nonetheless, as Herbert Kliebard argues, "historical circumstance and evolutionary lag" were seen as being able to be remediated through education.[40]

In 1910, Jones moved to the US Census Bureau, where he was put in charge of the census for African Americans. A year later he became director of the Phelps-Stokes Fund and was appointed "specialist in Negro education" at the US Bureau of Education. Then, after having been appointed chair of the National Education Association (NEA) Committee on Social Studies in 1912, Jones brought his brand of social education to the newly emerging curriculum. Under Jones's leadership, the Committee produced three reports: *A Preliminary Statement* (1914), *The Teaching of Community Civics* (1915), and *The Social Studies in Secondary Education* (1916). Historians Michael Lybarger and William H. Watkins argue that each document included elements of the Hampton social studies curriculum, and that the new social studies of the 1910s was indeed the Hampton social studies curriculum remade for the masses.[41] Lybarger, in particular, traces the parallels between the two. First, both curricula focused on social betterment and the well-being of the community as objectives. Next, what was called Civic Theory and Practice at Hampton became the Problems of Democracy course, virtually word for word. The topics the students were to study were the same: public commerce, corrections, charity, education, and health, and the new social studies education addressed students' needs as employees, much like the Hampton curriculum. However, one important difference was that the Hampton social studies course focused on the role of government in promoting the welfare of rural southerners, while in the NEA social studies documents, the focus was on residents of urban areas.[42]

Overall, historians have emphasized that Jones was a product of his times, and that he "repeatedly disassociated himself with the violent and barbaric deeds of the segregationist South, while simultaneously cautioning against independent black self-help."[43] Nonetheless, Jones aligned himself with the accommodationist thinking of Booker T. Washington and was frequently challenged by W. E. B. Du Bois, who called him "that evil genius of the Negro race."[44] Historians also have asserted that Jones is one of the most formidable figures in early twentieth-century education and, as Watkins argues, he was "arguably the most influential white theorist on black education."[45] Kliebard posits that his vision "became the prevailing doctrine for American education generally."[46] Indeed, Jones was instrumental in establishing the legacy of social studies education as a means to shape society, an understanding that is prevalent in the field today, although the goal of social justice has replaced the objective of social control or dominance.

It is difficult to pin down a central narrative in the development of social studies and the teaching of race and Black history, as evidenced by the contributions to this collection, which span the time period from the Emancipation of enslaved peoples to the closing decades of the twentieth century. In part, each chapter addresses change over time in social studies by considering when, where, and how transitions in the curriculum with respect to race occurred. Some evidence reveals schools and educators that were progressive in their approaches to teaching about race, as in the case of the Shortridge High School Senate. Other evidence, as in the case of the elementary geography textbooks used in South Carolina, reveals a retrograde approach to thinking about race and difference in the classroom. One conclusion that may be reached is that the evolution of teaching about race and Black history has been uneven across regions and nonlinear over time.

Histories of Social Studies and Race

When did social studies education move from emphasizing teaching students to fill a subservient role—whether they were immigrants, American Indians, or African Americans—to using curriculum and pedagogy to uplift? This collection reveals that the shift began early and that there are no easy conclusions about the path taken by social studies and its leaders in schools and communities that grappled with race and difference. Diverse chapters on the histories of social studies and race comprise this edited volume, which includes an assortment of American geographic locations. Likewise, the chapters include a multiplicity of pedagogical practices, subject areas, textbook content, curriculum initiatives, student organizations, and standards-based reform, as well as examination of both segregationist and integrationist policies in schools.

Ronald Butchart's thought-provoking first chapter opens the discussion with a historical analysis of the success of Reconstruction-Era segregated Black schools. These were the first generation of schools, teachers, and students for newly emancipated people in the American South. Providing artifacts from students and teachers, Butchart reveals the accomplishments of Reconstruction-Era southern Black schools. The curriculum, textbooks, and expectations were rigorous, although learning was largely rote and passive. Teaching and learning were not adapted to the conditions, experiences, or culture of newly freed slaves, but were modeled on teaching and learning in northern schools, from which many of the missionaries hailed. Missionaries comprised many of the teachers in the schools for Blacks. Butchart offers a cautionary meditation on contemporary theories that claim to explain the current achievement gap between Black and White students, especially on culturally relevant pedagogy.

In the second chapter, Thomas Fallace provides a framework for understanding several of the chapters where the authors examine social studies and race in the early twentieth century. Fallace discusses how the early social studies leaders, who authored the 1916 Report on Social Studies, were united in their linear historicist view of race and culture. He claims that these progressive scholars viewed African American and Native American populations as biologically and psychically equal to Whites, but socially, culturally, and ethically disadvantaged and deficient. Indeed, leaders such as Thomas Jesse Jones, John Dewey, Arthur Dunn, and James Harvey Robinson viewed non-White cultures largely as in need of development. Fallace uses historical evidence to construct his argument about the racial views of early social studies leaders and to describe how these perspectives helped to shape the curriculum in early social studies classrooms. The third chapter stands in sharp contrast. In this chapter, Sarah Bair examines the early years of Negro History Week, from its founding by Carter G. Woodson in 1926 through its growth in the postwar era. Bair's historical analysis also explores Woodson's rationale for the initiative and his vision for its implementation, which he planned to serve more extensive curricular goals.

Chapters Four, Five, and Six continue the examination of race and social studies education in specific contexts during the late nineteenth and early twentieth century. In Chapter Four, J. Spencer Clark describes the student government organization at Shortridge High School in Indianapolis, Indiana, and its students' frank and open discussions of race. The students' understandings of race expose not only notions of White racial superiority, but the complexity of subgroup stereotypes. For example, some students vocalized biases toward Southern European and Eastern European immigrants. Nonetheless, the student self-government group, led by teacher Laura Donnan, also reveals nascent concepts of Black equality and citizenry. In Chapter Five, Alana D. Murray uncovers the work of Nannie Helen Burroughs's Black history pageant, *When Truth Gets a Hearing*. Murray makes the case that this "unofficial" social studies curriculum served as a vehicle for African American racial uplift. Chapter Six spans the late nineteenth and early twentieth century time frame, in which Mindy Spearman examines portrayals of race in the American elementary geography textbooks that the state of South Carolina adopted for use. The language in these old textbooks, which included terms like *barbarism, savage, half-civilized,* and the visual depictions that Spearman has selected from the textbooks, reveal racial understandings of the time, in particular the esteem given to White superiority.

The last grouping of four chapters includes more contemporary analyses of race and social studies education. In Chapter Seven, Chara Haeussler Bohan and Patricia Randolph research conceptions of race in Georgia history textbooks that were adopted for use in the 1970s and 1980s, during the desegregation era of southern public schooling. As Spearman found in researching material of nearly a century earlier, Bohan and Randolph found stereotypical portrayals of African Americans engaged in physical labor and depictions of North American Indians dressed in traditional attire and living in provisional housing. The more modern textbooks told a more subtly veiled story of European progress and success. In Chapter Eight, Erica DeCuir explores the social studies curriculum in the era of standards-based reform in McDonogh #35 Senior High School in New Orleans. In 1917, McDonogh #35 was established as the first public high school for Black children in Louisiana. Despite the pressures of a state-mandated standardized curriculum and a corresponding accountability policy, in the late twentieth and early twenty-first centuries, McDonogh retained a strong academic curriculum that placed social justice and students at its center.

In Chapter Nine, Joseph Watras describes multicultural education in the context of desegregation-era schooling in Dayton, Ohio. *The New York Times* had heralded the city of Dayton as a model of desegregation. Watras suggests, however, that the subsequent purposeful teaching of Black history in Dayton schools failed to establish a more integrated residential pattern and failed to help students understand human potential. In Chapter Ten, Anne-Lise Halvorsen evaluates the successes and challenges of African-Centered Education, which was adopted in the

Detroit public schools in the late 1960s and lasted through the turn of twenty-first century. The program was supported and well received in the Detroit community, but unfortunately, in an era of increased demand for empirical evidence, the program did not substantiate its positive impact on student achievement and self-esteem. Nonetheless, Halvorsen uncovers educational benefits from African-Centered Education, especially in the Detroit Public Schools, which were nearly all-Black by the end of the twentieth century. Margaret Crocco provides concluding remarks in the Epilogue. The chapter points to the significance of race in social studies curriculum.

In conclusion, this volume on the intersection of the histories of social studies and race embodies a beginning point for research in this embryonic field. Certainly, the chapters all demonstrate the common challenges, successes, and changes over time that American schooling confronted with respect to race. The chapters focus in particular on the interplay of race and social studies faculty, students, administrators, community members, schools, textbooks, and curriculum. Commonalities between and among chapters, such as the dichotomous perception of race in social studies education, speak to more general lessons that can be derived from these case histories. No edited volume can be comprehensive, therefore gaps persist in this collection. For example, no discussion of race and social studies from localities in the western region of the United States is included. Thus, we welcome further investigation in the histories of social studies and race. We hope to inspire new directions in this area, to broaden the scope of research on the development, implementation, and interpretation of social studies within and among diverse communities and citizens.

We believe the chapters in this volume raise three key issues in the history of social studies. First, we see that teaching history *in* social studies was quite common in schools and communities, far more common than social studies replacing history in the school curriculum. The two coexisted and were frequently seen as one by practitioners. Next, we raise the question of the purposes of teaching about race and Black history. What were the intended purposes, and were they accomplished? If so, how were they accomplished? Were educators and curriculum designers more focused on racial uplift and individual identity or on the broader impact of shaping society and social justice? If it is both, when and where were these goals implemented? Finally, in what may come as no surprise to readers, the central finding of this collection is that there was great diversity in implementation of teaching about race and Black history over time and across place and region. The variances in different locales challenge the top-down histories that drive contemporary historiography and reveal a multifaceted history that often challenges preconceived notions of the purposes of teaching about race in social studies.

Notes

1. June R. Chapin and Richard E. Gross, "A Barometer of the Social Studies: Three Decades of Social Education," *Social Education* 34, no. 8 (1970): 794. See also Tyrone Howard, "The Dis(g)race of the Social Studies: The Need for Racial Dialogue in the Social Studies," in Gloria Ladson-Billings, ed., *Critical Race Theory Perspectives on Social Studies: The Profession, Policies, and Curriculum* (Greenwich, CT: Information Age Publishing, 2003), 27–44; Cynthia A. Tyson, "A Bridge over Troubled Water: Social Studies, Civic Education, and Critical Race Theory," in Gloria Ladson-Billings, ed., *Critical Race Theory Perspectives on Social Studies: The Profession, Policies, and Curriculum* (Greenwich, CT: Information Age Publishing, 2003), 15–26.
2. For examples of more traditional approaches to the history of social studies, see Ronald W. Evans, *The Social Studies Wars: What Should We Teach the Children?* (New York: Teachers College Press, 2004); David Warren Saxe, *Social Studies in Schools: A History of the Early Years* (Albany: State University of New York Press, 1991). Historiography that challenges traditional narratives include Avner Segall, "Social Studies and the Discourses of Postmodernity," in Christine Woyshner, Joseph Watras, and Margaret Smith Crocco, eds., *Social Education in the Twentieth Century: Curriculum and Context for Citizenship* (New York: Peter Lang Publishers, 2004), 160–175; Margaret Smith Crocco and O. L. Davis, Jr., eds., *"'Bending the Future to Their Will'": Civic Women, Social Education, and Democracy* (Lanham, MD: Rowman & Littlefield Publishers, 1999); Zoë Burkholder, "From 'Wops and Dagoes and Hunkies' to 'Caucasian': Changing Racial Discourse in American Classrooms during World War II," *History of Education Quarterly* 50, no. 3 (2010): 324–358.
3. Murry R. Nelson, *The Social Studies in Secondary Education: A Reprint of the Seminal 1916 Report with Annotations and Commentaries* (Bloomington, IN: Eric Publications, 1994).
4. Margaret Smith Crocco, "Dealing with Difference in the Social Studies: A Historical Perspective," *International Journal of Social Education* 18, no. 2 (2003/2004): 108.
5. For example, Sarah D. Bair, "Educating Black Girls in the Twentieth Century: The Pioneering Work of Nannie Helen Burroughs (1879–1961)," *Theory and Research in Social Education* 36, no. 1 (2008): 9–35; Sarah D. Bair, "The Struggle for Community and Respectability: Black Women School Founders and the Politics of Character Education in the Early Twentieth Century," *Theory and Research in Social Education* 37, no. 4 (2009): 570–599; Patrice Preston-Grimes, "Teaching Democracy before *Brown*: Civic Education in Georgia's African American Schools, 1930–1954," *Theory and Research in Social Education* 35, no. 1 (2007): 9–31.
6. Crocco, Introduction to *"'Bending the Future to Their Will,'"* 1.

7. Ritchie Witzig, "The Medicalization of Race: Scientific Legitimization of a Flawed Social Construct," *Annals of Internal Medicine* 125, no. 8 (1996): 675–679; Naomi Zack, *Race and Mixed Race* (Philadelphia: Temple University Press, 1993).
8. Herbert W. Harris, "Introduction: A Conceptual Overview of Race, Ethnicity, and Identity," in *Racial and Ethnic Identity: Psychological Development and Creative Expression*, eds., Herbert W. Harris, Howard C. Blue, and Ezra E. H. Griffith (New York: Routledge, 1995), 1–14.
9. Thomas D. Fallace, *Dewey and the Dilemma of Race: An Intellectual History* (New York: Teachers College Press, 2011), 6–9. See also Chapter Two of this book.
10. Ibid., 4.
11. Rudyard Kipling, "The White Man's Burden," *McClure's Magazine*, 12, 4 (February 1899): 290–291. Reprinted in Kevin Reilly, ed., *Readings in World Civilizations*, vol. 2, *The Development of the Modern World* (New York: St. Martin's Press, 1992), 199–200.
12. Naomi Zack, *Race and Mixed Race*; Sonia El Janis Carlyle, *Are You Mixed? A War Bride's Granddaughter's Narrative of Lives in-between Contested Race, Gender, Class, and Power*. PhD dissertation, Georgia Southern University, 2010; available online at http://dspaceprod.georgiasouthern.edu:8080/xmlui/handle/10518/2590; Maria P. P. Root, *Racially Mixed People in America* (Newbury Park, CA: Sage Publications, 1992).
13. Sonia El Janis Carlyle, *Are You Mixed?*, 19–20.
14. Luther Wright, Jr. "Who's Black, Who's White, and Who Cares: Reconceptualizing the United States's Definition of Race and Racial Classifications," *Vanderbilt Law Review*, 48 (1995): 513–570.
15. Cornel West, *Cornel West Reader* (New York: Basic Civitas Books, 1999), 258–259.
16. Herbert W. Harris, Introduction to *Racial and Ethnic Identity*, 8.
17. F. James Davis, *Who Is Black?* (University Park: Pennsylvania State University Press, 2001).
18. Herbert W. Harris, Introduction to *Racial and Ethnic Identity*, 9.
19. W. E. B. Du Bois, *The Souls of Black Folk: Essays and Sketches* (Chicago: A. G. McClurg, 1903; New York: Bantam Books, 1989), 3. Citations are to the Bantam edition, with introduction by Henry Louis Gates, Jr.
20. Richard Kluger, *Simple Justice: The History of Brown v. Board of Education and Black America's Struggle for Equality* (New York: Vintage Books, 1975), 315–59; Derek Bell, *Silent Covenants: Brown v. Board of Education and the Unfulfilled Hopes for Racial Reform* (New York: Oxford University Press, 2004), 114–129.
21. This section has been adapted from Christine Woyshner, "Notes toward a Historiography of the Social Studies: Recent Scholarship and Future Directions," in *Research Methods in Social Studies Education: Contemporary Issues and Perspectives*, ed. Keith Barton (Greenwich, CT: Information Age Publishing, 2006), 11–38.
22. Hazel W. Hertzberg, *Historical Parallels for the Sixties and Seventies: Primary Sources and Core Curriculum Revisited* (Boulder, CO: Social Science Education Consortium, 1971); Michael Lybarger, "The Historiography of

Social Studies: Retrospect, Circumspect, and Prospect," in *Handbook of Research on Social Studies Teaching and Learning,* James P. Shaver, ed. (New York: Macmillan, 1991), 3–15; National Council for the Social Studies, "Foundations of Social Studies SIG (1977–2004) Expires," *The Social Studies Professional* 186 (2005): 5.
23. Paul Robinson, "The Conventional Historians of the Social Studies," *Theory and Research in Social Education* 8 (1980): 65; Michael Lybarger, "The Historiography of Social Studies," 4.
24. Chara Haeussler Bohan, "Digging Trenches: Nationalism and the First National Report on the Elementary History Curriculum," *Theory and Research in Social Education,* 33, No. 2 (2005): 266–291; Ronald W. Evans, *The Social Studies Wars*; N. Ray Hiner, "Professions in Process: Changing Relations between Historians and Educators, 1896–1911," *History of Education Quarterly* 12 (1972): 34–56; Michael Lybarger, "The Historiography of Social Studies," 3–15; National Council for the Social Studies, "Foundations of Social Studies SIG (1977–2004) Expires," *The Social Studies Professional* 186 (2005): 5; David Warren Saxe, *Social Studies in Schools.*
25. See, for example, Chara Haeussler Bohan, "Early Vanguards of Progressive Education: The Committee of Ten, the Committee of Seven, and Social Education," in *Social Education in the Twentieth Century: Curriculum and Context for Citizenship* (New York: Peter Lang Publishers, 2004), 1–19; Oliver M. Keels, "The Collegiate Influence on the Early Social Studies Curriculum: A Reassessment of the Role of Historians," *Theory and Research in Social Education* 8 (1980): 105–120; David Warren Saxe, *Social Studies in Schools.*
26. For example, Ronald W. Evans, *The Social Studies Wars.*
27. See, for example, Herbert M. Kliebard, *Struggle for the American Curriculum, 1895–1958* (New York: Routledge, 1986); Ronald W. Evans, *The Social Studies Wars*; N. Ray Hiner, "Professions in Process; J. Wesley Null and Diane Ravitch, eds., *Forgotten Heroes of American Education: The Great Tradition of Teaching Teachers* (Greenwich, CT: Information Age Publishing, 2006); Diane Ravitch, *Left Back: A Century of Battles over School Reform* (New York: Touchstone, 2000).
28. Chara Haeussler Bohan and Joseph Feinberg, "New Social Studies Leaders: A Retrospective Analysis of Donald Oliver, Fred Newmann, and James Shaver's Contributions to Social Studies Education," *Social Studies Research and Practice,* 3, no. 2 (2008): 54–67; Chara Haeussler Bohan, "Digging Trenches," 266–291; Chara Haeussler Bohan, "Early Vanguards of Progressive Education: 73–94; O. L. Davis, Jr., ed. *NCSS in Retrospect* (Washington, DC: National Council for the Social Studies, 1996); Lybarger, "The Historiography of Social Studies," 11.
29. See, for example, Chara Haeussler Bohan, *Go to the Sources: Lucy Maynard Salmon and the Teaching of History* (New York: Peter Lang, 2004); George W. Chilcoat and Jerry A. Ligon, "'It Is Democratic Students We Are After:' The Possibilities and the Expectations for the Social Studies from the Writings of Shirley H. Engel," *International Journal of Social Education* 18, no. 2 (2003): 76–92; Stuart McAnnich, "The Educational Theory of Mary Sheldon Barnes: Inquiry Learning as Indoctrination to History Education,"*Educational Theory* 40 (1990): 45–52; Jared Stallones, *Paul Robert Hanna: A Life of Expanding*

Communities (Stanford, CA: Hoover Institution Press, 2002); Murry Nelson, "Merle R. Eppse and Studies of Blacks in American History Textbooks," *International Journal of Social Education* 3, no. 3 (1988): 84–90; Crocco, "'Bending the Future to Their Will.'"
30. Crocco, "'Bending the Future to Their Will,'" 3.
31. For example, Ronald Butchart, *Schooling the Freed People: Teaching, Learning, and the Struggle for Black Freedom 1861–1876* (Chapel Hill, NC: University of North Carolina Press, 2010); James D. Anderson, *The Education of Blacks in the South, 1860–1935* (Chapel Hill, NC: University of North Carolina Press, 1988).
32. See for example, Adam Fairclough, *A Class of Their Own: Black Teachers in the Segregated South* (Cambridge, MA: Belknap Press of Harvard University Press, 2007); Adam Fairclough, *Teaching Equality: Black Schools in the Age of Jim Crow* (Athens, GA: University of Georgia Press, 2001); Vanessa Siddle Walker, *Hello Professor: A Black Principal and Professional Leadership in the Segregated South* (Chapel Hill, NC: University of North Carolina Press, 2009); Vanessa Siddle Walker, *Their Highest Potential: An African American School Community in the Segregated South* (Chapel Hill, NC: University of North Carolina Press, 1996); Stephanie J. Shaw, *What a Woman Ought to Be and to Do: Black Professional Women Workers during the Jim Crow Era* (Chicago: University of Chicago Press, 1996).
33. For example, David S. Cecelski, *Along Freedom Road: Hyde County, North Carolina, and the Fate of Black Schools in the South* (Chapel Hill, NC: University of North Carolina Press, 1994); Derek Bell, *Silent Covenants: Brown v. Board of Education and the Unfulfilled Hopes for Racial Reform* (New York: Oxford University Press, 2004).
34. Michael Lybarger, "Origins of the Modern Social Studies: 1900–1916," *History of Education Quarterly* 23 (Winter 1983): 455–468; William H. Watkins, "Thomas Jesse Jones, Social Studies, and Race," *International Journal of Social Education* 10, no. 2 (1995–1996): 124–134.
35. Herbert M. Kliebard, "'That Evil Genius of the Negro Race:' Thomas Jesse Jones and Educational Reform," *Journal of Curriculum and Supervision* 10, no. 1 (1994): 11.
36. Thomas Jesse Jones, *Social Studies in the Hampton Curriculum* (Hampton, VA: Hampton Institute Press, 1908).
37. Jones, as quoted in Lybarger, "Origins of the Modern Social Studies," 458.
38. Watkins, "Thomas Jesse Jones, Social Studies, and Race," 127.
39. Lybarger, "Origins of the Modern Social Studies," 462; see also 461, 464, 458; Kliebard, 12.
40. Kliebard, "'That Evil Genius of the Negro Race,'" 11.
41. Lybarger, "Origins of the Modern Social Studies," 455; Watkins, "Thomas Jesse Jones, Social Studies, and Race," 124.
42. Lybarger, "Origins of the Modern Social Studies," 462–464.
43. Watkins, "Thomas Jesse Jones, Social Studies, and Race," 127–128. Likewise, Kliebard argues that "Jones embodied the ironies and contradictions that were part of educational reform generally from the turn of the twentieth century onward." See Herbert M. Kliebard, "'That Evil Genius of the Negro Race,'" 6.

44. W. E. B. Du Bois, "Returning Soldiers," *Crisis* 16 (May 1919): 281–287. In Lybarger, the quote reads "that evil genius of the Black race;" see Lybarger, "Origins of the Modern Social Studies," 461, while the title of Kliebard's essay shows the original framing: "'That Evil Genius of the Negro Race:' Thomas Jesse Jones and Educational Reform."
45. Watkins, "Thomas Jesse Jones, Social Studies, and Race," 128.
46. Kliebard, "'That Evil Genius of the Negro Race,'" 6.

Chapter One
Race, Social Studies, and Culturally Relevant Curriculum in Social Studies' Prehistory: A Cautionary Meditation

Ronald E. Butchart

Long before social studies emerged as a school subject, students studied social life in schools. They studied the social through the disciplines that would come to be subsumed under the social studies label. And race figured prominently, if only implicitly, in the subjects they studied in social studies prehistory. Race became more explicitly infused into proto–social studies curriculum and pedagogy in the United States as African Americans began emancipating themselves through schooling during and after the American Civil War. In that remarkable historical moment, extending well into the 1870s, African Americans acted on their freedom to demand access to literacy, to schooled knowledge, and to an understanding of the social world they were simultaneously creating and having thrust upon them. They built and sustained hundreds of schools in the face of implacable White opposition, educated thousands of Black teachers and supported even more White teachers, trebled their literacy rate in a decade, and established secondary schools and institutions of higher education, many of which continue a century and a half later. Black adults and Black children alike mastered a foreign curriculum and gave the American South the foundation for its eventual system of universal education.[1]

That unique historical moment set up a haunting contradiction; whereas it is now commonplace to note the achievement gap between Black and White students, in the 1860s and 1870s, the achievement gap was reversed—impoverished former slaves overwhelmed classrooms and teachers and achieved high levels, whereas poor southern Whites remained indifferent to educational opportunities until largely forced into schools by the Progressive Era's compulsory attendance laws.[2] To deal with the present-day achievement gap, educators and policy makers have offered many theories, from recycled claims of racial inferiority through worries about the deleterious effects of underclass youth culture, to arguments for greater cultural relevance in teaching and curriculum.[3] None of those theories, however, stands up when the historical evidence is examined. In this essay, I offer an historical argument to suggest the poverty of all of those theories, with particular attention to the currently popular focus on cultural relevance as a solution to minority youth's current learning problems. This meditation looks particularly at the prehistory of social studies curriculum and pedagogy in schools for Black youth in the American South, from 1861 to 1876.

Before turning to the historical narrative, however, I offer some definitions and explanations of contemporary thinking. In the ongoing effort to improve the educational performance of minority children and thereby to close the "achievement gap" between them and majority children, educators, researchers, and activists have, in the last two to three decades, turned to schooling strategies that take into account the gulf between the learners' native or home or neighborhood culture and the cultural allegiance most frequently manifested by the school. Scholars have given this educational strategy various names: culturally responsive pedagogy; culturally relevant pedagogy; culturally appropriate pedagogy; culturally congruent curriculum and pedagogy; culturally conscious classroom materials or curriculum, and, at least for African American learners, Afrocentric curriculum, among others.[4] While there may be differences of emphasis or orientation among those strategies, for the purposes of this inquiry, I refer to the general tendency as *aspects of culturally relevant curriculum and pedagogy.*

The notion of culturally relevant *curriculum* arises from a relatively simple pedagogical concept: learners can more easily engage with, and hence can more easily master, content that builds on what learners already know. Proponents of culturally relevant curriculum argue that the traditional curriculum of American schools contains language, images, symbols, and other carriers of culture and meaning that are familiar to middle-class and White students, but that are far less familiar or even alien to lower-class and minority students. It is the unfamiliarity of traditional school content, these educators assert, that accounts for much of the difficulty that less-privileged students have in school. They call, then, for curricular materials that reflect the diversity of US schools, from the physical depictions of children and adults in textbook illustrations, through the subjects of stories and poems in the literature curriculum, to the subjects and content of historical studies and other social studies. Equally accessible content, it is hoped, will yield more equal educational outcomes.[5]

Culturally relevant *pedagogy* expands on the same notion. Traditional pedagogical practices reflect culturally coded patterns, rituals, and routines that are not universal; they are patterns, rituals, and routines common to White middle-class life and culture. Learners whose home and community cultures differ significantly from that middle-class culture, particularly in their affective and communicative patterns, are therefore at a disadvantage in the classroom. For example, children from homes and communities that value communal reciprocity, mutuality, verbality, and physicality experience cultural dissonance in the traditional classroom, with its emphasis on hierarchical social relations, rationalized use of space and time, unidirectional teaching, individuality and competitiveness, silent study, and physical passivity. Middle-class home life, child-rearing practices, social relations, modes of self-presentation, and other aspects of middle-class life prepare White middle-class children to adapt readily to that environment. They are ready to learn immediately. Lower-class and minority children, on the other hand, enter a foreign environment where they must spend a good deal of time learning to negotiate hidden shoals and unexpected patterns of human interaction. Learning is thereby delayed and disrupted, and the children are immediately placed at a disadvantage. Thus, proponents of culturally relevant pedagogy call on teachers to become conscious of their usually unexamined cultural assumptions and to adopt interactional patterns that "tap into the home and community interaction patterns that are central to students' learning and relationships outside school...."[6]

In brief, then, the argument for a more inclusive, culturally relevant curriculum and pedagogy seeks to level the learning playing field by expanding the curriculum to include authentic curricular material that reflects the multiple cultures of contemporary, diverse schools, and by expanding teachers' classroom practices and expectations to embrace the interactional styles and codes that underlie the lived cultural practices of their students. A growing body of research literature appears to sustain the argument that such expansions of teaching materials and teaching styles have a positive impact on learning.[7] The hope is, of course, that schools broadly pursuing culturally relevant schooling will engage more—ideally all—students, particularly those who are currently most fully marginalized by and alienated from the school. Most proponents of culturally relevant pedagogy and curriculum would undoubtedly agree with Angela Valenzuela that concerns for social justice lie at the heart of their enterprise.[8]

The argument seems self-evident: the greater the gap between the language, images, and sanctioned social behavior in the classroom, on the one hand, and the social and learning experience of the learner, on the other, the more difficulty the learner will have in appropriating the curriculum. Time spent attempting to understand and navigate a foreign landscape—time inevitably diverted, in other words, in order to learn the implicit curriculum of the traditional classroom—is time lost to the task of learning the intentional curriculum. In the competitive classroom's war of all against all, such lost time is academically fatal for individuals and groups outside the White, middle-class mainstream.

All my deepest inclinations as a teacher educator, political progressive, and activist on behalf of radical change in the purposes and outcomes of public schools resonate with the logic and ends of culturally relevant pedagogy. Yet a historical parallel troubles me. An earlier example of culturally relevant curriculum and pedagogy, not least in early forms of social studies education, served very powerfully to limit the educational aspirations of African American learners. And at the same time that that particular experiment in culturally relevant curriculum and pedagogy was being perfected, an army of educators, many devoted to social justice, rejected culturally relevant pedagogy. They provided African American learners with a pedagogy and curriculum far removed from the students' cultural experiences. Those educators and their culturally inappropriate pedagogy and curriculum were enormously successful in promoting high achievement and expanding educational aspirations among their southern Black students. Indeed, they and their students proceeded to build the region's entire system of mass education. The former curriculum—the culturally relevant curriculum and pedagogy—meanwhile, demeaned the Black community and arguably contributed to setting back the struggle for social justice a century or more.

In brief, my argument is that we can study a point in time when the cultural gap between a virtual nation of learners and the dominant population was greater than it has ever been since. That nation of learners had been systematically excluded from participation in the dominant culture; had been culturally, intellectually, and spiritually isolated from the dominant community; and had, as a direct result, developed its own dynamic, rich culture, one that was in many ways a counterculture, a culture of resistance. When those learners gained access to formal education, they entered two distinct sorts of schools. One insisted that they deserved no less than the curriculum and pedagogy given to any learner, and it taught them exactly as the dominant society's learners were taught. The other insisted that the culture of these new learners was so foreign to that of the dominant group that a special, culturally relevant curriculum and pedagogy had to be provided, though of course those educators did not use the modern language of cultural relevance. The story of these competing modes of curriculum and pedagogy constitutes a cautionary tale in our struggle today to identify the best schooling for present-day minority children.

I am speaking, of course, about the first generation of schools, teachers, and learners after Emancipation in the American South. Southern African Americans flooded into day schools, night schools, and Sabbath schools by the tens of thousands as a central act of their self-emancipation. They sought out teachers from among their own literate ranks, overwhelmed the supply of northern teachers sent by philanthropic means, and even begged their former masters to provide schools. They mastered the curriculum with remarkable speed and demanded secondary schools, normal schools, and colleges within half a decade of Emancipation. Perhaps as many as fifteen thousand teachers served in southern Black schools between 1861 and 1876, yet they could not begin to meet the freed people's demand for access to knowledge.[9]

What did that nation of learners study in the schools they built? How did their teachers teach the curriculum? As noted, two competing models of curriculum and pedagogy had emerged by the mid-1860s. The first and most common model might be called culturally irrelevant curriculum and pedagogy. Most of the first generation of southern Black schools were indistinguishable, in curriculum and pedagogy, from contemporaneous northern common schools.

For example, in their first decade and beyond, most of the freed people's schools used textbooks commonly found throughout the country, including *Webster's Speller*, *Greenleaf's Arithmetic*, and *McGuffey's Readers*. An early meeting of the four leading aid societies supplying teachers to the southern schools discussed which national textbook series to adopt, but determined that all were equally appropriate and that "it would be hardly just treatment of publishers, should we adopt any one series...." One of the teachers, reminiscing five decades after her work in Charlottesville, Virginia, listed the many common texts used in her school, concluding, "In short we were not confined to special textbooks, but read and taught from what seemed to offer the best instruction."[10]

Likewise, the subjects studied were no different from the subjects studied in northern schools, reaching far beyond the hoary reading, writing, and arithmetic. Black students in the rough equivalent of the fourth grade in Charleston, South Carolina, studied

> Guyot's *Intermediate Geography*, Child's *Book of Nature*, Felter's *Intellectual Arithmetic*, and are about halfway through Payson & Dunton's *Writing Book, No. 3*. They write Compositions, and have oral lessons in Grammar.... They have already had a thorough training in the four rules in Arithmetic..., thus following out a simple course in Fractions and Denominate Numbers.[11]

Three years after her students began their studies on St. Helena Island, South Carolina, Laura Towne wrote in her private diary,

> The children have read through a history of the United States and an easy physiology, and they know all the parts of speech, and can make sentences,

being told to use a predicate, verb, and adverb, for instance. Ellen's class is writing compositions. We are going to have a grand school exhibition before we close, with dialogues, exercises in mathematics, in grammar, geography, spelling, reading, etc., etc.[12]

After only six years of access to schools, the African American students in the "colored" school of Petersburg, Virginia, passed a three-hour "examination in French, Latin, Algebra, Arithmetic, Geography, &c...."[13] The first principal of the South Carolina Normal School reported that his corps of prospective African American teachers had studied "Arithmetic, Geography, Grammar, Geometry, Reading, Writing, History, Drawing, Spelling, Map-Drawing, Latin, Algebra, Botany, Mineralogy, Physiology, Object Lessons, and Theory and Practice of Teaching, Constitution of South Carolina...."[14] From across the South, teachers consistently reported teaching languages, mathematics, sciences, geography, history, and other traditional subjects, in addition to reading and writing.

If there is any doubt as to the breadth of the gap between the curriculum in the freed people's schools and their life experiences, consider that throughout the slaveholding South, right up to the Civil War, African Americans were prohibited by law from attending school, and teaching even basic literacy to African Americans was a crime. Black literacy probably stood at no more than five percent by 1860, usually "stolen" by slaves and free Blacks when the opportunity allowed. Few ever traveled more than a few miles from their homes. The vast majority of slaves were confined to rural plantations and small farms, with little or no access to knowledge of or experiences with mainstream culture beyond what their owners allowed; the few slaves in towns and cities fared only somewhat better, severely limited by custom and law in where they could go and what they could do. Free Blacks were seldom much better off, usually living on the margins of poverty. The result was not cultural deprivation, by any means—free and enslaved Blacks created their own lively oppositional culture—but both their culture and their life experiences held little in common with the culture, knowledge, and expectations of the American common school that they began to attend at the outset of freedom.[15]

Yet despite the breadth of that gap, southern Black students persevered spectacularly in their schools. Two years after opening school in Charleston, South Carolina, long-time educator Arthur Sumner observed that his more advanced students were

> quite equal, in attainments, to the lower and middle classes of the Boston grammar-schools. They are very expert in mental arithmetic; can perform in hard examples the four rudiments, on the slate; are writing compositions; studying grammar by means of a book on composition; learning history;

and are just beginning Warren's *Common-School Geography*, after having already gone through another book on the subject.[16]

Jane Briggs Smith, working with former slaves only three years out of bondage, described "teaching them the parts of a circle (they can give you the geometrical definitions of the same, and—more than that—explain it) applying it to mathematical Geography, teaching them about the parallels, zones &c—always presenting the <u>thing</u> first and then the <u>name</u>, and when I give the name teaching them to spell it, and making all who can, write it on their slates."[17]

A year later, in 1869, Lucy Chase wrote of her students,

> I frequently call the attention of the whole school to illustrations of the meaning of familiar words. I spend a good deal of time in teaching Arithmetic both Mental and Written. Many of the children add, subtract, multiply and divide, units, tens, and even hundreds, with readiness. I spend so much time upon these exercises that I can mark the improvement, which is rapid. I have three classes in Geography, and I give, daily, lessons to the whole school on Maps. All the children can navigate the Gulfs and Bays of the Globe, and they are now journeying with pleasure through the U.S., halting at the capital cities and sailing on the pleasant rivers.[18]

In short, if the majority of the freed people were studying subjects common in northern common schools, academies, seminaries, and colleges, and working from the same texts found in Massachusetts, Ohio, Iowa, New Jersey, and Michigan, they were reading stories and considering illustrations drawn from experiences that could hardly have been further removed from their lives. The curriculum's language, imagery, settings, and ideas were drawn from a northern, industrializing, middle-class, White, pre-Victorian culture. It was a curriculum whose ideological bias was thoroughly Whig and Puritan, a curriculum whose literary canon was aristocratic and European, a curriculum whose language was formal, academic, and largely neutral in affect. The curriculum flattened expressiveness by parsing and categorizing language, neutralized history by silencing most of its narratives, and sucked the life out of geography through a fetish for memorizing place names and locations.[19]

Meanwhile, the pedagogy practiced in the majority of the first generation of southern Black schools was just as distant culturally from the lives of southern African Americans as was the curriculum. Many of the teachers in the early Black schools followed the traditional pedagogy of individual and small-group recitation that was still practiced by mid-century in schools throughout the South and in northern rural schools; others employed the more modern pedagogies then emerging in northern urban schools. Though distinct from one another in important ways, rooted in contrasting social relationships, both pedagogies were hierarchical, unidirectional, competitive, rationalized, and individualistic. Both privileged passive memorization over active participation, individual achievement over group acquisition, character over intellect.[20] Such a pedagogy, in other words, stood in sharp contrast to a culture that valued mutuality, community, and active engagement.[21]

Some of the teachers, both Black and White, who taught in the first generation of southern Black schools saw their work as serving the ends of social justice, though few used that exact language. They were deeply committed to Black empowerment through education. A few went so far as to include elements of African and African American history in their proto-social-studies curriculum, at least a nod toward an additive curriculum.[22] By far the majority of the freed people's teachers, however, made little if any accommodation in their curriculum or in their pedagogy. They taught the same curriculum, from the same textbooks, following the same pedagogical strategies, as teachers used in northern White schools. Yet the evidence is overwhelming that their students learned rapidly and accurately. By 1864, only two years after the first schools opened on the Sea Islands of South Carolina, William Allen observed privately that some of the schools "would rank fairly with northern schools."[23] In that same year, the fastest students in New Orleans' Black schools had "finished the primary books of reading and geography and are now reading the third and fourth readers with facility. They have acquired the knowledge of arithmetic as far as long division and fractions, the multiplication tables, the use of outline maps, and can write with commendable neatness."[24] An observer of a public examination of the pupils at the Butler School, Fortress Monroe, Virginia, remarked,

> Questions in Geography, asked by both teachers & visitors, were, with few exceptions, answered promptly and accurately; but the examination in Arithmetic, and especially in fractions was the most interesting. It surprised me; and I think I never heard a class of the same age, who gave so clearly & understandingly the rules, and the reasons for them, by which fractions are changed in adding, subtracting, multiplying & reducing them.[25]

After six years of school, the Black students studying Latin in Petersburg, Virginia, "none of them over 14 years of age and the youngest apparently about 6," demonstrated in a public examination "great acquaintance with the rules of Latin grammar and were much more ready in construing the Exercises than could have been expected...."[26] Scores more examples could be provided. Nor can these testimonies be dismissed as the predictable comments of teachers ingratiating themselves to their sponsors; the observations were consistent across private entries in diaries, letters to families and friends never intended for publication, grudging observations in southern papers otherwise hostile to Black education, and letters sent by observers to the aid organizations and the Freedmen's Bureau.[27]

To reiterate, then, one group of educators working with southern African Americans as the sun set on American slavery taught the same subjects in the same ways that they had taught in northern schools. Their students mastered that foreign curriculum, under those foreign forms of pedagogy, with a rapidity and grace that astounded even their detractors. Yet those students were immersed in a culture that bore little resemblance to the culture undergirding the curriculum and pedagogy. In other words, despite a culturally inappropriate, if not a culturally hostile, curriculum and pedagogy, nearly a century and a half ago African American children flourished in schools.

Another model of curriculum and pedagogy competed with the model described above, however. Its exponents explicitly considered the freed people's culture and experiences when choosing their curriculum, materials, and classroom practices. They were, then, educators who wrote and mobilized an early form of culturally relevant curriculum and practiced an early form of culturally relevant pedagogy. The contrast is troubling.

This second group of educators believed that a people so culturally different from the White norm needed special schoolbooks tailored to their special condition, experiences, and future. Mere months after the start of the Civil War, the American Tract Society established a school in Washington, D. C., "precisely for the purpose of determining what kind of books were needed to teach the freedmen," in the words of historian Samuel L. Horst.[28] Based on its experience with Black students in that school, the society published in 1863 the first culturally relevant curriculum for the schools of the freed people in the form of a didactic textbook. Over the next four or five years, a full range of primers, readers, inexpensive elementary monthly papers, and textbooks rolled from the American Tract Society presses, written expressly for the freed people, drawing explicitly from experiences presumed to be relevant to southern Black life, with illustrations drawn specifically for a Black audience. The tract society's *Freedmen's Library* series constructed the freed people as an ignorant, docile, apolitical southern Black mass looking to godly White teachers and ministers for advice and direction, speaking a stereotyped ungrammatical patois, and striving pathetically to mimic their White superiors.[29] This was a curriculum that might have built upon past experiences and communicated in a language that might have seemed familiar, and consequently might have facilitated learning. The messages embedded in the lessons and language and images, however, were deeply demeaning and the goals were deeply conservative. This was culturally relevant curriculum intended to demonstrate the place of African Americans in a hierarchical, racist society.[30]

Similarly, within less than a decade of the inauguration of the first southern Black schools, a fully articulated, culturally relevant school emerged, combining a self-consciously culturally relevant curriculum with an equally self-consciously culturally relevant pedagogy. Hampton Normal and Industrial Institute, founded in 1868 by Samuel Chapman Armstrong, insisted that the freed people would learn best in a comprehensive institution that took African American culture as its first consideration. For Armstrong, prominent African American cultural traits included sloth, emotionality, irrationality, and immorality, and the task of education was to impose the routines and didactic teachings that would tamp down and attempt to pave over those traits with an allegiance to the superior traits of the White race. Of the freed people he wrote, "it is true that not mere ignorance but deficiency of character is the chief difficulty, and that to build up character is the true objective point in education." He continued,

> Morality and industry generally go together. Especially in the weak tropical races idleness, like ignorance, breeds vice. The best of sermons and school amount to little when hearers and pupils are thriftless, live from hand to mouth, and are packed at night either in savage huts or in dirty tenement houses. Morality, though founded in spiritual life, depends very much upon outward and social conditions; and, if man is to work out his own salvation, he must learn how to work.[31]

Thus, Hampton was to be, from its founding, a boarding school, not a community school, in order to isolate its inmates from social conditions of the Black community. It was to have a curriculum explicitly designed and carefully organized to root out specific aspects of African American cultural traits, especially idleness and thriftlessness, through routinized labor that constituted half the students' daily routine. Its early social studies curriculum preached the historical virtues of individualism and self-sufficiency, the backwardness of mutuality and community, and the social geography of progress and power, always located anywhere but in Africa. It was to follow a pedagogical regimen calibrated precisely to the presumed cultural capacities of its students. A mere quarter of a century later, an unrepentant and unchanged Hampton would welcome into its faculty the man that Anson Phelps Stokes would label "the evil genius of the Black race," Thomas Jesse Jones. Jones would go on to move Hampton, and the nation, into the modern social studies curriculum. As designed for Hampton, the social studies curriculum was intended to extend and rationalize a culturally relevant curriculum of subordination and cultural imperialism. Jones invented the explicit curriculum, but the implicit curriculum simply awaited his arrival.[32]

What can we say of the success of these two contrasting modes of teaching African American learners? First, in both settings, African Americans learned with an alacrity and agility that continually surprised their supporters and, reluctantly, their detractors. Whether studying botany and the lives of Black abolitionists under Caroline F. Putnam, or carpentry and housekeeping under Armstrong, at Excelsior School or Hampton, Black students mastered the respective curricula through contrasting pedagogies. Less than a decade after the first schools opened their doors, their graduates were establishing schools of their own, assuming positions in state governments, opening businesses, and establishing farms. The newly minted teachers reproduced with remarkable accuracy the modes of pedagogy and forms of curriculum under which they had learned.[33] The majority created traditional schools with little regard for their students' culture; the minority reproduced Armstrong's model of a culturally relevant pedagogy and curriculum.

There is nothing in the historical evidence to suggest that newly freed slaves, whether cotton hands on the isolated South Carolina Sea Islands, immersed in a culture with many African survivals, or Black urban workers with multiple opportunities to observe and absorb White culture, learned less effectively when taught by committed but culturally insensitive teachers than when taught by those who sought culturally appropriate curricula and teaching modalities. But we have reason to wonder whether those who learned in schools with a traditional, Eurocentric curriculum and pedagogy did not get the better of the bargain. They were taught by teachers convinced that they could master anything a White learner could master. They were immersed in a curriculum more likely to prepare them to "penetrate the given world;" they were more powerfully educated in the curriculum of power; and they were more fully invested with the cultural capital that would allow them, within the brutal realities of the emerging age, to create spaces for action and thought. As James D. Anderson has argued, Armstrong and Hampton were highly successful in preparing a cadre of Black leaders, but especially Black teachers, who went back into their communities to reproduce a deeply conservative, racist ideology, one that placed the blame for Black immobility and poverty squarely on the imputed racial and cultural traits of African Americans.[34]

Both approaches to teaching Black learners worked, though they worked to achieve very different ends. An empirical question worth pursuing would be: Which mode of Black education under Jim Crow produced the greater proportion of women and men who challenged Jim Crow most effectively? But until we have the studies that can answer that question, the best we can do is to note that at a point in history when African American learners were culturally distant from mainstream culture, their academic achievement was splendid, no matter the mode of teaching or the cultural relevance of what was taught.

What does this story of early universal southern Black education tell us today about the necessity for or efficacy of culturally relevant curriculum and pedagogy? First, it can serve as a salutary warning that making curriculum or pedagogy culturally relevant does not, of itself, guarantee socially progressive results. The example of Samuel Chapman Armstrong must remind us that curriculum and pedagogy are means to an end, not the end itself. Purpose matters. Certainly, those who employ the language of cultural relevance today have social justice and liberatory ends in mind; Armstrong had very different ends in mind.

As progressive educators seek to extend the language of cultural relevance, they must always ask, toward what ends will other educators employ these means? And what beliefs about our children do these other educators hold? Will their ends and beliefs become simply another "tool" in the teacher's box of teacher tools, serving primarily to contain and pacify another generation of learners? Armstrong believed African American culture and its carriers were a millennium or more behind, and inferior to, European American culture and its carriers; he mobilized his belief about those cultures to create a schooling calibrated quite precisely to mete out correct dosages of what he took to be the core cultural traits needed by Black learners as they traversed that millennium. Of course, he conveniently ignored the fact that his culture had no intention of standing still and waiting while its presumed inferiors strove to catch up.

Second, in regard to African American education specifically, this history raises troubling questions about where the struggle for African American education stands in the post-*Brown* era. Irrefutably, a century and a half ago African Americans emerged from the nightmare of human bondage with a vibrant culture that equipped them to demand access to the master's curriculum, in the master's language, even when that curriculum was packaged in arcane language and expressed in images and illustrations that bore virtually no connection to the lived experiences of an impoverished and exploited people. They mastered that curriculum, to the chagrin of their former masters.

Yet a century and a half later, too many of the descendants of those same people, with minds as keen as their forebears, surrounded by media that give unparalleled access to mainstream culture, do not master the curriculum. Despite the manifest academic success of tens of thousands of Black youths,[35] Black achievement overall remains the target of media scrutiny and social science theorizing, much of it seeking explanations in theories of cultural poverty not far removed ideologically from the thinking of Samuel Chapman Armstrong and Thomas Jesse Jones. What this analysis demonstrates, in contrast to culturalist theories, is that we cannot explain the achievement gap and the problem of minority learners primarily in terms of culturally inaccessible curricula and pedagogies, for historically we know that learners whose culture would have made the school's curriculum and pedagogy even more inaccessible were able to penetrate and master their schooling regardless. Today, many cannot or do not. Why? Where else must we look to gain insight, if culture-blaming is inadequate? What has happened in schools, in the hearts of teachers, in the recent history of Black America, in the economy, in the structure and ideological effects of the social class system that begins to explain our objective conditions in the opening years of the twenty-first century? Until we gain insight into those issues and their links to the achievement gap, adopting culturally relevant curricula and pedagogies is doubtlessly better than doing nothing, but it may be little more than tinkering on the margin.

Notes

1. Ronald E. Butchart, *Schooling the Freed People: Teaching, Learning, and the Struggle for Black Freedom, 1861–1876* (Chapel Hill: University of North Carolina Press, 2010); James D. Anderson, *The Education of Blacks in the South, 1865–1935* (Chapel Hill: University of North Carolina Press, 1988). A portion of the research reported in this paper was made possible in part by a grant from the Spencer Foundation.
2. Butchart, "Black Hope, White Power: Emancipation, Reconstruction and the Legacy of Unequal Schooling in the U.S. South, 1861–1880," *Paedagogica Historica* 46, no. 1–2 (February–April 2010): 33–50; James L. Leloudis, *Schooling in the New South: Pedagogy, Self, and Society in North Carolina, 1880–1920* (Chapel Hill: University of North Carolina Press, 1996); William A. Link, *The Paradox of Southern Progressivism, 1880–1930* (Chapel Hill: University of North Carolina Press, 1992); Mathew D. Davis, "Stimulation, Sustenance, Subversion: The General Education Board and Southern U.S. Public Education," *Journal of Educational Administration and History* 38 (December 2006): 313–22; Rebecca S. Montgomery, *The Politics of Education in the New South: Women and Reform in Georgia, 1890–1930* (Baton Rouge: Louisiana State University, 2006).
3. Richard J. Herrnstein, Charles Murray, *The Bell Curve* (New York: Free Press, 1994); John Charles Boger and Gary Orfield, eds., *School Resegregation: Must the South Turn Back?* (Chapel Hill: University of North Carolina Press, 2005); Janice E. Hale-Benson, *Black Children: Their Roots, Culture, and Learning Styles* (Baltimore: The Johns Hopkins University Press, 1982); John U. Ogbu, *Black American Students in an Affluent Suburb: A Study of*

Academic Disengagement (Mahwah, NJ: Lawrence Erlbaum, 2003); John H. McWhorter, *Losing the Race: Self-Sabotage in Black America* (New York: HarperCollins, 2000). Citations regarding cultural relevance follow in note 4.

4. Gloria Ladson-Billings, *The Dreamkeepers: Successful Teachers of African American Children* (San Francisco: Jossey-Bass, 1994); Ladson-Billings, "But That's Just Good Teaching! The Case for Culturally Relevant Pedagogy," *Theory into Practice* 34 (1995): 159–65; Molefi K. Asante, *Afrocentricity: The Theory of Social Change* (Buffalo, NY: Amulefi Publishing Co., 1980); and Molefi K. Asante, *Afrocentricity and Knowledge* (Trenton, NJ: Africa World Press, 1990).

5. Although I deal here with culturally relevant curriculum and pedagogy in schools for African Americans, the concept has been applied to students from a variety of minority communities. See, for example, Eileen Carlton, Crystall Travis Parsons, and Jamila Smith Simpson, "The Black Cultural Ethos, Students' Instructional Context Preferences, and Student Achievement: An Examination of Culturally Congruent Science Instruction in the Eighth Grade Classes of One African American and One Euro-American Teacher," "*Negro Educational Review* 56 (July 2005): 183–203; Mary M. Clare and Danielle Torres, "Sí! Se Puede! Culturally Congruent Special Education Evaluation for Migrant Students," *Multiple Voices for Ethnically Diverse Exceptional Learners* 9 (August 2006): 122–34; Beverly J. Klug and Patricia T. Whitfield, *Widening the Circle: Culturally Relevant Pedagogy for American Indian Children* (New York: RoutledgeFalmer, 2003); Velma D. Menchaca, "Providing a Culturally Relevant Curriculum for Hispanic Children," *Multicultural Education* 8 (Spring 2001): 18–21; Stanton Wortham and Margaret Contreras, "Struggling Toward Culturally Relevant Pedagogy in the Latino Diaspora," *Journal of Latinos and Education* 1, No. 2 (2002): 133–44.

6. Bena R. Hefflin, "Learning to Develop Culturally Relevant Pedagogy: A Lesson about Cornrowed Lives," *Urban Review* 34 (September 2002): 233. See also, for example, Norvella P. Carter, Torrance N. Hawkins, and Prathiba Natesan, "The Relationship between Verve and the Academic Achievement of African American Students in Reading and Mathematics in an Urban Middle School," *Educational Foundations* 22 (Winter–Spring 2008): 29–46. For examples of culturally relevant pedagogy in various disciplines and levels of learning, see, among many others, Okhee Lee and Cory Buxton, "Science Curriculum and Student Diversity: A Framework for Equitable Learning Opportunities," *Elementary School Journal* 109 (November 2008): 123–37; Robin Averill, Dayle Anderson, Herewini Easton, Pania TeMaro, Derek Smith, and Anne Hynds, "Culturally Responsive Teaching of Mathematics: Three Models from Linked Studies," *Journal for Research in Mathematics Education* 40 (March 2009): 157–86; Julie K. Kidd, Sylvia Y. Sanchez, and Eva K. Thorp, "Defining Moments: Developing Culturally Responsive Dispositions and Teaching Practices in Early Childhood Preservice Teachers," *Teaching and Teacher Education: An International Journal of Research and Studies* 24 (February 2008): 316–29. Even adult learners have their advocates for culturally relevant pedagogy: Talmadge C. Guy, ed., *Providing Culturally Relevant Adult Education: A Challenge for the Twenty-First Century* (San Francisco: Jossey-Bass, 1999).

7. In addition to the sources cited earlier, see also, for example, Elizabeth Bondy, Dorene D. Ross, Caitlin Gallingane, and Elyse Hambacher, "Creating

Environments of Success and Resilience: Culturally Responsive Classroom Management and More," *Urban Education* 42 (no. 4, 2007): 326–48; Terri Patchen and Anne Cox-Petersen, "Constructing Cultural Relevance in Science: A Case Study of Two Elementary Teachers," *Science Education* 92 (November 2008): 994–1014; D. L. Shallert and J. H. Reed, "The Pull of the Text and the Process of Involvement in Reading," in J. T. Guthrie and A. Wigfield, eds., *Reading Engagement: Motivating Readers Through Integrated Instruction* (Newark, DE: International Reading Association, 1997), 68–85; Jacque Ensign, "Including Culturally Relevant Math in an Urban School," *Educational Studies* 34, no. 4 (Winter 2003): 414–23.

8. Angela Valenzuela, "Reflections on the Subtractive Underpinnings of Education Research and Policy," *Journal of Teacher Education* 53 (May/June 2002): 235–41. See also Jacqueline Leonard, Wanda Brooks, Joy Barnes-Johnson, and Robert Q. Berry, III, "The Nuances and Complexities of Teaching Mathematics for Cultural Relevance and Social Justice," *Journal of Teacher Education* 61, No. 3 (2010): 261–70.

9. Ronald Butchart, *Schooling the Freedpeople*; Anderson, *Education of Blacks in the South*; Butchart, *Northern Schools, Southern Blacks, and Reconstruction* (Westport, CT.: Greenwood Press, 1980); Robert C. Morris, *Reading, 'Riting, and Reconstruction* (Chicago: University of Chicago Press, 1981); Ronald Butchart, "Perspectives on Gender, Race, Calling, and Commitment in Nineteenth-Century America: A Collective Biography of the Teachers of the Freedpeople, 1862–1875," *Vitae Scholastica* 13 (Spring 1994): 15–32.

10. *American Freedman* 1 (January 1867): 154; *National Freedman* 1 (August 1865): 214–15; Delaware Association for the Moral Improvement and Education of the Colored People, "Minutes," 12 October 1867; New England Educational Commission, *First Annual Report of the Educational Commission for Freedmen* (Boston: NEFAS, 1863): 33–34; "The Freedmen at Port Royal," *Atlantic Monthly* 12 (September 1963): 303; quotations from J. A. Lane, "Minutes of Meeting of 9–10 June 1865," in American Missionary Association Archives, item #88806, Amistad Research Center, Tulane University (hereafter: AMA and item number); Philena Carkin, "Reminiscences of My Life and Work among the Freedmen of Charlottesville, Virginia, From March 1st, 1866 to July 1st, 1875," unpublished ms., 1910, in Special Collections, University of Virginia.

11. Arthur Sumner to Ednah Dow Cheney, 6 November 1873, New England Freedmen's Aid Society Collection, Box #3 1862–1876, Massachusetts Historical Society, Boston, MA.

12. Laura M. Towne, *Letters and Diary of Laura M. Towne, Written from the Sea Islands of South Carolina, 1862–1884*, edited by Rupert S. Holland (Cambridge, MA: Riverside, 1912), entry for 13 June 1865, pp. 163–64.

13. Petersburg, VA, *Daily Appeal*, July 1873, p. 3.

14. Mortimer A. Warren, "The State Normal School, South Carolina....," manuscript First Annual Report of the South Carolina State Normal School, 1875, South Caroliniana Library, University of South Carolina.

15. For an introduction to aspects of Black culture in the slave South, see, among others, Lawrence W. Levine, *Black Culture and Black Consciousness: Afro-American Folk Thought from Slavery to Freedom* (New York: Oxford University Press, 1977); John W. Blassingame, *The Slave Community: Plantation Life*

in the Antebellum South (New York: Oxford University Press, 1972); Gilbert Osofsky, ed., *Puttin' on Ole Massa* (New York: Harper Torchbooks, 1969), esp. 9–44; Eugene D. Genovese, *Roll, Jordan, Roll: The World the Slaves Made* (New York: Vintage, 1972); Ira Berlin, *Slaves without Masters: The Free Negro in the Antebellum South* (New York: New Press, 1974); and Ira Berlin, *Many Thousands Gone: The First Two Centuries of Slavery in North America* (Cambridge, MA: Harvard University Press, 1998).

16. *Fourth Annual Report of the Barnard Freedmen's Aid Society of Dorchester* (n.p.: Barnard Freedmen's Aid Society, 1867), p. 4.
17. Jane Briggs Smith to Fuller Fiske, 12 January 1868, writing from Sumter, SC, Jane Briggs Smith Fuller Papers, American Antiquarian Society (emphasis in original).
18. Lucy Chase to Miss Lowell, December 14, 1869, Chase Family Papers, American Antiquarian Society.
19. The best study of nineteenth century textbooks remains Ruth Miller Elson, *Guardians of Tradition: American Schoolbooks of the Nineteenth Century* (Lincoln: University of Nebraska Press, 1964); on the curriculum in northern schools, see Lawrence Cremin, *American Education: The National Experience, 1783–1876* (New York: Harper and Row, 1980), although Cremin would probably not agree fully with my characterization of the curriculum.
20. A preliminary sketch of these competing pedagogies preliminarily appears in Ronald E. Butchart and Amy F. Rolleri, "Modern Schools in a Pre-Modern Context: Schools for Ex-Slaves in the United States during Reconstruction," unpublished paper presented to the International Standing Conference on the History of Education, 2003.
21. There is a growing literature from which such a characterization can be distilled, although all of that literature paints a far richer portrait of the culture than can be elaborated here. The sources that have been foundational for me include Lawrence W. Levine, *Black Culture and Black Consciousness* (New York: Oxford University Press, 1977); Thomas W. Webber, *Deep Like the Rivers* (New York: W. W. Norton and Co., 1978); Tera W. Hunter, *To 'Joy My Freedom* (Cambridge, MA: Harvard University Press, 1997); Patricia C. Click, *Time Full of Trial* (Chapel Hill, NC: University of North Carolina Press, 2001); Michele Foster, "Educating for Competence in Community and Culture: Exploring the Views of Exemplary African-American Teachers," *Urban Education* 27 (1992): 370–94; Beverly M. Gordon, "African-American Cultural Knowledge and Liberatory Education: Dilemmas, Problems, and Potentials in a Post-Modern American Society," *Urban Education* 27, No. 4 (1993): 448–70; Vivian L. Gadsden, "Literacy, Education, and Identity among African Americans: The Communal Nature of Learning," *Urban Education* 27 (1993): 352–69.
22. See for example Ronald Butchart, "'We Best Can Instruct Our Own People': New York African Americans in the Freedmen's Schools, 1861–1875," *Afro-Americans in New York Life and History* 12 (January 1988): 27–49; Ronald Butchart, "Caroline F. Putnam," in *Women Educators in the United States, 1820–1993: A Bio-Bibliographical Sourcebook*, edited by Maxine Seller (Westport, CT: Greenwood Press, 1994), 389–96; Ronald Butchart, "Lydia Maria Francis Child," ibid., 111–18; and Ronald Butchart, "Edmonia G.

and Caroline V. Highgate: Black Teachers, Freed Slaves, and the Betrayal of Black Hearts," in *Portraits of African American Life Since 1865, The Human Tradition in America,* No. 16, edited by Nina Mjagkij (Wilmington, DE: Scholarly Resources, Inc., 2003), 1–13. The term "additive curriculum" is drawn from the work of James A. Banks, who considered an additive curriculum the second level or stage (out of four) in school reform toward equity; see James A Banks, *Multiethnic Education: Theory and Practice,* 3rd ed. (Boston: Allyn and Bacon, 1994).
23. Willliam F. Allen, diary, 19 June 1864, typescript, William F. Allen Collection, Wisconsin Historical Society.
24. [Edwin Miller Wheelock], "Education of the Freedmen," *New Orleans Times,* September 2, 1864, quoted in Charles Kassel, "Educating the Slave—A Forgotten Chapter of Civil War History," *Open Court* 41 (April 1927): 249.
25. George Whipple to Michael Strieby, 8 July 1867, AMA #90940.
26. Petersburg, Va., *Daily Index,* July 7, 1871, page 3.
27. See, among many other examples, Carkin, "Reminiscences...;" Towne, *Letters and Diary...;* Wayne E. Reilly, ed. *Sarah Jane Foster, Teacher of the Freedmen* (Charlottesville: University Press of Virginia, 1990), 76, 128–29; Jane Briggs Smith Fiske Collection, American Antiquarian Society, Worcester, MA; Lydia Atkinson, "Diary of Lydia Atkinson," Friends Historical Library, Swarthmore College; Cornelia Hancock Manuscripts, Friends Historical Library, Swarthmore College; letters of Josephine Elizabeth Strong in Strong Family Papers, Yale University Library, Manuscripts and Archives, Petersburg, Virginia, *Daily Courier,* July 7, 1871, 3.
28. Samuel L. Horst, *Education for Manhood: The Education of Blacks in Virginia during the Civil War* (Lanham, MD: University Press of America, 1987), 195. The society transferred control of the school to another group once its purpose had been accomplished.
29. The *Freedmen's Library* included *The Freedmen's Primer* [1864]; *The Lincoln Primer* [1866]; *The Freedmen's Spelling Book* [1865]; *The Freedmen's Readers* series [1866]; Isaac W. Brinckerhoff, *Advice to Freedmen* [1863]; Brinckerhoff, *A Warning to Freedmen against Intoxicating Drinks* [1865]; Helen E. Brown, *John Freeman and His Family* (1864); Jared Bell Waterbury, *Southern Planters and the Freedmen* [1866?]; Clinton B. Fisk, *Plain Counsels for Freedmen: In Sixteen Brief Lectures* [1866], among others. All were published in New York by the American Tract Society.
30. For a full description and analysis of the American Tract Society texts, see Ronald Butchart, *Northern Schools, Southern Blacks, and Reconstruction,* 136–51.
31. Samuel Chapman Armstrong, "Lessons from the Hawaiian Islands," in Edith Armstrong Talbot, *Samuel Chapman Armstrong: A Biographical Study* (New York: Doubleday, Page and Co., 1904), 213–14.
32. Anderson, *Education of Blacks in the South,* 33–78; William H. Watkins, *The White Architects of Black Education: Ideology and Power in America, 1865– 1954* (New York: Teachers College Press, 2001), 43–61 and 98–117.
33. The careers and practices of the early graduates of Black teacher training can be pieced together from H. W. Ludlow, ed., *Twenty-Two Years' Work of the Hampton Normal and Agricultural Institute at Hampton, Virginia.* (Hampton,

VA: Normal School Press, 1893); Carkin, "Reminiscences...," especially the letters reproduced in vol. 2; the thousands of "Teacher's Monthly Reports" in the records of the Bureau of Refugees, Freedmen, and Abandoned Lands; teachers' reports in state archives; and many other sources.
34. Anderson, *Education of Blacks in the South*, 33–78.
35. See, for example, Jerome E. Morris and Carla R. Monroe, "Why Study the U.S. South? The Nexus of Race and Place in Investigating Black Student Achievement," *Educational Researcher* 38 (January/February 2009): 21–36; Morris, *Troubling the Waters: Fulfilling the Promise of Quality Public Schooling for Black Children* (New York: Teachers College Press, 2009); David W. Stinson, "Negotiating Sociocultural Discourses: The Counter-Storytelling of Academically (and Mathematically) Successful African American Male Students," *American Educational Research Journal* 45 (December 2008): 975–1010; Stinson, "African American Male Adolescents, Schooling (and Mathematics): Deficiency, Rejection, and Achievement," *Review of Educational Research* 76 (Winter 2006): 477–506.

CHAPTER TWO

THE RACIAL AND CULTURAL ASSUMPTIONS
OF THE EARLY SOCIAL STUDIES
EDUCATORS, 1901–1922

Thomas D. Fallace

For curriculum historians hoping to dismiss the idea of the social studies, there has been no easier target than sociologist Thomas Jesse Jones, who headed the 1916 National Education Association (NEA) Committee on Social Studies. The narrative posited by William Watkins, Diane Ravitch, Michael Lybarger, and Herbert Kliebard generally includes the following: Jones studied sociology under the mentorship of the Spencerian positivist Franklin Giddings.¹ Based on this racist sociology, Jones constructed the social studies program at the Hampton Institute for Southern Blacks and Native Americans to teach these groups to be submissive and accept the inferior roles they were destined to fill in the emerging modern economy. Rather than empower these minorities with an academic curriculum—as W. E. B. Du Bois was proposing—Jones, and the Northern philanthropists who supported him, chose to offer a vocational curriculum meant to keep these groups in their place. Having achieved praise and success with the Hampton model, the NEA called upon Jones to implement this program in all United States schools in order to inculcate immigrant and non-college-bound students with the very same values of submissiveness and assimilation he had used at Hampton. Consequently, the 1916 Committee on Social Studies Report—the document generally believed to have launched the social studies movement in US public schools—is viewed by Watkins, Ravitch, Lybarger, and Kliebard as elitist, because it was aimed at preparing immigrants and the urban poor to work submissively in the emerging industrial economy; conservative, because it was aimed at recreating, not challenging, existing class structures; and perhaps even inherently racist, because it denied college preparatory academic content to those who were regarded as biologically and culturally inferior.²

This assessment is not necessarily wrong, but it is too simplistic and tidy. Asserting that Jones was elitist and racist tells us very little, because so were virtually all progressive White scholars at the time, including the other major influences on the 1916 report, Arthur Dunn, James Harvey Robinson, and even, to an extent, John Dewey.[3] In this chapter, I demonstrate that the influential members of the Committee on Social Studies were united in their linear historicist view of race and culture. Specifically, I demonstrate how these progressive scholars all viewed African American and Native American populations as biologically and psychically equal, but socially, culturally, and ethically disadvantaged and deficient. The founders of the social studies approached these non-White cultures as being in need of development, as prior steps towards the industrialized, democratic society of the West. This position was not only reflected in the written work and curricula of the founders, but it also found its way into the most popular textbooks, including those used in the Problems of Democracy course—the senior capstone class recommended by the 1916 NEA Committee on Social Studies, which was designed to engage students in interdisciplinary explorations of current issues and problems.[4] However, unlike many scholars of the period, Jones, Dunn, Robinson, and Dewey espoused a faith in education as a means of improving the cultural deficiencies of racial groups. At the time, the belief in the power of education to transform "inferior" groups was a moderate position, not a conservative one.

Unlike Giddings, the founders believed in the plasticity of racial types and in the ability of education to overcome racial inequality over time. By current standards, this notion was indeed racist, because it denied that African Americans and Native Americans had any cultural contributions to make to American society; it reinforced the idea that these groups were not yet ready to take on the full responsibility of citizenship; and it confirmed the supremacy of White culture and justified racial segregation. But when viewed against the standards of their own time, the authors of the 1916 social studies report held more progressive views than many of their peers.

Race, History, and Progress

The field of the social studies is generally believed to have begun with the publication of the NEA Committee on Social Studies Report in 1916.[5] In the years leading up to that date, there was a continuum of views on the cultural and biological potential of racial minorities. On one end of the spectrum were those who argued that the differences among the races were completely biological, hereditary, deterministic, and fixed. Further along the continuum were those who believed that biology and social environment both played a role in determining racial types and that these types were, in the short term at least, more or less fixed. Further along were those who believed in the psychical and biological equality of all races, but who still considered certain races to be culturally and socially deficient. This cultural deficiency was learned, but in practice it was considered just as debilitating as biological inferiority, because culture exerted such a powerful sociological force on individuals and groups. Finally, there were those who, while maintaining some biological basis for racial types, considered all races to be culturally equal. These pluralists demanded that the cultural contributions of all races be recognized, valued, and celebrated.[6] Of the major authors and influences of the 1916 Social Studies Report, only Dewey ever reached the pluralistic position, and he did so after the field had essentially been established.

Many scholars of the late nineteenth century subscribed to the view that African Americans and American Indians represented earlier, more primitive forms of living that had been abandoned by the more civilized societies. The racial traits of these groups were considered fixed and biologically determined. Drawing upon the work of Charles Darwin and Herbert Spencer, most scholars insisted that all the societies of the world could be placed upon a single continuum of racial development that led from savagery to barbarianism to civilization. As Franklin Giddings explained, "The beliefs and customs of civilized peoples contain many survivals of beliefs and practices that still exist in full force in savage communities. These indicate not only that the civilized nations have developed from savagery, but that existing savage hordes are in a stage of arrested development, and therefore approximate the condition of primitive man."[7] Similarly, leading sociologist Charles Ellwood insisted that socialization of minorities was "at every turn limited, controlled, and modified by a series of instinctive impulses which have become relatively fixed"—a point exemplified by "the negro child, [who] even when reared by a White family under the most favorable conditions, fails to take on the mental and moral characteristics of the Caucasian race."[8] For these influential sociologists, educating racial minorities for professional life was useless, because they did not have the psychological and biological potential to ever achieve the level of civilization necessary for modern democratic living.

Further along the continuum were those scholars who suggested that, although biology indeed played a role in the divergence of races, the cultural and physical environment exerted an equal if not more powerful influence on racial development. Many social scientists, including John Dewey, William I. Thomas, Lester F. Ward, Albion Small, James Mark Baldwin, and Thomas Jesse Jones, believed that these races could be educated and integrated, but they disagreed about the pace and method of this process. "The Negro, for instance, had not been properly prepared for freedom," leading sociologist William I. Thomas explained in 1912, "Enthusiasts for Negro and peasant emancipation did not foresee the loss of control involved in the disturbance of old habits, nor make a proper allowance for the time elements involved in education into new habits."[9] That is, the power of biological and social instincts could be overcome through education, but it would be decades before Blacks would be ready for citizenship, because their inherited instincts would need to be reconditioned through exposure to a more advanced, civilized social environment. At the policy level, careful systemic intervention would be required to allow this transformation to occur.

The third, pluralistic view expressed the belief in the full cultural equality among races. This perspective, expressed most by African American scholars such as W. E. B. Du Bois and Alain Locke, by progressive White scholars such as cultural anthropologist Franz Boas, and by political philosophers Randolph Bourne and Horace Kallen, asserted that racial inferiority was purely the product of socially imposed inequality. Its proponents insisted that there was nothing biologically, inherently, or even culturally inferior about non-White cultures whatsoever. In *The Souls of Black Folk*, Du Bois dismissed the superiority of European civilization as a product of the "arrogance of peoples irreverent toward Time and ignorant of the deeds of man."[10] In 1897, Du Bois defiantly proclaimed, "We believe that the Negro people, as a race, have a contribution to make to civilization and humanity, which no other race can make... it is our duty to conserve our physical powers, our intellectual endowments, our spiritual ideals."[11] Likewise, the ethnographic fieldwork of Boas had demonstrated the complexity and richness of so-called primitive cultures, thereby debunking the Spencerian theory that civilized nations represented more complicated versions of savage and barbarian ones.[12] Bourne and Kallen both directly challenged the idea that newly arrived immigrants needed to assimilate into Anglo-Saxonism.[13] These pluralist scholars posited that cultures of immigrant and native minority populations were equal to that of the majority White Protestant one, and that these groups had cultural contributions to make. However, very few scholars belonged in the pluralist camp. Dewey arrived at the pluralist position only after 1916, and the other founders of the social studies never did.

The Racial Views of Thomas Jesse Jones

Thomas Jesse Jones is generally credited with coining the term "social studies" and with exerting a large influence on the recommendations of the

1916 Committee on Social Studies. Throughout the early twentieth century, Jones was considered the world's foremost authority on the education of African Americans. Although Ravitch, Lybarger, Watkins, and Kliebard have cast Jones's views as similar to, if not identical with, those of Franklin Giddings, his views actually progressed beyond the deterministic thinking of his mentor. Jones agreed that all races could eventually be culturally equal, but believed that one had to respect the biological and social restraints they inherited. According to Jones, in his overview of the social studies program at the Hampton Institute, African and Native Americans were socially backward races; they were unfortunate but innocent victims of history. Through no fault of their own, they had been left behind early in human development, while the cultures of Europe continued to progress beyond them. Reformers needed to be patient, because Native and African Americans had "suddenly been transferred from an earlier form of society into a later one without the necessary time of preparation." As Jones explained, "Natural evolution from one social stage to another requires time."[14] As a result, exposing these "primitive" students to an academic curriculum would be futile and wasteful, because they had not socially evolved far enough to make use of such knowledge and responsibility. Jones reported how, by studying historical development of the races and the sociological study of present races, his Hampton students arrived at this same conclusion.

Jones's view of the political limitations of Blacks must be considered in light of the Dunning historiographical school of Reconstruction, which dominated the field in the early part of the twentieth century. William Dunning, a history professor at Columbia University who was considered the foremost authority on the subject, argued that southern Blacks were innocent victims and pawns in the northern radicals' game of political revenge upon southern Whites. Reconstruction had failed, he argued, because, immediately after the Civil War, illiterate and backward southern Blacks were given political power for which they were not ready. As a result, the South quickly unraveled into chaos and disarray. Having squandered any chance of a peaceful transition to postwar society, the northerners virtually forced southern Whites to implement Black codes and Jim Crow laws to reestablish order.[15] Thus, Dunning's racist historical narrative not only reinforced perceived racial hierarchies, but it depicted southern Blacks as victims of history and confirmed the perception that they were unable to engage in the kind of thinking and action necessary for informed citizenship. This narrative made an enormous impact on the sociological view of African Americans and on race relations. According to Dunning and Jones, the Black race had simply not arrived at the intellectual level necessary for self-governance, a point that the history of the Reconstruction had allegedly proven empirically.

Nevertheless, Jones specifically positioned himself as a moderate between the southerner who thought that African Americans could never catch up and the pluralist who asserted that, "his race is the equal of any race." Jones also demonstrated his belief in the biological restraints of African and Native Americans. "The White youth grows to manhood without feeling any of the limitations which the colored youth feels," he explained, but, on the other hand, Blacks had to cope with the natural inherited impulses that made socialization difficult.

However, the limitations of Blacks and American Indians were not solely due to their inherited impulses. Jones also believed that it was due to the inadequacies of their social environment. Employing Giddings's "law of sympathy," Jones argued that social groups would emulate one another in proportion to the quantity and intensity of a particular trait found in the group. "An appreciation of this law of sympathy," Jones insisted, "contributes greatly to a knowledge of all race divisions."[16] This theory of sympathy was reinforced by one of the most influential books of the 1890s, French sociologist Gabriel Tarde's *The Laws of Imitation*. In this study, Tarde asserted that "Society may...be defined as a group of beings who are apt to imitate one another," an argument that not only reinforced the views of Giddings, but also those of leading social scientists Franz Boas, James Mark Baldwin, Josiah Royce, William I. Thomas, and George Herbert Mead.[17]

According to Jones, imitation via the law of sympathy explained why the limitations of southern Blacks were greater than those of northern Blacks. The law of sympathy acted more intensely upon them because there was a greater concentration of Blacks in the South and a greater intensity of historical persecution.[18] Likewise, the law of sympathy explained why American Indians who had left reservations achieved a higher level of civilization than those who had remained. Only complete immersion in civilized culture, it was believed, could undo hundreds of years of savagery. Consequently, Jones concluded that racial progress occurred only when certain members of the race were isolated from the rest, so they would not regress to their earlier forms. This law of sympathy explained why progress was such a slow, incremental process. This historical narrative of differentiated racial development not only informed the policy of what to teach American Indian and African American students, but also constituted the substance of the curriculum. As Jones explained:

> The study of [the] stages in the development of the social mind and character is of great value to the pupil in that it gives him confidence that the present condition of his people is merely a stage and not a permanent condition; in that it enables him to recognize the weaknesses of his people

the more readily, especially those faults, usually overloaded in eagerness to develop the economic side; and in that it calls his attention to the highest stage towards which he must strive to educate his people, by correcting their faults and encouraging their virtues.[19]

Thus, Jones used history to inform his Hampton students how and why they had arrived at a certain level of inequality and also to inspire them to achieve to higher levels. Inequality was not simply the result of the purely biological inheritance of the race, a theory that Jones believed would hopelessly demoralize his minority students. Instead, the social inferiority of Blacks and American Indians could be explained by their historical circumstances. Social and cultural growth would require sustained access to the moral and cultural milieu of White, civilized society. Only the passage of time could remedy social inequalities, not necessarily individual initiative. The most efficient way to accomplish this progress was to prepare his Hampton students for the inferior roles they would likely take in the integrated society. As misguided as this perspective may seem, the version of history Jones presented was specifically intended to inspire and empower his minority students, not to oppress them.

The Racial Views of John Dewey

In contrast to Jones and Giddings, Dewey rejected the theory that there was an inherent, latent, and predetermined inferiority of any racial or cultural group. In other words, for Dewey all humans, regardless of race, were psychically and biologically equal. In addition, Dewey rejected the theory of the inheritance of acquired characteristics known as neo-Lamarckianism, which many scholars employed to ascribe biological superiority to Whites. He also rejected the imitation-suggestion theory of French sociologist Gabriel Tarde, who argued that societies passively imitated one another, thus leading to distinct cultural types. For Dewey, humans were not born to achieve any necessary end, nor were they biologically or sociologically predestined to fulfill any cultural role or level. Instead, humans developed through interactions mediated by their social environment. However, like Jones, prior to 1916 Dewey believed that the degree of civilization contained in the mediating environment—arranged hierarchically and coordinated with the psychological stages of the child—determined whether one would develop to be savage or civilized. Consequently, those who were denied access to a civilized, scientific, democratic degree of culture were stuck in an earlier form. All of these earlier cultural groups happened to be non-White. In fact, in Dewey's *Ethics* textbook, coauthored with James Tufts, these earlier groups were identified specifically as "the so-called totem group, which is found among North American Indians, Africans and Australians, and was perhaps the early form of Semitic groups."[20]

Like Jones, Dewey subscribed to the view that the stages of sociological growth corresponded with the psychological stages of child development, and that these earlier, childlike forms still existed as primitive tribes.[21] Dewey wrote to University of Chicago laboratory schoolteacher Clara Mitchell in 1895 that, "practically all stages of civilization are **now** presented somewhere on earth's surface.[22] In *School and Society*, Dewey argued that geography "presents the earth as the enduring home of the occupations of man."[23] Dewey believed that the world still contained all the sociological stages through which Western culture had passed. Therefore, geography should be approached by studying the locations of the occupations representing each stage. As James Tufts explained in the *Ethics* textbook he co-authored with Dewey, "It is beyond question that the ancestors of modern civilized races lived under the general types of group life which will be outlined, and these types of their survivals are found among the great mass of peoples today."[24] To Dewey and Tufts, the world was like a living museum of previous and current stages of racial development (or social occupations), which could be arranged hierarchically along a single continuum from the primitive to barbarian to the civilized.[25]

Dewey translated his historicist ideas into practical suggestions for dealing with racial diversity in classrooms and schools. Specifically, in 1902 he praised "the power of public schools to assimilate different races to our own institutions, through the education given to the younger generation." Dewey even addressed the issue of immigrant parents who resented the acculturative function of US schools because it denigrated their cultural heritage. To solve this problem, Dewey proposed that schools could recognize the cultural elements of students' countries of origin by celebrating the "*historic* meaning in the industrial habits of the older generations—modes of spinning, weaving, metal working, etc.... [that were] disregarded in this country because there was no place for them in our industrial system [italics added]."[26] When these abandoned occupations were appreciated in their own context as "historic," Dewey argued, immigrants would be more likely to adapt to modern ways. Thus, Dewey considered the lifestyles of immigrant families as psychically equivalent, but socially deficient. That is, the immigrant cultures were to be appreciated as prior steps towards the more advanced modern, scientific, democratic culture of the United States, but not as culturally unique perspectives to be celebrated, valued, and maintained, as pluralists like Du Bois and Boas suggested. Because Dewey equated culture with social occupations, all the cultures of the world could be arranged hierarchically, based upon the degree to which they had subordinated their environment and contributed to social progress.

However, after 1916, Dewey began to focus more on the significance of plurality in the environment as a necessity for actualizing potentials. In Chapter Seven of *Democracy and Education*, Dewey outlined his pluralist vision for a democratic society, one in which the ideas and cultures of multiple groups were "mutually interpenetrating."[27] He revised his philosophical approach to make the preservation of cultural difference a necessity for actualizing the potentials of the individual and the society. After 1916, the linear historicist aspects of his work became less important, and the genetic psychological aspects of his work dropped out altogether. His pedagogy became less historical and more presentist, his philosophy became less psychological and more anthropological, and his views of evolution and race became less linear and more pluralist. As a result, he reconstructed his views into a form more palatable to readers of the twenty-first century. However, this significant transformation did not take place until after Dewey had already exerted his influence on the founders of the social studies, especially on Arthur Dunn.

The Racial Views of Arthur Dunn and James Harvey Robinson

Arthur Dunn served as the secretary for the Commission on Social Studies, and in 1916 was the United States Bureau of Education Specialist in Civic Education. Many of the ideas he had helped implement in Indianapolis schools made their way into the 1916 NEA Committee on Social Studies Report. Dunn wrote little about race, but the reader can infer some of his views from how and why he cited Dewey and the specific pedagogical recommendations he made. In his 1907 text *The Community and Citizen*, Dunn declared that "no better preparation can be made" for the reading of his text than "a careful reading of Professor Dewey's 'Ethical Principles Underlying Education,' quoted in the preface, and 'The School and Society' by the same author."[28] In both of these texts, Dewey outlined his rationale for setting up the curriculum as a historical reenactment of the history of the human race. That is, Dewey outlined how and why children should retrace the history of the race from savagery to barbarianism to civilization.[29]

In *School and Society*, Dewey explained the pedagogical significance of his repeating the race experience approach. "We can trace and follow the progress of mankind in history, getting an insight also into the materials used and the mechanical principles involved," Dewey reasoned, "In connection with these occupations[,] the historic development of man is recapitulated." Dewey argued that his linear historicist approach aligned with the latest psychological and anthropological research on primitive societies. Like developing savages, Dewey related how students "go on through imagination through the hunting to the semi-agricultural stage, through the nomadic to the settled agricultural stage."[30] Similarly, in *Ethical Principles Underlying Education*, Dewey insisted that "a study of still simpler forms of hunting, nomadic and agricultural life in the beginnings of civilization; a study of the effects of the introduction of iron, iron tools, and so forth, serves to reduce the existing complexity to its simple forms."[31] The idea was that the historical content presented to students would not be historical as such, but rather would be presented as immediate problems, which also happened to have historical and scientific significance. After students had mastered the corresponding form and content for each psychological and sociological stage, they would eventually arrive at the modernist stage of civilization, which included the introduction of the techniques of the professional and/or expert. However, this content was to be taught sequentially in the same order that the race had originally discovered it. As a result, the cultures of non-White "primitive" societies (semi-agricultural, agricultural, nomadic) were approached as prior steps towards the culture of the industrialized West.

Drawing upon the ideas Dewey presented in these two works, Dunn subscribed to a similar linear view of cultural development. For example, in *The Community and the Citizen*, Dunn made reference to shortcomings of the "savage tribes" who put to death their sick. But "as men become civilized," Dunn assured his readers, civilized man learned to be more compassionate for the weak and helpless.[32] Most readers of the time would have read the term "savage" not only as a reference to the ancestors of Western civilization, but also as a reference to the present native and aboriginal societies of Africa, North and South America, and Australia. Dunn incorporated these ideas into his recommendations for the Indianapolis public schools, for which he served as a consultant. Dunn argued that the Indianapolis schools had not been doing an adequate job of making the content of civic education relevant to students, especially in the elementary grades.

To reform the curriculum in light of Dewey's psychology, Dunn suggested the use of the book *Robinson Crusoe*, so students could identify with the "story of a single-handed struggle with nature, emphasizing by contrast our dependence upon community life." To underscore the contrast between primitive and civilized culture, Dunn suggested that the students should study the superiority of the social nature of "their own home life." After *Robinson Crusoe*, Dunn explained, students should study "Hiawatha's childhood...giving opportunity for a study of Indian family life and a comparison of it with their own home life and the life of Robinson Crusoe." They should follow these activities by engaging "in clay work and basketry, making objects suggested by the story of Robinson Crusoe and Hiawatha"—not to learn from these primitive examples on their own terms, but rather to appreciate their *historic* significance and to understand how modern White society had advanced far beyond savagery by engaging in social and cooperative work.[33] Dunn believed that by comparing primitive and modern life, students would grow to see the advantages of industrialization and socialization; therefore, the study of the cultural history of the entire human race, which Dewey advocated, served as the organizational scheme for the entire elementary curriculum that Dunn recommended. The curriculum was meant to justify and idealize the industrializing modern economy and the students' place at the forefront of this process.

In addition to Dewey and Dunn, James Harvey Robinson also believed that savage societies still roamed the earth, were culturally equivalent to children, and could provide insight into the development of Western civilization. Robinson, who also served on the NEA Committee on Social Studies, was one of the most respected historians in the United States, and his textbooks on European and world history were widely used. In his book *The New History*, which was quoted repeatedly in the 1916 social studies report, Robinson argued that much could be learned about the evolution of the civilized society by studying "the savage that exists on the earth at the present time." Like Dewey, Robinson argued that "inferences...may be made [between] the reasoning of the savage and the progressive unfolding of the infant's mind."[34] In his popular textbook *Medieval and Modern Times*, in which Robinson employed his "new" historical approach of tracing the social and cultural—instead of merely the political and military—history of Western Europe, he referenced the encounters between European explorers and the "savage natives" and "savage red men."[35] These interactions were not merely clashes of cultures, but rather clashes between a civilized culture and a socially backward one.

In summary, the racial views of Jones, Dewey, Robinson, and Dunn shared five common themes. First, all of the societies of the world, past and present, could be subsumed in a single linear scale of cultural development, beginning with savagery, moving to barbarianism, and culminating with civilization. That is, all the cultures of the world were not merely different, but instead were different degrees of a single transracial culture that just happened to have been authored and led by civilized Whites. Second, all native, aboriginal, and African American societies were culturally deficient; they represented earlier, historic steps towards the West and so, as a result, they were considered undeveloped, underdeveloped, inchoate, and primitive by the standards of White civilization. Next, the stages of sociological development more or less corresponded with the stages of psychological development of a human being from childhood to adulthood. Consequently, non-White societies were considered the cultural equivalent of children or adolescents. Fourth, even though all humans were more or less biologically and psychically equivalent, the social and cultural environment exerted a powerful force on the individual. Therefore, individuals from culturally deficient societies and races were not yet ready to take on the full responsibilities of citizenship until they transcended the limitations of their cultural deficiency. Finally, the founders of the social studies believed that education was the only force that could eventually civilize the deficient American races and the only way to solve the race problem. However, the political equality of Native and African Americans was a goal to be achieved at some undetermined future time, when the different races were fully "ready."

Although the Committee on Social Studies' 1916 report was not about race and did not address race directly, these five ideas represented the hidden assumptions the authors brought to the influential document. It would be an exaggeration to say that the authors of the social studies report deliberately sought to perpetuate racial inequality, but their ideas did reflect and reinforce a set of cultural assumptions about the cultural inferiority of non-White social groups. These assumptions, in turn, created a context in which the social oppression and political disenfranchisement of Native and African Americans could be maintained into the near future. Even though the members of the Committee on Social Studies endorsed a curricular vision based on critical thinking, social problems, and relevance, they did not identify racial inequality as major issue to be critically analyzed. In fact, most social scientists of the time agreed that the race problem, as it was called, was overwhelming and unsolvable in the short term.

Race and the Problems of Democracy Course

The logical place for the authors of the social studies report to address the race problem was in the recommended senior capstone class, the Problems of Democracy (POD). The National Education Association Committee on Social Studies specifically designed the POD course to address relevant and enduring social problems. Its purpose was for high school seniors to explore contemporary social problems through interdisciplinary study. However, it did not specifically list the inequality of Native Americans and African Americans as an issue or a relevant topic to be covered. In fact, the report was completely silent on issues of race and racial inequality.

As outlined, both Dewey and Dunn made pedagogical recommendations based on the ethnocentric, linear approach to cultural development. The curricula described in *Schools of To-morrow* by John and Evelyn Dewey demonstrate that innovative schools in Indiana, Missouri, and Illinois had also set up their curricula as historical reenactments of the human race, which traced cultural development from the primitive stage to the civilized stage.[36] However, it is difficult to determine to what degree schools adopted this ethnocentric curriculum framework at the local level, beyond these documented examples. Evidence of classroom practice during this time is rare.

There were several prejudice-reduction programs associated with the intercultural education movement in the 1920s that were adopted at the local level. Intercultural education directly targeted ethnocentric and stereotypical perceptions about racial/national groups by teaching the cultural contributions each group had to offer to American life. These materials eventually made their way into hundreds of classrooms.[37] In addition, educational materials produced by immigrant groups themselves reflected a perspective dubbed "patriotic pluralism" by historian Jeffrey Mirel, in which the immigrants' desire to assimilate coexisted with the effort to retain many cultural attributes of their native country.[38] However, "patriotic pluralism" and intercultural education did not really take hold until the late 1920s. Furthermore, both movements largely ignored the cultural contributions of non-White communities, and both movements tended to reinforce an essentialist view of culture that reduced racial groups to the "cultural gifts" of their nations of origin. Despite these efforts at teaching racial and cultural tolerance, prior to 1922 most teaching materials continued to reflect the hierarchical view of cultures outlined above. As a result, social studies materials of the period largely reinforced the ethnocentric assumptions of the founders.

We have already seen the dismissive use of the term "savage" by James Harvey Robinson; his textbooks were some of the most widely used of the period. However, Robinson never stated his racial views as baldly as David Saville Muzzey. In his textbook *An American History*, by far the most widely adopted text in the United States around the time of the founding of the social studies program, Muzzey espoused similar ethnocentric and racist views. He insisted that Native Americans "had generally reached a stage of development called 'lower barbarianism,' a stage of pottery making and rude agricultural science...like the Mississippi negro of today." Muzzey believed that both Native Americans and African Americans were stuck in an earlier form of development. At the end of the book, Muzzey specifically reflected on the "growing problem of relations to inferior races." He lamented how "we" [White Americans], have a "race problem" greater than any other nation, because negroes are "perhaps a century behind whites in civilization."[39] Muzzey was a historian who only commented on the race problem when it related to the history of Whites. Many historians, on the other hand, simply ignored the "race problem" altogether. The discipline that dealt most directly with the race problem was sociology.

Sociologists generally subscribed to the same five assumptions about race and culture outlined earlier, and these ideas found their way into the textbooks used in social studies classrooms, including the POD course.[40] The POD course was the most original and progressive idea presented by the Committee on Social Studies. Because it took nearly a decade for authors to publish books specifically for the POD class, most schools used civics textbooks such as Howard Copeland Hill's *Community Life and Civic Problems* and Ray Oswald Hughes's *Community Civics,* and sociology textbooks such as Charles Ellwood's *Sociology and Modern Social Problems* and Henry Reed Burch and S. Howard Patterson's *American Social Problems*.[41]

The most popular textbooks of the period included references to the cultural deficiency of non-White social groups. For example, Hill's civics text noted that one of the chief causes of the "lack of progress among backwards peoples of the earth," such as African Americans, was their failure to overcome their immediate bodily needs.[42] Hughes's civics text included a section on the "melting pot" in which the author listed the problems of assimilating "the Yellow Man," the "Black Man," and the "Red Man." He explained, "Some Indians, especially the tribes now living in Oklahoma, have shown great capacity for progress in civilization." Yet other Indians, Hughes lamented, such as those who refused to wear white collars and who continued to "live as they did a thousand years ago" would never be assimilated. He concluded that Native Americans had progressed the farthest toward civilization because "no one thinks of the race difference between them and the whites as he does between the whites and the yellow or black men."[43] Thus, Hughes reinforced a racial hierarchy of progress that extended from White to Red to Yellow to Black. In addition, these books related the assumptions of the Dunning historiographical school, either directly or indirectly, by explaining how during Reconstruction, Blacks had demonstrated that they were not prepared for the responsibility of full citizenship because they were socially and culturally backward.

Charles Ellwood's sociology text devoted an entire chapter to "The Negro Problem," in which he asserted his belief that heredity played a bigger role in racial differentiation than many other scholars had acknowledged. "It is obvious," he insisted, "...that the Negro may, on the side of his instinctive and hereditary equipment, be inferior to the White man in his natural adaptiveness to a complex civilization..."[44] Ellwood traced many of the undesirable traits Blacks allegedly had to their historic African and enslaved lifestyles. Thus, he argued that they were not inherently inferior; they were just not a good fit with modern society, because their instincts had been formed under such different social and cultural conditions. Burch and Patterson's sociology text also devoted a chapter specifically to the race problem. They reiterated Ellwood's view that "the natural selection of a tropical environment... has produced in the Negro qualities which cannot be overcome by a few centuries of civilization." The authors explained how the African slave's "moral ideals were low and their conception of family undeveloped," and how slavery "hindered the development of [Black men's] independent manhood." As a result, Negroes were "childish" and were characterized by "an unconscious exaggeration and untruthfulness." Ultimately, the authors of the textbooks commonly assigned in the POD course reinforced the conception of Native Americans and African Americans as underdeveloped, childlike races in need of social development. These races were, in the words of Burch and Patterson, "a natural people" who might "lapse into barbarism."[45] Not only did these authors lament the unfortunate political power provided Blacks during Reconstruction, but they consistently praised the work being done at Jones's Hampton Institute, as well as the vocational orientation of Booker T. Washington. They supported the education being provided for African Americans, but doubted that they would culturally progress towards civilization any time in the near future.

Conclusion

Jones, Dewey, Dunn, and Robinson believed that Native American and African American societies were culturally deficient because they represented earlier primitive forms of living that had been surpassed and abandoned by Western culture. Although they disagreed about the degree to which these deficiencies were biologically based, they agreed that these deficient groups were in need of careful and deliberate development under the supervision of the "civilized," before they could contribute positively to American society. However, the fact that the founders believed in education as a means of helping these groups achieve full acculturation reflected their conviction that all races had the potential to arrive at social equality eventually. This belief in education as a means of uplifting racial groups put the founders of the social studies at odds with proponents of the eugenics movement, who found popular support through such books as Madison Grant's *Passing of the Great Race* and Lothrop Stoddard's *The Rising Tide of Color*.[46] It also reflected a more liberal position than the sociologist authors of POD textbooks such as Ellwood, Burch, and Patterson. In other words, Jones, Robinson, Dunn, and Dewey were less ethnocentric than many of their contemporaries, because they largely denied the biological constraints of race, but they were, nevertheless, ethnocentric in their belief in the social deficiency of non-White groups. The belief in the cultural deficiency of non-White groups rationalized and reinforced the political and social disenfranchisement of African Americans and Native Americans.

To what extent were the racial and cultural views of the founders of the social studies reflected in classroom materials? Although race was never a central issue in most White schools, these ideas did find their way into the classroom. The average US student in a social studies class may have very likely have read Robinson's *Medieval and Modern Times,* Muzzey's *An American History,* and Ellwood's *Sociology and Modern Social Problems* over the course of their schooling, because these were some of the most widely adopted texts in the country. As a result, s/he would have been exposed to repeated references to the "savagery" and "primitiveness" of contemporary African Americans and American Indians. In addition, had the student attended an elementary school like those described by Dewey and Dunn, his or her curriculum might very well have been set up as a linear reenactment of the cultural development of the human race through the stages of savagery, barbarianism, and civilization. Therefore, many students would have viewed the cultures of African Americans and Native Americans as lifestyles that had been deliberately abandoned and overcome by the more civilized Western world. The ethnocentric, racist idea that all of the world's societies could be placed hierarchically on a single, linear scale of cultural development heavily influenced the content and pedagogy of nearly all scholars of the period, including the first generation of social studies educators. Scholars who have pointed to the elitist and ethnocentric views of the early social studies educators are correct in their assessment. However, they overlook some of the complexity, fluidity, and inconsistency of their views. Then, as now, racism and ethnocentrism were not dichotomous either/or positions, but rather qualified, nuanced arguments. Although the founders of the social studies fell short of the pluralism of Du Bois and Boas, they were still more progressive than many of their peers including, as evident from this research, the sociologist authors of the first textbooks used in the Problems of Democracy course.

Notes

1. Franklin H. Giddings was a leading nineteenth-century American sociologist at Columbia University. Giddings was best known for his theory of "consciousness of kind" as the basis of all social development and differentiation.
2. See William Watkins, *The White Architects of Black Education: Ideology and Power in America, 1865–1954* (New York: Teachers College Press, 2001); Diane Ravitch, *Left Back: A Century of Battles over School Reform* (New York: Simon & Schuster, 2000); Michael Lybarger, "The Political Context of the Social Studies: Creating a Constituency for Municipal Reform," *Theory and*

Research in Social Education, 8 (Fall 1980), 1–28; Herbert Kliebard, *Changing Course: American Curriculum Reform in the 20th Century* (New York: Teachers College Press, 2002).
3. Thomas Fallace, "John Dewey and the Origins of the Social Studies: An Analysis of the Historiography and New Interpretation," *Review of Educational Research,* 79 (June 2009): 601–624.
4. By the 1930s, the Problems of Democracy course had been adopted by about a third of US schools. See Thomas D. Fallace, "Did the Social Studies Really Replace History in American Secondary Schools?" *Teachers College Record,* 109 (December 2008): 2245–2270.
5. The Committee on Social Studies report was published in 1916 as part of the Commission on the Reorganization of Secondary Education, commonly referred to as the *Cardinal Principles.* The 1916 report recommended a new scope and sequence of history and civics courses, which was meant to replace the existing curriculum, which most schools had based on the recommendations of the NEA's 1893 Committee of Ten and/or the American Historical Association's (AHA) 1899 Committee of Seven. Thomas Jesse Jones, James Harvey Robinson, Arthur Dunn, and John Dewey are generally regarded as the biggest influences on the contents of the report.
6. See Alex R. Schafer, "W. E. B. Du Bois, German Social Thought, and the Racial Divide in American Progressivism," *Journal of American History* 88 (Dec 2001): 925–949; Mathew Frye Jacobson, *Whiteness of a Different Color: European Immigrants and the Alchemy of Race* (Cambridge, MA: Harvard University Press, 1998); James B. McKee, *Sociology and the Race Problem: Failure of a Perspective* (Urbana, IL: University of Illinois Press, 1993); Dorothy Ross, *The Origins of American Social Science* (New York: Cambridge University Press, 1991); Robert Richards, *Darwin and the Emergence of Evolutionary Theories of Mind and Behavior* (Chicago: University of Chicago Press, 1987); Stephen Jay Gould, *Ontogeny and Phylogeny* (Cambridge, MA: Belnap, 1977); George Stocking Jr., *Race, Culture and Evolution: Essays in the History of Anthropology* (Chicago: University of Chicago Press, 1968); Thomas F. Gossett, *Race: The History of an Idea in America* (New York: Shocken, 1963).
7. Quoted in Watkins, *The White Architects of Black Education,* 73, 75.
8. Charles Ellwood, "The Theory of Imitation in Social Psychology," *American Journal of Sociology* 6 (May 1901); 735.
9. William I. Thomas, "Race Psychology: Standpoint and Questionnaire, With Particular Reference to the Immigrant and the Negro," *American Journal of Sociology* 17 (May 1912), 726, 736.
10. Quoted in David Levering Lewis, *W. E. B. Du Bois: Biography of a Race* (New York: Henry Holt, 1993), 286.
11. W. E. B. Du Bois, "The Conservation of the Races (1897)," in *W. E. B. Du Bois: Writings,* ed. Nathan Hughes (New York: Viking Press, 1986), 825, 822.
12. Franz Boas, *The Mind of Primitive Man,* revised 2nd edition (New York: Macmillan, 1938).
13. See Louis Menand, *The Metaphysical Club: A Story of Ideas in America* (New York: Farrar, Straus, and Giroux, 2001).
14. Thomas Jesse Jones, *Social Studies in the Hampton Curriculum* (Hampton, VA: Hampton Institute Press, 1908), 4.

15. William Archibald Dunning, *Reconstruction: Political and Economic, 1865–1877* (New York: Harper and Brothers, 1907).
16. Jones, *Social Studies*, 5, 47.
17. On Tarde's influence, see Ruth Leys, "Mead's Voices: Imitation as Foundation; or the Struggle against Mimesis," in *Modernist Impulses in the Human Sciences 1870–1930*, ed., Dorothy Ross (Baltimore: Johns Hopkins University Press, 1991), 213.
18. Jones, *Social Studies*, 5, 47.
19. Ibid., 47.
20. John Dewey and James H. Tufts, *Ethics*, in *John Dewey: The Middle Works*, vol. 5 of *The Collected Works of John Dewey*, ed. Jo Ann Boydston (Carbondale: Southern Illinois University Press, 1976), 25, 26. [original publ. date 1908]
21. See Watkins, *The White Architects of Black Education*; McKee, *Sociology and the Race Problem*; Gould, *Ontogeny and Phylogeny*; Stocking, *Race, Culture and Evolution*.
22. John Dewey, to Clara Mitchell, 29 Nov. 1895 (record 00272) in *The Correspondence of John Dewey, Vol 1: 1871–1918*. Third edition CD-ROM version, ed. Larry Hickman (Carbondale: Center for Dewey Studies, Southern Illinois University, 2005). Underline was in the original letter.
23. John Dewey, *The Child and the Curriculum and The School and Society* (Chicago: University of Chicago Press, 1969), 19. [*The School and Society* was originally published in 1899; *The Child and the Curriculum* was originally published in 1902.]
24. John Dewey and James H. Tufts, "Ethics," 23.
25. Thomas Fallace, "John Dewey and the Savage Mind: Uniting Anthropological, Psychological and Pedagogical Thought, 1894–1902," *The Journal of the History of Behavioral Sciences*, 44 (Summer 2008): 335–349, and "Repeating the Race Experience: John Dewey and the History Curriculum at the University of Chicago Laboratory School," *Curriculum Inquiry*, 39 (June 2009): 381–405.
26. John Dewey, "The School as Social Centre (1902)," in *John Dewey: The Middle Works*, vol. 2 of *The Collected Works of John Dewey*, ed. Jo Ann Boydston (Carbondale: Southern Illinois University Press, 1979), 85–86.
27. John Dewey, *Democracy and Education: An Introduction to Philosophy of Education* (New York: Free Press, 1916), 87.
28. Arthur Dunn, *The Community and the Citizen* (New York: Heath and Company, 1907), vi.
29. See Fallace, "Repeating the Race Experience."
30. John Dewey, *The School and Society*, 20, 19, 53. Evidence of linear historicism at the Dewey School can also be found in Katherine Camp Mayhew and Alice Camp Edwards, *The Dewey School: The Laboratory School of the Univeristy of Chicago, 1896–1903* (New York: Appleton-Century, 1936).
31. Ibid., 21.
32. Dunn, *The Community and the Citizen*, 153–54.
33. Department of the Interior, Bureau of Education, *Educational Survey of Elyria, Ohio* (Washington, DC: Government Printing Office, 1918), 181.
34. James Harvey Robinson, *New History: Essays Illustrating the Modern Historical Outlook* (New York: Macmillan, 1912), 252, 108.

35. James Harvey Robinson, *Medieval and Modern Times* (Ginn and Company, 1916), 221, 431.
36. John and Evelyn Dewey, "Schools of To-Morrow (1915)," in *John Dewey: The Middle Works*, vol. 8 of *The Collected Works of John Dewey*, ed. Jo Ann Boydston (Carbondale: Southern Illinois University Press, 1979), 244, 260, 369–70.
37. See Zoe Burkholder, *Color in the Classroom: How American Schools Taught Race, 1900–1954* (New York: Oxford University Press, 2011), 15–43; Diana Selig, *Americans All: The Cultural Gifts Movement* (Cambridge, MA: Harvard University Press, 2008), 68–112.
38. See Jeffrey Mirel, *Patriotic Pluralism: Americanization Education and European Immigrants* (Cambridge, MA: Harvard University Press, 2010).
39. David Saville Muzzey, *An American History* (New York: Ginn and Company, 1911), 23, 619.
40. See McKee, *Sociology and the Race Problem*.
41. These texts were selected because they were the most popular in the North Central States according to a 1922 survey. This region was not necessarily representative of the entire nation. See Walter Monroe and I.O. Foster, *The Status of the Social Sciences in High Schools and the North Central Association* (Urbana, IL: University of Illinois Press, 1922), 30–36.
42. Howard Copeland Hill, *Community Life and Civic Problems* (New York: Ginn and Company, 1922), 333.
43. Ray Oswald Hughes, *Community Civics* (New York: Allyn and Bacon, 1917), 403.
44. Charles A. Ellwood, *Sociology and Modern Social Problems* (New York: American Book Company, 1919), 249.
45. Henry Reed Burch and S. Howard Patterson, *American Social Problems: An Introduction to The Study of Society* (New York: Macmillan, 1920), 126, 128, 129, 136.
46. Madison Grant, *The Passing of the Great Race, or the Racial Basis for European History* (New York: Charles Scribner's Sons, 1916); Lothrop Stoddard's *The Rising Tide of Color: Against White World Supremacy* (New York: Charles Scribner's Sons, 1920).

Chapter Three
The Early Years of Negro History Week, 1926–1950

Sarah Bair

In February 1926, a broad collection of schools and communities in the United States celebrated Negro History Week for the first time. For the next 50 years, Negro History Week continued to grow in scope and to develop as a launching pad for other initiatives designed to popularize the study of African American history. In 1976, as the United States commemorated its bicentennial, Negro History Week expanded to Afro-American History Month. Since then, each February, schools around the country have continued to recognize an annual celebration of what is now called Black History Month. Like other "set-aside" months (for example, Women's History Month), Black History Month has its share of supporters and detractors. Its advocates do not consider Black History Month an end in itself; they continue to work toward the goal of a social studies curriculum that fully integrates Black history within courses taught throughout the year. Carter G. Woodson, the educator and historian who first developed the idea of Negro History Week in 1926, spent much of his professional life working toward this same goal. In this chapter, I explore the early years of Negro History Week and examine both Woodson's rationale for the initiative as well as his vision for its implementation as a platform to serve more far-reaching curricular goals.

Many of his contemporaries considered Woodson's Negro History Week to be among his most important achievements, but this initiative represented only a fraction of his work as a historian and a promoter of Black history.[1] Thus, Woodson biographers and other scholars interested in his work typically describe Negro History Week in general terms within the context of his roles as a writer, fund-raiser, and leader of the Association for the Study of Negro Life and History (ASNLH), an organization that he founded in 1915 in Chicago.[2] Maghan Keita in *Race and the Writing of History: Riddling the Sphinx* and August Meier and Elliot Rudwick in *Black History and the Historical Profession*, for example, devote chapters to Woodson in which they describe his approach to Black history and credit him with a central role in the Black history movement in the first half of the twentieth century.[3] Meier and Rudwick's work is especially helpful in detailing the establishment of the ASNLH, in explaining Woodson's fund-raising challenges and describing compromises he made in order to maintain autonomy and raise funds simultaneously, and in situating Woodson within the spectrum of Black scholars of his day, including W. E. B. Du Bois and Booker T. Washington. According to Meier and Rudwick, Woodson's reluctance to espouse a strong philosophical stance on racial advancement, a fact that activists such as Du Bois found puzzling, reflected not so much an acceptance of racial oppression, but rather his scientific approach to writing history and his belief that the facts, properly recorded, would tell their own story.[4]

In his 2007 book, *The Early Black History Movement, Carter G. Woodson, and Lorenzo Greene,* Pero Gaglo Dagbovie takes perhaps the closest look at Negro History Week of any Woodson scholar. Building on an earlier article written for the *Western Journal of Black Studies,* in which he describes how Woodson sought to popularize the study of Black history and to make it more practical and accessible for teachers and community groups, Dagbovie analyzes Negro History Week more fully and calls it Woodson's "most famous and perhaps most effective effort in attracting a mass following and popularizing the study of black history."[5] Dagbovie provides several examples of Negro History Week activities and argues that critics, both in Woodson's day and later, who viewed Woodson's approach as too gradual or conservative failed to accurately assess his goals and to appreciate why he chose the strategies that he did. In his more recent book, *African American History Reconsidered* (2010), Dagbovie suggests that Woodson did indeed become more radical over time, but the author agrees with Meier and Rudwick that the historian's early appearance of conservatism was less a reflection of his political views and more a manifestation of his scientific approach to the study of history.[6] In this chapter, using Woodson's journals, the *Journal of Negro History,* and the *Negro History Bulletin,* as the primary texts, I build on Dagbovie's work and argue that Woodson largely achieved his three primary goals for Negro History Week, which included developing and distributing high-quality resources on African American history, stimulating interest and an appetite for further study and understanding among both Blacks and Whites, and creating a forum in which educators around the country could share ideas and practices.

My analysis of Woodson's program is informed by an examination of the context in which he worked, in addition to literature on his life and work and Dagbovie's descriptions of Negro History Week. Woodson developed his career during a period when many educators and political leaders debated how history should be taught in schools, how textbooks should be written and chosen, and who should be included in the American narrative. Jonathan Zimmerman's *Whose America? Culture Wars in the Public Schools* provides an invaluable, detailed description of these debates. He explains how disagreements among historians, educators, community groups, and civic organizations surrounding the "New History" movement in the 1920s, as well as controversies over specific textbooks such as those by David Muzzey and Charles and Mary Beard, which were deemed overly critical of the founding fathers and too pro-British, led many ethnic groups to weigh in on their respective treatments in history textbooks.[7] Zimmerman describes how a wide array of groups coalesced around the belief that a critique of the nation's founders "weakened the Revolution" and called into question the roles played by other ethnicities in the United States.[8] Even as they concurred in their attack on seemingly pro-British narratives, however, different ethnic groups fought among themselves over a variety of fundamental historical questions, including ones such as who discovered America, Christopher Columbus or Leif Eriksson, Zimmerman notes.[9] Despite their differences, however, these ethnic groups shared European ancestry. For Black Americans and American Indians, history textbooks presented a different set of challenges due not only to omissions, but to obvious inaccuracies and portrayals of inferiority. Zimmerman explains that many individuals and groups, including the NAACP's textbook committee, established in 1932, sought to redress biases, stereotypes, and inaccuracies within the historical record of African Americans.[10] Still, no single individual embodied the cause of Black history more than Carter Woodson.

By 1926, when he initiated the first Negro History Week, Carter Woodson was 51 and had been working for the cause of Black history for almost two decades. After graduating from Berea College, near his hometown of Huntington, West Virginia, in 1903, Woodson began his teaching career, first in West Virginia and later in the Philippines. Between 1907 and 1915, Woodson's growing passion for history, and for Black history in particular, began to emerge fully. He spent six months of 1907 traveling the world and studying history in Europe, which he followed by a year of graduate studies at the University of Chicago. In 1908, he began a doctoral program in history and government at Harvard University. With Albert Bushnell Hart as his advisor, Woodson became well-schooled in the "techniques of professional history" with their emphasis on using evidence and a scientific approach to historical inquiry.[11] While still working on his doctorate, Woodson accepted a teaching position in 1909 in the Washington, DC, public schools and conducted his research at the Library of Congress. After officially completing his doctorate in 1912, Woodson continued to teach at M Street High School in Washington, DC, until 1917.[12]

Both his graduate studies and his teaching experiences shaped Woodson's views on the importance of Black history. During this period in his life, he began to publish his own work on African American history, including his first major book, *The Education of the Negro Prior to 1861: A History of the Education of the Colored People of the United States from the Beginning of Slavery to the Civil War*, which came out in 1915. He also encouraged other Black scholars to help construct the historical record of African Americans in the United States. In 1915, Woodson founded the Association for the Study of Negro Life and History (ASNLH) and began publishing its journal, *The Journal of Negro History*. According to W. D. Wright in his *Black History and Black Identity: A Call for a New Historiography*, Woodson at this time began to envision a movement among both Black and White historians that would promote interest in Black history.[13] Negro History Week emerged under the auspices of the ASNLH a decade later.

Woodson took several concrete steps to ensure the success of the first Negro History Week in 1926. First, he used the press—both Black newspapers and widely distributed mainstream ones such as the *New York Times*—to spread the word of the ASNLH's new initiative. Hoping to cast as wide a net as possible, Woodson sent notices to Black newspapers around the country, including the *Chicago Defender*, the *Pittsburgh Courier*, the *Washington Tribune*, and the *Norfolk Journal and Guide*. These papers continued to cover Negro History Week and other ASNLH events on a regular basis. Second, he appealed directly to historically Black colleges, to state boards of education, and to major school districts, asking that they plan events for the celebration.[14] Finally, he distributed useful Negro History Week materials to schools, colleges, and community groups around the country at no cost, in an effort to build initial support. Recognizing that he could not continue to provide materials in the long run without raising additional funds for the ASNLH, Woodson organized a major fund-raising drive immediately following the first Negro History Week in 1926 and called upon other Black educators to support his efforts. For example, in a February 1926 letter to John Hope, president of Morehouse College in Atlanta, Woodson described the success of the first Negro History Week, explained his plans for a nationwide effort to raise $20,000 to support future events, and encouraged Hope to join his cause.[15] He also enlisted Black newspapers to track the progress of the campaign.[16]

In addition to gaining publicity, raising money, and distributing materials, Woodson recommended a basic, practical structure for Negro History Week that could be widely adopted. First, he encouraged communities to form local chapters of the ASNLH and to set up committees to plan Negro History Week events. Committee membership was to include representatives from schools, churches, clubs, and lodges, with the hope that each of these groups would plan events for the week. Suggested events included speeches, special sermons, concerts, plays, and conferences. Woodson also encouraged local committees to petition their school districts and state boards of education to adopt textbooks on African American history and to encourage their local libraries to purchase appropriate materials, as well. Recognizing the power of visual images, the ASNLH distributed posters and photographs of distinguished African Americans and asked local communities to display them prominently in schools and community centers.[17] In all cases, Woodson viewed Negro History Week events as vehicles for supporting his broader rationale and goals for the study of Black history.

Rationale for Negro History Week

We must tell the story with continually accruing detail from the cradle to the grave. From the mother's knee and the fireside of the home, through the nursery, the kindergarten and the grade school, high school, college and university—through the technical journals, studies and bulletins of the Association—through newspaper, storybook and pictures, we must tell the thrilling story.[18]
—Mary McLeod Bethune, 1938

With these words, written for an article published in Woodson's *Negro History Bulletin* in February 1938, educator and activist Mary McLeod Bethune captures the essence of Woodson's push for the study of Black history generally and for Negro History Week specifically.[19] Strikingly, Bethune's message, like Woodson's earlier calls for a Negro History Week celebration, suggests a multipronged approach to Black history and one that underscores the desire to popularize the movement. Woodson, Bethune, and other supporters of Black history saw that the story of Black people—from their roots in African civilizations, to their resistance and fight against slavery, to their numerous contributions to American society—needed to be researched, published, distributed, and learned by Blacks and Whites alike. This effort would be neither easy nor inexpensive, but, according to Woodson, it was the only way to carry out the important process of racial uplift. Before examining why Woodson viewed the seemingly narrow approach of Negro History Week as an important step in this process, it is useful to review his broader arguments for the study of Black history. An analysis of these arguments will allow the reader to see more clearly how Woodson structured Negro History Week to support these larger goals.

As Meier and Rudwick point out, Woodson, in his support for Black history as a tool for exposing the fallacies within "popular and scientific racism," represented the "convergence of two distinct streams of historical publication: the long tradition of writing on the black past on the part of black intellectuals and polemicists, on the one hand, and the professionalization of American historical study and the triumph of 'scientific history' on the other."[20] Woodson, like his contemporaries across the ideological spectrum, believed in the power of history to promote racial pride and to diminish the impact, especially among schoolchildren, of negative racial stereotyping. At the same time, Woodson, having come of age intellectually in conjunction with the professionalization of history as a field of study, insisted that the best standards of historical scholarship be maintained and that historians of Black history resist the pull of propaganda.[21] Both of these traditions are evident in Woodson's rationale for the study of Black history and in his advocacy of Negro History Week.

At the most basic level, Woodson argued that African Americans needed their history in order to ensure their survival and ability to thrive. He believed that the absence of a written record rendered any group of people vulnerable to marginalization and invisibility at best and to virtual extinction at worst. With no history, Woodson contended, Blacks would have no voice and thus no way to refute the false assumptions, prejudices, and silences that so characterized mainstream history in the first half of the twentieth century, a point he learned well during his studies at Harvard and addressed in his *The Mis-Education of the Negro*, published in 1933.[22] In an April 1926 article for *The Journal of Negro History,* in which Woodson commented on the inaugural Negro History Week, he stated, "If a race has no history, if it has no worth-while tradition, it becomes a negligible factor in the thought of the world, and it stands in danger of being exterminated."[23] Using other groups as examples, he made this case repeatedly in his effort to gain support for his cause. Most often, he lamented the case of American Indians who, with little written record of their own traditions, had been written out of mainstream American history almost entirely. Without significant intervention, Blacks, he believed, were in danger of being on a similar path.[24]

Second, Woodson argued that the traditional historical record, taught in both White and Black schools at the time, severely distorted reality and needed to be corrected in the name of historical accuracy. As an important first step in mitigating this problem, Woodson called for increased attention to the development of Black history archives. He often used Negro History Week literature as a platform to reinforce this position and to encourage local communities across the country to take on the responsibility of gathering historical artifacts. In the Negro History Week pamphlet produced in 1936, for example, Woodson included a lengthy excerpt from a September 9, 1935, speech given in Chicago by his longtime associate, Charles H. Wesley, to commemorate the twentieth anniversary of the founding of the ASNLH. Emphasizing the need for a "reconstruction of history," Wesley explained that there would be no hope of refuting false assumptions and supplying relevant facts about the lives and achievements of Blacks if the facts had been thrown away.[25] In his early appeals for money, Woodson argued that Whites were spending $1,000,000 per year toward archiving materials and writing history while Blacks could not seem to raise a mere $20,000 for their efforts. For rhetorical effect he would ask, "Are our needs only 1/50 of theirs?"[26] Only through the collection, organization, and distribution of historical artifacts, an effort that would require financial resources, could Blacks begin to correct the record.

In his 1936 report on Negro History Week, Woodson noted that the records of other peoples had been well preserved in capitals around the world, but that nothing of the sort had been done for African Americans. By 1936, the Association had established a small collection at the Library of Congress, but Woodson hoped that this "nucleus" could be significantly expanded and that local communities as well as colleges and universities would begin to build their own collections by recovering and cataloging letters, wills, diaries, deeds, and other unpublished manuscripts. At the same time, Woodson cautioned his readers to be discriminating in their evaluation of sources and to be sure to "separate the dross from the gold" as they sought to reconstruct family and community histories. In keeping with his support of "scientific history," Woodson routinely emphasized that minor facts should not be exaggerated in importance.[27]

Finding the correct balance between one end of the spectrum that ignored Black history altogether and the other that gave disproportionate credit to minor achievements became a point of emphasis for Woodson. In his very first report on Negro History Week in 1926, he noted that history shows all races to be imbued with vices and virtues and that no good comes from overstating the accomplishments of one race at the expense of another. Noting that there should be "no undue eulogy of the Negro," Woodson argued that the purpose of Negro History Week should be to correct the record, but not to overcorrect it.[28] He believed that if a complete rendition of the facts could be clearly and compellingly stated, they would speak for themselves. Writing of Negro History Week in 1928, he offered the following cautionary words to educators:

> Any tendency to eulogize the Negro unduly or to leave the impression that the race has done more than some other group that has done its best would be decidedly unwise. The purpose of this celebration is to disabuse the public mind of this very sort of bias. The record of the Negro is well taken care of if the race is given the same consideration which is accorded to others.[29]

Throughout his career, in reports on Negro History Week published in the *Journal of Negro History* and later in the teacher-oriented *Negro History Bulletin*, Woodson maintained that Black history should be told without the bias that had so long characterized mainstream history.

Finally, Woodson argued that a better understanding of Black history could begin to undo the harm of negative racial stereotyping and the resultant inferiority complex among Black children that had been caused by poor schooling. Woodson worked especially hard, through Negro History Week and other initiatives, to bring the voices of Black historians into schools in order to mitigate some of the damage being inflicted on Black students. While being taught to "admire the Hebrew, the Greek, the Latin, and the Teuton and to despise the African," an African American child, Woodson argued, had "the thought of the inferiority of the Negro drilled into him directly or indirectly in almost every social science subject which he studied."[30] Ironically, Woodson believed that, in terms of racial identity, a Black child who left school after mastering the fundamentals might be better off than one who continued in school, because the biases would be less deeply ingrained. In fact, in his 1931 report on Negro History Week in *The Journal of Negro History*, Woodson argued that the very people who would be in the best position to move the race forward—that is, Blacks who had spent the most time in top colleges—rarely took up the cause for racial uplift because they had been taught nothing of their own history and had learned only that the way to advance was to emulate Whites.[31] Because educated Blacks were taught in ways that emphasized classical historical learning, they did not have the expertise in Black History to refute claims of historical White superiority. In many cases, they perpetuated these claims and felt no obligation to "give back" to their communities.

Woodson considered it sadly ironic that large Historically Black Colleges and Universities were often the ones with the least interest in Negro History Week because, according to him, the leaders of these institutions had been trained to teach the Negro "only about others."[32] Woodson claimed that because they themselves have been "educated away from the race rather than to the race," they were inclined to "mis-educate" their students, leaving them with no knowledge of "what their people have done or what they have the capacity to do."[33] In an October 1927 letter to John Hope, Woodson bitterly related a story of a Black college instructor who, when asked to teach a course on Negro History, considered it a joke and continued his "so-called teaching" of propaganda.[34] This same "miseducation" afflicted White students, who were left with the "tendency of man to hate those whom he does not know" and to assume that Blacks had done nothing to contribute to American society.[35]

In his 1932 report on Negro History Week, Woodson emphasized this point with a critique of the directors of the George Washington Bicentennial Celebration, who left Blacks out of the literature produced to celebrate the event, except to briefly mention their participation as slaves. Frustrated by the fact that few people knew enough to question this version of the "facts," Woodson, in his role as Director of the ASNLH, made it his mission to publicize the work and contributions of many free Blacks during the period.[36] An editorial writer for the *Pittsburgh Courier* had made a similar point in January 1927, noting that if a teacher made a preposterous claim about a member of another race such as that Columbus had been an American Indian or that Woodrow Wilson was a Republican, it would be met with immediate outrage and correction. This kind of swift and indignant response was not the case, the writer argued, with the misrepresentation of Blacks. Because the average African American child was taught that his race had no history and that none of his/her race's accomplishments were worthy of being recorded, there were few people to question the record, no matter how biased, inaccurate, or incomplete.[37] An announcement in the *New York Times* for Negro History Week in February 1927 made a similar point, adding that it was not enough for scholars to learn the truth about Negro history if word never reached the broader community, especially children.[38]

In his efforts both to correct the record and to bolster racial pride, Woodson saw an important role for Black scholars. Because White historians had either neglected Blacks altogether or had written only of their inferior status and subjugation, he believed that Black history, first and foremost, had to be written by Blacks. Pleased with how a February 1928 editorial in the *Philadelphia Tribune* addressed this point, Woodson printed excerpts from it in the April 1928 issue of the *Journal of Negro History*. The editorial writer argued that the majority of people, Black and White alike, "accept the pap dished out by others" and rarely raise critical questions about what they read.[39] With no Negro history to counterbalance the White version, Blacks, the *Tribune* writer noted, were left with an "inferiority complex" that could only be remedied by a more complete and fair version of the facts.[40] If this was to be done, the "Negro must do it."[41]

While Woodson's arguments for studying Black history resonated with many Black educators in his day and continue to be compelling more than 50 years after his death, the decision to place so much emphasis on the celebration of a Negro History Week each year raised the same kinds of questions that the recognition of Black History Month and Women's History Month does today. Shouldn't Black history be studied all year? Doesn't the designation of a single week minimize or trivialize the broader goal of integrating Black history into the curriculum? Might these efforts do more harm than good? Woodson clearly grappled with these questions and worried that his intentions for Negro History Week would be misunderstood. He routinely repeated his goals and spent as much time explaining what Negro History Week should *not* be as he did describing what could be accomplished. In an article he wrote for the *Negro History Bulletin* in 1938, Woodson stated,

> Some teachers and their students have misunderstood the celebration of Negro History Week. They work up enthusiasm during these few days, stage a popular play, present an orator of the day, or render exercises of a literary order; but they forget the Negro thereafter throughout the year. To proceed in such fashion may do as much harm as good. It is a reflection on the record of the race to leave the impression that its history can be thus disposed of in a few days.[42]

Woodson proposed a much different vision for Negro History Week. Initially Woodson viewed Negro History Week as a vehicle through which he and other members of the ASNLH could focus their efforts, generate interest, and galvanize support. It was an intermediate step, designed to encourage a sustained commitment and to provide a manageable structure that could be replicated in a variety of settings. Furthermore, Woodson understood that schools and communities deciding to participate in Negro History Week would need resources and literature for their programs. The ASNLH, eager to supply these resources at a reasonable cost, knew that once widely distributed, the materials could be used well beyond a single week in February. For example, Woodson reported in 1927 that the Carnegie Corporation had provided funds for the New York Public Library to purchase the A. A. Schomburg Collection of 4,000 books on African Americans. This collection, he noted, not only facilitated the growth of Negro History Week in New York, but also stimulated the ongoing desire for Blacks to learn more about their own history.[43] Noting the poor performance of White students on tests of Negro history, early advocates of Negro History Week further hoped that schools with predominantly White students also would benefit from the materials provided by the ASNLH.[44]

Ideally, in Woodson's view, Negro History Week would be a celebration to cap a year-long study of Black history. He encouraged schools to plan programs throughout the year, pointing out that the "expedient" of Negro History Week would not be required if Black history was incorporated into the curriculum in the same way that the history of other groups was. Using the pages of the *Negro History Bulletin*, he held up as exemplars those schools who sustained year-long efforts. The Indiana Negro History Society in Terre Haute received praise in the inaugural 1937 volume for supporting schools in the effort to use opening exercises, assemblies, special reports, and current events in the teaching of Negro art, music, and history and to connect these to other activities in the school, such as building up picture galleries and literary clubs throughout the year.[45] Woodson urged schools at the secondary level to adopt textbooks on Negro history and reported that one such text, his own, *The Negro in Our History*, was being used in at least some schools in 21 different states by 1929.[46]

Celebrating Negro History Week

Based on a clear rationale in support of the study of Black history in schools and communities, Carter Woodson and other early supporters of Negro History Week developed a well-articulated vision of how Negro History Week should be implemented. While recognizing the need for some flexibility at the local level, Woodson used the organizational structure of the ASNLH to shape Negro History Week around the priorities he considered most vital to his movement. Given the obstacles and resistance in his path, Woodson moved forward gradually and pragmatically. From the start, however, he made it clear that Negro History Week should encompass far more than a handful of speeches given over the course of a few days in February. Woodson's correspondence and annual reports on Negro History Week reveal that he held many priorities, but they can be broadly grouped around three primary goals: (1) to develop and distribute as widely as possible high-quality resources on African American history; (2) to stimulate interest and an appetite for further study and understanding among both Blacks and Whites; and (3) to create a forum through which educators around the country could share ideas and practices.[47] Each of these implementation goals, if met, would further Woodson's broader aim of transforming the way that students, both Black and White, learned Black history.

By 1926, the first year that Negro History Week was observed, the ASNLH was well positioned to work toward the goal of collecting and distributing resources. From the start, Woodson had encouraged scholars of Black history to be members of the Association and to contribute well-researched articles to its journals, but the designation of a Negro History Week helped to create a demand for the articles and for other high-quality materials produced by the ASNLH. The resources contained historical content and images as well as suggestions for specific activities. In the earliest years, Woodson distributed pamphlets and circulars to ASNLH members and to state departments of education, large city school systems, historically Black colleges, civic organizations, women's clubs, and major newspapers and radio stations.[48] By the 1940s, Woodson had begun distributing, at a cost of $2.00, Negro History Week kits that included writings, speeches, plays, and photographs that could be used by teachers.[49] In addition, beginning in 1937, Woodson used the teacher-friendly *Negro History Bulletin* as a mechanism for distributing resources.

While the *Journal of Negro History*, read widely by members of the ASNLH and made available through public and college libraries around the country, provided a research outlet for Woodson and other scholars of Black history, ten years into the celebration of Negro History Week, Woodson needed an effective and affordable way to provide ongoing resources to teachers and students around the country. Although the Association already provided pamphlets and circulars for Negro History Week and published new books each year that could be used in classrooms, Woodson hoped that a practical, engaging journal, published each month during the school year, would keep teachers focused on Black history throughout the year and would allow Negro History Week to become what he had truly intended it to be, a culmination of studies conducted all year long. With this in mind, Woodson launched *The Negro History Bulletin (NHB)* in October 1937. Initially, he charged $1.00 for a yearly subscription or 12 cents per issue, but schools or clubs who ordered five or more copies could obtain them for 45 cents per year.[50] Even when he increased the number of pages from 8 to 16 in October 1939, Woodson maintained the same price, in an effort to keep the journal accessible.[51]

The *NHB* followed a basic format in its early years. Each issue began with an introductory article focusing on an important person or event from African American history. The first issue, for example, opened with an article detailing William and Ellen Craft's escape from slavery. The lead article was followed by two or three pages of biographical sketches under the heading "Persons and Achievements To Be Remembered." This section included information on people born in that particular month. Most often "notable" African Americans such as Phillis Wheatley or Frederick Douglass were included here, but Woodson also included Whites known for their work on behalf of Black causes. In November 1937, for example, Andrew Carnegie was recognized for always making "provisions for

Negroes" in his libraries and for his $600,000 donation to the Tuskegee Institute. Author Louisa May Alcott appeared in the same issue and was credited for her work as a Union nurse, for her advocacy of women's rights and temperance, and for her antislavery sympathies.[52] Following this section, the *NHB*s included notes on books that could be used by classroom teachers, as well as special praise for a Book of the Month. Finally, each issue included a section entitled "School News," which provided examples of successful activities being carried out by schools around the country. Beginning with the second issue, Woodson added a list of questions based on content covered in the previous issue, with the hope that teachers could have their students answer the questions each month in order to reinforce what they were learning.

Because Woodson believed it was critical for Black history to be accurate, and because he wanted educators to refute the record implying that Blacks had little history to call their own, Woodson used the opening articles in each issue of the *Negro History Bulletin* to demonstrate that Blacks had always been powerful actors in the making of their own history. Often, he highlighted the stories of Black business leaders or of individuals who fought against slavery and succeeded as free men. One of the best examples of this focus can be seen in an article entitled "The Struggle of the Negro Against Bondage" in the February 1938 issue. The article provided an overview of the role of the Negro in the abolition movement and critiqued accounts in mainstream history that suggested that Blacks depended on Whites to fight for abolition and that they had little to do with it themselves. Using empowering language, the article emphasized that from the very beginning slaves struggled to be free by working on holidays, Sundays, and at night to save extra money to buy freedom; by running away to free territories; and, in a few cases, through rebellion.[53]

Woodson granted that Black abolitionists—with a few exceptions—had been hampered by lack of educational opportunities, but he wanted teachers to emphasize to their students that abolitionism was not a White movement. In the article, he stated his argument this way: "The abolition movement was not a movement by others for the Negro. It was to some extent a movement by the Negro for himself. The Negroes from the very beginning were the first abolitionists. They had never sat down and waited for someone to bring them freedom."[54] Woodson further pointed out that in addition to giving speeches for the cause of abolition, Blacks raised money to support the effort. Those who were doing well in the North, he explained, were counted on to provide funds. According to Woodson, some of the large sums obtained in antislavery meetings in New York, Philadelphia, Boston, Pittsburgh, and Cincinnati were raised not among White people, but among African Americans. He also noted that many of the subscribers to abolitionist newspapers were Blacks, and he argued that William Lloyd Garrison could not have succeeded with *The Liberator* had it not been for the large number of Blacks who subscribed themselves and paid for subscriptions for others, although they themselves could not read.[55]

Just as Woodson used articles written in a way accessible to teachers and students alike to correct the record and to show Blacks in positions of agency, he included book reviews in the *Negro History Bulletin* to make teachers aware of credible resources that they could use with their students. Along with reviews of books written by Woodson's fellow scholars of Black history and published by The Associated Publishers, Inc., the ASNLH's publishing branch, established in 1921, Woodson included reviews of books intended for elementaryschool-aged children. In fact, Woodson often lamented the lack of quality resources appropriate for young children and tried to encourage their publication and use.[56] Some books, like Helen E. Whiting's *Negro Folk Tales*, featured as "The Book of the Month" in the first *NHB* issue, were sold in low-cost school editions for 75 cents. Whiting's book, designed as a supplement to the traditional curriculum and geared to students in first grade, told stories of life in Africa.[57] Other books chosen as "Book of the Month," such as Jane D. Shackelford's *The Child's Story of the Negro*, offered "simple but complete" histories of African Americans to students in upper elementary grades.[58]

Each February, *The Negro History Bulletin* published an issue devoted specifically to Negro History Week. In the December 1937 issue, Woodson announced that the February 1938 issue would be devoted almost entirely to Negro History Week and that it would include 16 pages rather than the usual 8. It would also come out in early January, so that schools could use it to plan their programs. These special issues each February included several articles that provided concrete suggestions for Negro History Week activities. Whether Woodson wrote the articles himself or they were submitted by colleagues in the ASNLH or by educators around the country, they reflected Woodson's vision and goals. For example, articles with titles such as "Timely Suggestions for Negro History Week" and "Making Negro History Week Count" encouraged teachers to move beyond a "great men" approach and to teach their students about significant movements in Black history. Contributors also urged teachers to have their students work on school histories and church histories within their local communities and to encourage awareness campaigns on the importance of saving local records.[59] Some of the articles offered specific guidelines, such as one that called for pictures of distinguished African Americans to hang on the walls of every school classroom.[60]

In addition to using Negro History Week as a mechanism for widely distributing resources, Woodson hoped it could be used to stimulate interest in Black history throughout the country. As a first step to ensure that this interest would be generated, he saw to it that the press, on both local and national levels, widely covered Negro History Week events. He made himself and other members of the ASNLH available for interviews with radio stations and newspapers; he sent copies of Negro History Week materials to major newspapers around the country; and he advised community committees to contact their local presses as they planned events each year. He also used the Black press to support fund-raising efforts needed for the ongoing implementation of Negro History Week. During Woodson's initial $20,000 fund-raising drive, launched in 1926, Black newspapers such as the *Pittsburgh Courier*, the *Norfolk Journal and Guide*, and the *Chicago Defender* listed the goal amounts for each state. An April 1927 follow-up article in the *Chicago Defender* revealed how far short of the established goals states were falling and provided an address for sending contributions.[61] In its coverage of the 1927 Negro History Week, the *Pittsburgh Courier* offered an endorsement, saying that its paper "joins readily in spreading the news to its readers and urging them to join heartily in this week of celebration."[62] Although mainstream newspapers such as the *New York Times* and the *Washington Post* did not offer explicit endorsements of Woodson's efforts, they did regularly cover Negro History Week events.

As part of his effort to use press coverage to popularize Negro History Week, Woodson sought to balance local events, largely carried out by committees on the ground and covered by community newspapers, with more ambitious ones that would draw national attention. One of the most significant national events came during the 1930 celebration of Negro History Week in Washington, DC. After weeks of planning, the ASNLH hosted a banquet for more than 300 people to honor three living former African American members of Congress as well as Oscar De Priest, who was then representing a Congressional district in the Illinois House of Representatives. After dinner and speeches from leaders within the Black community, the guests left the banquet hall and traveled to the Washington Auditorium at Nineteenth and E Streets for a gathering of five thousand people, assembled to honor the congressmen. Here, Oscar De Priest himself treated the audience to a rousing speech, during which he described his role in Congress and discussed the importance of human rights and the true protection of all amendments to the US Constitution. Noting a degree of irony, he stated, "It is worse than a crime to witness in the United States the gross intolerance which exists in a country famed for its foundation on the rock of liberty."[63] Although the evening turned out to be a great success and drew the kind of attention Woodson was seeking, it involved an enormous amount of planning, which taxed Woodson and his colleagues. Thirty-five years later, in a special issue of the *Negro History Bulletin*, Lorenzo J. Greene, who served as one of Woodson's assistants during the planning and later went on to be a professor of history at Lincoln University, published excerpts of his diary from the period leading up to the banquet. Greene portrayed Woodson as a man with enormous drive and energy who worked 18-hour days and could be seen doing everything from writing and editing books and articles, to mailing countless letters and parcels, to serving as the building janitor when needed.[64]

In addition to encouraging press coverage and to planning national events designed to garner widespread publicity, Woodson sought to stimulate further interest in Black history through the use of well-placed visual images. He asked local Negro History Week committees throughout the country to post photographs of prominent African Americans in their schools and community centers and to set up bulletin boards featuring African American writers in local libraries. The ASNLH played an important role in this campaign. By 1934 the Association had secured and made available for reproduction approximately 150 photographs of "outstanding Negroes," but Woodson noted in his annual report of the same year that his organization could not keep up with the growing demand, and he encouraged other groups to join the effort.[65] In addition, Woodson argued that displaying books by and about African Americans in prominent places within community libraries would give patrons the message that rich collections of African American literature and history existed. This awareness, in turn, would prompt their interest in learning more.

Finally, in addition to distributing resources and stimulating interest, Woodson envisioned Negro History Week as a catalyst for collaboration among educators. It was partly with this in mind that he launched the *Negro History Bulletin* and incorporated a section entitled "School News." Here, the *Bulletin* featured stories of what schools around the country were doing to celebrate Negro History Week. Editors also included accounts of initiatives held throughout the year and applauded the efforts of those districts who implemented this kind of sustained approach. For example, in one of the earliest issues, the New Orleans School District was held up as an exemplar of community outreach for its regular public exercises, which were designed to encourage interest in the study of African American history and culture at home as well as in school.[66] The *Bulletin* also encouraged readers to provide feedback on activities shared by schools and teachers. In one illustrative case, under a headline entitled "Criticism of the Children Invited," the editor asked students to give feedback on a Negro History Week program submitted by Halsey Junior High School in New York City. After listing several questions to which readers could respond, the article noted that intelligent criticism would be helpful to other communities as well as to teachers at Halsey.[67] This type of collaborative and interactive approach, by which schools around the country shared lesson plans, pageant scripts, and Negro History Week programs, typified early issues of the *Bulletin*.

Over time, this sharing of expertise and the resultant increased knowledge base among teachers and other community educators caused Woodson to become more comfortable with local control of Negro History Week activities. His annual reports in the 1940s reflect this shift in his thinking. Pleased to see the fruits of the ASNLH's early labors, Woodson pointed out that the popularization of Black history had led to the development of "considerable local talent." Gone were the days when a small handful of Black historians had to travel the country, trying to cover Negro History Week events. Rather, local educators could plan and execute meaningful and worthwhile programs on their own. By the 1940s, local committees had also become somewhat less reliant on ASNLH materials, because they had developed many of their own exhibits, posters, and scrapbooks.[68]

Conclusion

Carter Woodson and his supporters always saw Negro History Week as one important plank of a much larger platform, but never as an end in itself. Woodson, a man known for working 18-hour days over several decades for the cause of Black history, quickly recognized the need for a manageable and accessible vehicle through which to focus the educational efforts of the ASNLH. In the first half of the twentieth century, a period shaped by Jim Crow laws and institutional racism, it was a daunting task to rectify the historical record and bring a true understanding of African American history to the general public. Although Negro History Week had its drawbacks, including a susceptibility to trivialization, Woodson saw its potential as a vehicle for improving the study of history and for making history more inclusive and accurate.

Woodson was able to promote the concept of Negro History Week to educators more easily than he could other more radical strategies. By providing materials for free in the first year and at low costs after that, by offering clear guidelines to local communities, and by making himself and other scholars available for speeches and programs, Woodson could promote a "doable" project. He was confident that early successes would generate both interest in Black history and the financial support needed to extend the ASNLH's efforts. Although often frustrated by the challenges of fund-raising, Woodson reported steady growth in the reach of Negro History Week throughout his life.

In Negro History Week, Woodson also saw the potential for gathering and distributing African American history materials on a broad scale.

Initially, this effort would be primarily in one direction, with the ASNLH producing and distributing materials to schools and communities to be used during Negro History Week and throughout the year. Books distributed by the ASNLH's publishing arm could be sold at low cost to schools and libraries, thus making them available to the general public. Posters and photographs distributed by Woodson's organization and displayed in communities around the country would generate interest and promote further study. Eventually, Woodson believed, communities preparing for Negro History Week would begin to produce their own materials and to develop their own local archives. Slowly, as local committees and study groups around the country replicated these efforts, African American history could be constructed and brought to the public. At the same time, educators within these communities would be encouraged to share their resources and ideas through outlets such as the *Negro History Bulletin*. By exchanging resources and deepening their own understanding of Black history, teachers, Woodson argued, would be better positioned to undo damage caused by inaccurate and incomplete history and racial stereotyping.

Throughout his career, Woodson worked on many fronts to promote the study of Black history. For schools, both those attended by Blacks and ones attended by Whites, he advocated full integration of Black history in the curriculum at the elementary and high school levels. Short of that, he recommended stand-alone courses in African American history, and he wrote textbooks specifically for that purpose. In all cases, he urged schools, universities, and community groups to celebrate Negro History Week each February, ideally as a concluding event to a year of ongoing study. Although Negro History Week never became a steppingstone to the more fully developed curriculum that Woodson imagined, few initiatives have had a greater impact on the popularization of Black history.

Notes

1. In his *The Early Black History Movement, Carter G. Woodson, and Lorenzo Greene* (Chicago, IL: University of Illinois Press, 2007), 52–53, Pero Gaglo Dagbovie quotes several of Woodson's colleagues, who laud his efforts with Negro History Week and testify to its impact. He also notes that in 1949, the American Jewish Historical Society followed Woodson's model and established a Jewish History Week.
2. For the most complete biography of Woodson see Jacqueline Goggin, *Carter G. Woodson: A Life in Black History* (Baton Rouge, LA: Louisiana State University Press, 1993).
3. Maghan Keita, *Race and the Writing of History: Riddling the Sphinx* (Oxford: Oxford University Press, 2000), 51–69; August Meier and Elliot Rudwick,

Black History and the Historical Profession (Urbana, IL: University of Illinois Press, 1986).
4. Meier and Rudwick, *Black History and the Historical Profession*, 10–11. Meier and Rudwick provide a fascinating overview of the political, social, and personal motives that shaped relationships among Black intellectuals in the first half of the twentieth century and describe how Woodson's personal traits made him gravitate toward more conservative Black leaders. Their research, based largely on Woodson's writings and correspondence and on interviews with people who knew him, make it clear, however, that Woodson, especially in his private interactions within the ASNLH, could be quite outspoken on racial issues.
5. Pero Gaglo Dagbovie, "Making Black History Practical and Popular: Carter G. Woodson, the Proto Black Studies Movement and the Struggle for Black Liberation," *Western Journal of Black Studies* 28, no. 2 (2004): 372–383; Dagbovie, *The Early Black History Movement*, 47.
6. Pero Gaglo Dagbovie, *African American History Reconsidered* (Urbana, IL: University of Illinois Press, 2010), 77–81.
7. Jonathan Zimmerman, *Whose America? Culture Wars in the Public Schools* (Cambridge, MA: Harvard University Press, 2002), 16–31.
8. Ibid., 20.
9. Ibid., 22.
10. Ibid., 42–54.
11. Ibid., 44.
12. Jacqueline Goggin, *Carter G. Woodson: A Life in Black History*, 18–31.
13. W. D. Wright, *Black History and Black Identity: A Call for a New Historiography* (Westport, CT: Praeger, 2002), 34–35.
14. Carter G. Woodson, "Negro History Week," *The Journal of Negro History* 11 (April 1926): 238.
15. Woodson to Hope, February 17, 1926; Carter G. Woodson Papers, box 4, folder 7, Emory University Archives.
16. See for example "Negro History Week to be Celebrated Each Year the Second Week of February," *The Pittsburgh Courier* (1911–1950), Feb. 27, 1926, Proquest Historical Newspapers online at: http://envoy.dickinson.edu:2048/login?url=http://envoy.dickinson.edu:4736/docview/492133648?accountid=10506; and "History Association Announces Returns from Financial Drive," *The Chicago Defender,* National Edition (1921–1967), Apr. 30, 1927; ProQuest Historical Newspapers; available online: Pittsburgh Courier Article: HERE
ProQuest document ID
201869182
Document URL
http://envoy.dickinson.edu:2048/login?url=http://envoy.dickinson.edu:4736/docview/201869182?accountid=10506

Chicago Defender Article:
ProQuest document ID
492133648
Document URL
http://envoy.dickinson.edu:2048/login?url=http://envoy.dickinson.edu:4736/docview/492133648?accountid=10506

17. Woodson's annual articles on Negro History Week, published each April from 1926 to 1940 in the *Journal of Negro History,* provide an excellent overview of his structural goals for Negro History Week. After 1940, Woodson reports on Negro History Week as part of his Annual Report in each October issue of the *JNH.*
18. Mary McLeod Bethune, "Clarifying Our Vision with the Facts," *Negro History Bulletin* 1 (February 1938): 8.
19. Woodson launched the *Negro History Bulletin* in 1937 as a practitioner-oriented journal published monthly during the school year. It became a major source of information for Negro History Week activities.
20. Meier and Rudwick, *Black History and the Historical Profession*, 2.
21. Ibid., 2–3.
22. Carter G. Woodson, *The Mis-Education of the Negro* (Washington, DC: The Associated Publishers, Inc., 1933), 151–152.
23. Carter G. Woodson, "Negro History Week," *The Journal of Negro History* 11 (April 1926): 239.
24. Ibid., 239–240.
25. Carter G. Woodson, "Negro History Week—The Eleventh Year," *The Journal of Negro History* 21 (April 1936); 105.
26. See for example Woodson to Hope, April 26, 1926, and Woodson to James Robinson, May 12, 1965, Woodson Papers, box 4, folder 7, Emory University.
27. Carter G. Woodson, "Negro History Week—The Eleventh Year," *The Journal of Negro History* 21 (April 1936): 106.
28. Carter G. Woodson, "Negro History Week," *The Journal of Negro History* 11 (April 1926): 241.
29. Carter G. Woodson, "Negro History Week—The Third Year," *The Journal of Negro History* 13 (April 1928): 122.
30. Carter G. Woodson, "Negro History Week—The Fifth Year," *The Journal of Negro History* 16 (April 1931): 126.
31. Ibid., 127.
32. Carter G. Woodson, "Negro History Week—The Tenth Year, *The Journal of Negro History* 20 (April 1935): 124.
33. Ibid., 124–125.
34. Woodson to Hope, October 1, 1927, Woodson Papers, box 4, folder 7, Emory University. Yes, it's Hope.
35. Carter G. Woodson, "Negro History Week—The Tenth Year," *The Journal of Negro History* 20 (April 1935): 126.
36. Carter G. Woodson, "Negro History Week—The Sixth Year," *The Journal of Negro History* 17 (April 1932): 119–120.
37. "Negro History Week," *The Pittsburgh Courier (1911–1950)*, January 29, 1927, A8; Proquest Historical Newspapers, *Pittsburgh Courier,* 1911–2002.
38. "Negro History Week to Begin Here Today: Achievements of Race and Its Leaders to Be Taught as Lesson to Its Youth," *New York Times (1923–current file)*, February 20, 1927, E2; Proquest Historical Newspapers, *New York Times,* 1851–2006.
39. Quoted in "Negro History Week—The Third Year," *The Journal of Negro History* 13 (April 1928): 124.

40. Ibid.
41. Ibid.
42. Carter G. Woodson, "Starting Right," *The Negro History Bulletin* 1 (February 1938): 12.
43. Carter G. Woodson, "The Celebration of Negro History Week," *The Journal of Negro History* 12 (April 1927): 108.
44. Carter G. Woodson, "Negro History Week—the Tenth Year," *The Journal of Negro History* 20 (April 1935): 125–126.
45. Carter G. Woodson, "What Schools Are Doing," *The Negro History Bulletin* 1 (October 1937): 7–8.
46. Carter G. Woodson, "Negro History Week—the Fourth Year," *The Journal of Negro History* 14 (April 1929): 113.
47. See Woodson's early annual reports published in April issues of *The Journal of Negro History* as well as Woodson to Hope, February 17, 1926, Woodson Papers, box 4, folder 7, Emory University.
48. Carter G. Woodson, "Negro History Week," *The Journal of Negro History* 11 (April 1926): 238; Goggin, *Carter G. Woodson*, 85; Dagbovie, *The Early Black History Movement*, 50.
49. Pero Gaglo Dagbovie, "Making Black History Practical and Popular," 376.
50. *The Negro History Bulletin* 1 (October 1937): 8.
51. Pero Gaglo Dagbovie, *The Early Black History Movement*, 61.
52. *The Negro History Bulletin* 2 (November 1937): 5, 7.
53. Carter G. Woodson, "The Struggle of the Negro against Bondage," *The Negro History Bulletin* 1 (February 1938): 2–3.
54. Ibid., 3.
55. Ibid.
56. "Books," *The Negro History Bulletin* 1 (February 1938): 16.
57. "Book of the Month," *The Negro History Bulletin* 1 (October 1937): 8.
58. "Book of the Month," *The Negro History Bulletin* 1 (February 1938): 16.
59. *The Negro History Bulletin* 1 (February 1938): 11–12.
60. Ibid., 12.
61. "History Association Announces Returns from Financial Drive," *The Chicago Defender*, National Edition (1921–1967), Apr. 30, 1927; ProQuest Historical Newspapers.
62. "Negro History Week," *The Pittsburgh Courier* (1911–1950), Jan. 29, 1927; Proquest Historical Newspapers.
63. Carter G. Woodson, "Negro History Week Celebration," *The Journal of Negro History* 15 (April 1930): 131.
64. Lorenzo J. Greene, "Dr. Woodson Prepares for Negro History Week, 1930," *The Negro History Bulletin*, 28 (Summer 1965): 195.
65. Carter G. Woodson, "Negro History Week—the Ninth Year," *The Journal of Negro History* 19 (April 1934): 116.
66. "School News," *The Negro History Bulletin* 1 (February 1938): 7.
67. "Criticism of the Children Invited," *The Negro History Bulletin* 13 (January 1950): 91.
68. Carter G. Woodson, "Annual Report of the Director," *The Journal of Negro History* 28 (October 1943): 377–378.

CHAPTER FOUR

NOTIONS OF CITIZENSHIP: DISCUSSING
RACE IN THE SHORTRIDGE HIGH SCHOOL
SENATE, 1900–1928

J. Spencer Clark

At Shortridge High School from 1900–1928, the student senate was among the most popular extracurricular school activities, if not the most popular. Shortridge was the only high school in Indianapolis until 1900—it was known as Indianapolis High School until then—and it was located on the north side of the city, between several affluent neighborhoods and the city center. The senate met after school every Friday afternoon, with an average attendance of 100 to 150 students from all over Indianapolis. It not only drew a large number of students, but students could follow coverage of its proceedings weekly in the school newspaper. The Shortridge Senate was praised and touted annually in the school yearbook; it received local, state, and national press; and it regularly hosted visitors to observe the proceedings. The senate was very much a part of the school culture, and students seemingly took pride in their participation, reminiscing for years to come in memoirs and journals about their experience.[1]

A social studies teacher named Laura Donnan developed the Shortridge Senate as a self-governing student body in 1883. Its structure imitated the United States Senate in its organization and procedures; the students even took the names of actual US senators. In the senate proceedings, the students proposed bills and discussed a wide range of controversial issues that were associated with the proposed legislation. Inevitably, some of the most common and recurring discussions in the senate from this period involved popular notions of citizenship. In these discussions about citizenship, race was often discussed and was used as justification for a wide range of perspectives about what constituted an American citizen. In this chapter, I investigate these discussions and examine minutes from the Shortridge

Senate proceedings, articles from the school newspaper, and articles in the school yearbook. This chapter focuses on the question, How were the students' understandings of race characterized in their discussions of citizenship in the Shortridge Senate?

A student honored Laura Donnan in the Shortridge yearbook, *The Annual*, one year before Donnan retired in 1926. The student focused on Donnan's work with the senate and wrote, "She has inculcated into hundreds of its members a respect for law, a love of democracy, and a toleration for ideals. She has insisted that the senate make no discrimination in race, sex, color, or religion."[2] Donnan was commonly remembered for instilling in her students the value of equal rights for all citizens. The senate was one piece of a civics program that she implemented at Shortridge High School that focused on promoting liberal ideals within a republican government. As Virginia Cox, another student, remembered, "The equality of persons that is so sought for in governments was prevalent in the Senate."[3] In general, by 1887, all Shortridge students were required to take Donnan's civil government course; over the next 40 years, Donnan's civil government course became among the most popular and influential courses at Shortridge. The students' engagement in her courses often sparked their participation in her related extracurricular activities, such as the senate.

Donnan had designed the Shortridge Senate to be a simulative and participatory form of curriculum that would provide students with an opportunity to model the legislative process and apply what they had learned in her civil government courses. Donnan wanted her students to gain awareness of controversial issues that faced the country and to deliberate these issues, expressing their own personal convictions. She had clearly defined outcomes for the senate, yet many students simply remembered it as an autonomous self-governing body. For example, Virginia Cox wrote:

> The senate was, in reality, a "self-government" class. The members had charge of the meetings, with Miss Donnan interrupting only when absolutely necessary. There was no constraint upon them in the attitude of teacher–pupil, and that they appreciated this is shown by the fact that with few exceptions, they governed themselves well.[4]

Donnan intended to promote a more liberal and participatory notion of government and citizenship in her students. However, the proceedings of the Shortridge Senate often resulted in reinforcing notions of citizenship that perceived Americans as the sole proprietors of self-government in the world, notions that distinguished the Teutonic people who founded the United States from other races. This chapter will focus on the discussions that Shortridge students had about issues of citizenship and how they used race to justify their views. I will begin by briefly discussing the context of Shortridge High School and some of the competing views of citizenship pertaining to race in the Progressive Era.[5]

Laura Donnan's Early History

Donnan was born to abolitionist parents in 1854. Donnan was originally from Indianapolis and was a graduate of the high school herself. Donnan attended the Normal School at Indianapolis and taught elementary school in two small communities before attending the University of Michigan. There she received her master's degree in constitutional history. Her master's thesis was titled "Duties of a Private Citizen in a Republic;"[6] a title that befitted her activity in the civic education program she implemented at Shortridge. Donnan returned to teach at her alma mater, where she would be remembered as one of the "Shortridge Immortals," teaching there for 45 years.[7]

At Shortridge, Donnan quickly became very popular with her students because of the classes she taught, her pedagogy, and the extracurricular activities she initiated and sponsored. She had sponsored or helped nearly every school activity over the span of her career, and her efforts were very well known.[8] One article in the school newspaper noted, "I need not tell you what Miss Donnan is doing for the *Echo*, Oratorical Association and the Senate."[9] Donnan was founder and longtime sponsor of the Shortridge Oratorical Society; the John Quincy Adams Club, which provided an impromptu forum to debate school and governmental issues pertinent to students; the Keyes Association, which discussed patriotic topics and coordinated patriotic events and activities in the community; and the Shortridge *Daily Echo*, which was the first daily high school newspaper in the country. Donnan was involved with nearly every field trip; she chaperoned the girls because "she did not want the girls to miss out on anything," and she also showed her support at nearly every sporting event and school activity.[10]

Donnan was an advocate for woman's suffrage and was outspoken on equality for all men and women, as one former student remembered, "She was a strong advocate for the rights of blacks."[11] The only racial incident that happened at Shortridge during its integrated period, prior to segregation in 1927, occurred in the spring of 1904 in Donnan's civil government classroom. The incident involved a White male student who did not want to take his newly assigned seat next to a Black female student. After the student disobeyed her in front of the class, Donnan dismissed the White student. He appealed to both the principal and the school board, both of which supported and upheld her decision. Both students reportedly transferred out of Donnan's class, and the White student eventually dropped out of school.[12] Donnan was known for her equal treatment of all students. As Virginia Cox recalled:

> It made no difference to Laura Donnan from what part of the city a child came. She often made the remark that children who lived on the 'boo-lee-vard' need not expect any partiality. She neither upheld nor discriminated against those who lived either in poverty or wealth.[13]

Shortridge students were very aware of Donnan's strong convictions regarding equal rights for all citizens.

After being established in 1883, the Shortridge Senate quickly became the most popular club in the school, drawing not only participants, but also observers from inside and outside of the school.[14] As an extracurricular activity, the senate provided an extension of Donnan's civil government courses and, more specifically, of the weekly debates that were conducted in those courses. The senate's underlying purpose was to prepare students to be active citizens, to inform them of issues facing the nation, and to demonstrate how to engage in public discourse upon leaving high school.

The Shortridge Senate was not only unique as a method of educating young citizens, but it was also a unique association of young citizens. The Shortridge Senate may have imitated the United States Senate in its processes and content; however, the students who took on the names of the White male US senators were in some cases not White and in many cases were not male, as female students often constituted the majority. The only requirement to participate in the Shortridge Senate was passing Donnan's civil government course, which was typically taken in freshman year as a course required for graduation. Academic performance, then, was the reason for exclusion from the extracurricular activity.[15]

The Shortridge Senate provided a forum to discuss the most controversial issues of the day including Black citizen's rights, immigration issues, and woman's rights. The discussions brought to the forefront the economic, political, and social implications of these controversial issues. The inclusiveness of the Shortridge Senate and its regular discussions of issues of exclusion provided a context of educational practice that promoted liberal democratic citizenship at a time when the attributes of citizenship were highly contested.

Notions of Citizenship in Progressive Era Society and Schools

During the Progressive Era, urban school enrollments climbed, as did the number of immigrants who attended urban schools. Policy makers realized that schools were vital spaces in the effort to shape new democratic citizens, both domestic and foreign-born. A majority of these efforts could be viewed as part of the movement that emphasized Americanization curriculum and activities. There were several different views in regard to what Americanization should entail in schools. This difference was partly tied to the varying notions of what attributes were required to be an American citizen. Historian of education Jeffrey Mirel identified three distinct views on Americanization: assimilationist, cultural pluralist, and amalgamationist.[16] Each perspective on Americanization envisioned, to differing degrees, that foreign-born individuals would discard aspects of their own culture, and then adopt or contribute to a distinctive American culture.

The Americanization efforts drew upon several nationalist ideals that were in contention to determine which groups would be included and excluded as American citizens. Scholar Gary Gerstle identified two nationalistic ideologies that contended for social prevalence in the Progressive Era: civic nationalism and racial nationalism.[17] Civic nationalism embodied a more liberal stance in regard to citizenship. A civic nationalist would see the nation as "a community of equal, rights-bearing citizens united in patriotic attachment to a shared set of political practices and values."[18] A racial nationalist would see the nation in "ethnoracial terms, as a people held together by common blood and skin color and by an inherited fitness for self-government."[19] Gerstle argued that the pursuit of the contradictory ideals of civic and racial nationalism shaped American history, especially in the Progressive Era.[20] The contradiction was best evinced in the politics of President Theodore Roosevelt, a politician whom the Shortridge students respected and often quoted. President Roosevelt believed in the principles of civic nationalism, but he also had deeply seated reservations about certain races and nationalities gaining American citizenship. For example, Gerstle noted that Roosevelt simply argued that certain races— notably Asians and African Americans—could not meet the fundamental requirements of American citizenship. "Only the very highest races have been able to make success of self government, and it would be foolish, even contemptible, to assume that 'utterly undeveloped races' could function on an even footing with whites in a democracy,"[21] Roosevelt said. Shortridge students' comments demonstrated both civic nationalist and racial nationalist ideologies in their discussions. They used aspects of these ideologies to justify their beliefs about which groups were fit and unfit for citizenship.

Rogers Smith discussed the ideal of racial nationalism in a different manner and called it ethnocultural Americanism. This view of citizenship was rooted in two distinct historical traditions: liberalism and republicanism. Smith noted that ethnocultural Americanism at its extreme was "nativism," and embodied a distinctive American character. Its advocates utilized aspects of the liberal and republican traditions to justify their claims, and as Smith described:

> From the revolutionary era on, many American leaders deliberately promoted the popular notion that Americans had a distinctive character, born of their freedom-loving Anglo-Saxon ancestors and heightened by the favorable conditions of the new world. This character made them the last hope to preserve human freedom—and it also set them above blacks and truly Native Americans, and later Mexicans, Chinese, Filipinos, and others who were labeled unfit for self-government.[22]

Many Americanization efforts used the supposedly distinctive American character as a means of assessing the attributes of potential citizens, and they utilized nationality and race to justify a group's perceived capabilities for democratic citizenship and self-government.

These notions of citizenship, along with Progressive Era state-building efforts, contributed to curricular efforts to Americanize students from other cultures.[23] As Julie Reuben notes, these efforts were the result of Progressive Era debates that attempted to clarify exactly what constituted an American citizen and, more specifically, who was capable of democratic self-government.[24] These debates were important because they considered the citizenship not only of new immigrants, but also of previously excluded and disenfranchised groups. Many policy makers and social reformers looked to history and civics courses, which in 1916 would collectively become known as the social studies, to undertake a major role in shaping young citizens. Arthur W. Dunn was one such reformer, who contributed to the 1916 committee that created the social studies during his tenure as civic education specialist for the United States Bureau of Education. Dunn actually taught at Shortridge from 1900 until 1910. During this time, he served as Donnan's department head, conducted a study on civic education, and wrote his first textbook, *Community Civics*, which would become synonymous with the new social studies curriculum outlined in 1916.

Well before Dunn's arrival at Shortridge, students debated competing conceptions of citizenship in Donnan's classroom, in the newspaper, and in the senate. Furthermore, students commonly discussed excluded groups and exhibited a wide range of views related to those groups in the senate sessions. Donnan clearly encouraged her students to share their views, no matter the degree of prejudice they had, and she advocated for this approach in her 1889 speech to the National Education Association (NEA): "The pupils should be encouraged to express fully their opinions, however unusual or unpopular they may be."[25] In her speech, Donnan advocated for the teaching of civics in every high school, and she wanted to create a space where students' unpopular views regarding democratic citizenship for immigrants and previously excluded groups could be voiced.

At Shortridge during this period, however, the unpopular views regarding democratic citizenship came from students who supported a more liberal and civic nationalist perspective regarding American citizenship. These types of views were considered unpopular because many Progressive Era Americans viewed millions of recent immigrants, African Americans, and most Asian Americans "as inherently unfit for citizenship in a democracy," and believed that citizenship was reserved for those who fit the distinctive American character.[26] As Zoë Burkholder notes, discussion of race in schools was confined almost entirely to racial minorities who were White, and who commonly originated from Eastern and Southern Europe.[27] In the Shortridge Senate, students discussed the citizenship capabilities of White Europeans, but often less frequently than they discussed several other races or nationalities. The groups that Shortridge students discussed in the senate may not have been typical of other schools, but they justified the capabilities of these groups based on their nationality, which was typical in other schools. It was common during the Progressive Era for one's race to be signified by nationality. Burkholder explains that in schools, teachers often constructed *race-as-nation* as a way to discuss the individual attributes of people.[28] This characterization of race benefited certain White nationalities, as they were considered to have an innate ability to be citizens in a democracy, despite being racially inferior to other Whites. On the other hand, however, non-Whites were believed to not "possess the inherent capabilities for participatory democratic citizenship."[29] Thus, a people's nationality, and their corresponding implicit race, had distinct implications for their perceived capabilities as democratic citizens in the United States.

Notions of Citizenship in the Shortridge Senate

As explained by Burkholder, talking about race-as-nation was a consistent means for students in the Shortridge Senate to discuss who was fit for American citizenship. Students at Shortridge were also well versed in the liberal and republican traditions of their country, due to Donnan's civic program.[30] The students at Shortridge often justified their arguments with these traditions in their senate discussions on an array of issues. However, when discussing citizenship, the distinctive American character often trumped the liberal and republican traditions in their discussions.[31] The discussion of citizenship reflected so strongly on the students' own social identity as Americans that their notion of American citizenship limited their thinking of race as nation. In the minds of the students, very few of the groups discussed in the Shortridge Senate were fit to become fully realized American citizens. Students used their thinking about race-as-nation to determine how closely a group of people could come to embodying the distinctively American notion of citizenship. In the following sections, I describe how Shortridge students discussed citizenship in terms of race as nation.

Asian Nationalities

Chinese immigrants were one of the most discussed groups in the Shortridge Senate and were commonly mentioned in a negative and exclusionary manner. The senate minutes indicated that attitudes toward the Chinese were negative to such an extent that the students never even considered the possibility of their citizenship in the United States. The Chinese were discussed solely in terms of labor issues, often as a side note to restrictive immigration bills, such as the Chinese Exclusion Act of 1882. The students wanted to ensure that such legislation remained intact, especially when they passed any new legislation regarding immigration. In the course of these discussions, the Chinese were the target of some of the most stereotypical and derogatory comments recorded in the senate and were commonly described as "coolies," "lovers of rice," or the "yellow race." [32] The Chinese were repeatedly denigrated, along with Eastern and Southern European immigrants.[33] The students repeatedly called for regulation of Chinese immigration, because Chinese immigrants purportedly accepted lower wages than other groups in America. For example, the secretary of the senate recorded that one student "objected to the coolie class because of their tendency to work for exceedingly low wages."[34] When students sought to pass restrictive immigration bills targeted at European groups, they would add sections to the bill just to uphold the Chinese Exclusion Act and noted that "to allow Chinese to immigrate as other nations...would greatly demoralize the country."[35] In general, students thought that the Chinese were the preeminent scapegoat for countrywide labor issues and added that the money earned by immigrants did not benefit America in any way, thus ruining opportunities for American laborers.[36]

The senate minutes indicated that the Philippines were discussed every year and that students' attitudes varied in regard to Filipinos as a race. However, Shortridge students never thought Filipino citizenship was a possibility, which was similar to their attitude to the Chinese. The students often discussed the possibility of Philippine independence, yet the prevailing attitude towards Filipinos, as political scientist Rogers Smith explained, was that they were "too racially distinct, inferior, and troublesome to possess any form of US citizenship or nationality."[37] This perspective was reflected in the Shortridge Senate, where students noted that Filipinos lacked an innate of ability to self-govern and were ultimately dependent on "superior races" for social advancement as a group of people.

Filipinos, while equally distinct from the American identity, received a slightly more balanced discussion in Shortridge Senate than the Chinese did. Much of the legislation related to Filipinos dealt with the question of their independence. While the Shortridge students thought "The Filipinos are better able to govern themselves than China," most did not think that Filipinos were ready for self-government.[38] The minutes noted that the students argued that "the Filipinos are an unproved race of people.... they have been mothered too much and are absolutely helpless".... "The Filipinos do not know the real fundamentals of citizenship"[39] ...and "the race in general lacked power of organization, which denied them the right to republicanism."[40] Yet there were some differing opinions among the students, such as the following comment: "The inhabitants of the Philippine Islands deserve self-government for they have become well-educated and civilized.... Besides, if this bill is passed, the United States will still supervise the most important affairs of the islands."[41] One student even compared Filipinos directly to Americans and said, "many educated men in the islands would establish schools when they gain their independence...they have good ideals as do the Americans."[42] While these comments reflected a more positive regard for Filipinos, the perception remained that they were only capable of self-governance in their own nation, and only due to the guidance of Americans or their imitation of Americans.

Discussions about Japanese immigrants provided a unique example of Shortridge students' thinking about citizenship because the students' views of the Japanese changed over this period of time. This change was most likely due to President Theodore Roosevelt's popularity and his well-known opinion of the Japanese.[43] Prior to 1907, when President Roosevelt signed the Gentlemen's Agreement, the Shortridge students had most often equated the Japanese with the Chinese laborers. For example, in 1907, the senate minutes indicated that students discussed a "Japanese Coolie Bill."[44] In this case, the students passed the bill in accordance with the Gentlemen's Agreement, which only allowed certain classes of Japanese to come to the United States to seek citizenship. Therefore, a certain class of Japanese people was excluded, but the students believed that other classes could share American ideals. After the Gentlemen's Agreement, the Japanese disappeared from the Shortridge Senate records. They were only discussed as aggressors in debates about protecting the Philippines as a US territory. Overall, discussions of the Japanese in the Shortridge Senate demonstrated the students' awareness of the predominant social perceptions concerning race and government policies.

Latin American Nationalities

The Shortridge students also found some Latin American nationalities, such as Cubans and Mexicans, unable to self-govern and considered them unfit for American citizenship. Cubans and Mexicans were usually discussed in relation to annexation, and students discussed their ability to possibly be US citizens. For example, students claimed, "Cubans are not in a condition to warrant their annexation" and "Cuba must work out her own salvation."[45] The students even compared Cubans to Filipinos in regard to their capability of self-government and said, "The Philippines are far more capable of self-government than were the Cubans when they were granted their independence."[46] The Shortridge students discussed Mexicans differently, as students' justified their ability to become US citizens based on their behavior as a nation. One student argued, "Mexico has always been an unruly neighbor, and has always encroached on our borders."[47] Shortridge students viewed the presence of Cubans and Mexicans in the United States as imminent, but they did not think that these groups would ever be fit for self-government.

European Nationalities

When Shortridge students discussed Europeans, they primarily talked about Eastern and Southern Europeans, and they thought that Europeans held potential for citizenship. Shortridge students often argued that the only ways these groups would effectively be able to participate as full citizens would be through increased education, English language development, and/or elimination of criminal behavior. These groups were commonly referred to simply as "immigrants" in much of the legislation. Eastern and Southern Europeans were often compared as counterexamples to other specific groups—for example, the Chinese or Japanese, Russians or Germans, Mexicans or Pacific Islanders. The legislation related to Eastern and Southern Europeans was usually proposed to restrict immigrant labor or to institute some sort of language proficiency standard or literacy test. Other proposed legislation included mandates that charged immigrants a fee for entering the US.[48] Southern Europeans were noted most frequently; students made comments like, "Our immigrants are chiefly from southern Europe.... The objection to them is that they go to the slums and lower the morality of the nation," or "We could not get along without Italian labor," and "We don't need an illiteracy test.... The people of southern Europe come here for opportunity."[49]

The concept of opportunity was often used to advocate for fewer restrictions on immigration. Many students were willing to overlook the lack of education if they believed certain groups of immigrants were willing to take advantage of the plethora of opportunities in America. This rationale supported the distinctive American character, because it placed value on the purported work ethic of Americans and the ability to transcend social ranks through hard work. However, some Americanization advocates who cited preservation, assimilation, and/or the inevitable degradation of the distinctive American character challenged the argument that valued opportunity. For example, students argued, "Immigration is a detriment to the U. S. financially.... we should restrict immigration so as to preserve the nation." They commented, "Our trouble with foreigners is our own fault.... We should assimilate them," and "American characteristics will soon be lost if immigration continues to such a large extent."[50] Many students also believed that immigrants were the sole inhabitants of the slums.[51] Students often criticized the literacy level that Eastern Europeans and Southern Europeans had in their native language, in English, or in both. Language and accent were often the most distinctive characteristics of immigrants in a city such as Indianapolis, with its largely German and Western European population. This student understanding of accent could be seen in a story in the yearbook that involved an Italian woman who used phrases like, "You say-a you teach us to love-a your flag."[52] The Eastern and Southern Europeans had a distinct notion of citizenship, the Shortridge students believed. According to many Shortridge students, the willingness to take advantage of opportunity in America was an important goal for this group of immigrants and served as their validation for citizenship.

The Shortridge Senate discussed other European groups, including Germans and Russians. Shortridge students proposed legislation to require all immigrants to take a literacy test. In a discussion about this legislation, one student spoke in favor of it solely because it favored German immigrants and kept out "less desirable" Eastern and Southern Europeans. He said, "America wants people with energy enough to learn English. Germany... affords all a chance to learn English in night school. Italians, Hungarians, Austrians, and Greeks are not wanted in America."[53] In regard to Russians, the Shortridge students were sympathetic and thought that Russians were capable of US citizenship because they immigrated for political reasons. One student even opposed the legislation regarding literacy tests because, "The Russians... came here for political freedom and had no time to learn English."[54] The discussions about these Europeans groups demonstrated how easily race as nation could open doors to citizenship in America, especially in comparison to the Asian and Latin American nationalities.

Americans without Citizenship

Shortridge students thought that African American citizens, like Eastern Europeans and Southern Europeans, had the potential to be full-fledged citizens. Similarly, students argued that the only way that Black citizens could effectively participate as full citizens was through increased education and decreased engagement in criminal behavior. While students believed there were exemplary Black citizens and individuals, these individuals were often not considered to be representative of the entire race, and thus many of the Shortridge Senators thought that full citizenship was not yet attainable for the group.

Shortridge students discussed the rights of Black citizens in several ways. Proposed legislation often dealt with Black citizens' education and suffrage, White congressional representation in states that disenfranchised Black citizens, and lynching. Curiously, Shortridge students did not record much of the actual discussions that concerned the deliberations about Black citizens' issues. It was apparent, however, that these issues were discussed, because the secretary of the senate often noted that legislation related to Black citizens' issues had been introduced and discussed on the senate floor. However, there was one exception that appeared in the senate minutes in 1902. The students had proposed legislation that limited the representation in Congress for states that had disenfranchised their Black citizens. This legislation was deliberated over six sessions and sparked a wide array of speeches by Shortbridge students.

In the second session in which this legislation was deliberated, the discussion began with speeches that justified the disenfranchisement of Black citizens. One student said, "the states in question were justified in the disenfranchising of their Negroes since their doing so was decided in the education and taxes," while another student noted that the Black citizens were susceptible to bribery and criminal activity, and would therefore prove detrimental to self-government.[55] Three White students spoke in support of Black citizens and one student stated: "The injustice of the argument is that the criminal tendencies of the race should debar them from the privilege of participation in government." He resented the criminal Negro being taken as a representative of his people. He expressed his belief that this extensive deprivation of the Negroes, of their privileges, would result in a rebellion. "Our country," he said, "can never lay claim to a representative government as long as White legislators represent the Negro citizens. Disenfranchisement deprives the Negro of the opportunity and desire to develop, and as a result, he becomes a hindrance instead of a help in the management of public affairs."[56]

This speech prompted two other White students to share a variety comments on Black leaders and the credit they bring to their race. They also blamed White citizens for the bribery of Black citizens and asserted that slavery still virtually existed in South Carolina, in consideration of how Black citizens were treated there.[57] These comments triggered responses from other White students that discredited Black citizens as a race. One student commented on criminal behavior and said "the Negro who is bribed is far more culpable than the briber since in sight of the law the former could be punished while the latter was wholly exempt."[58] Another student commented that Booker T. Washington was hardly representative of the entire race and that Black citizens were not only incapable of exercising the right to vote, but that they would abuse such privileges.[59] The last student to speak at this session put the notion of second-class citizenship into perspective. The secretary recorded his comment:

> The two questions involved in the consideration of the measure were liberty and representative government. Of the Negro race itself the Senator said he was heartily in favor; he saw in it great possibilities. But it was not liberty, he held, to extend to them in their present condition the privileges of suffrage. Representation should be of brain and not mass, and the Negroes are yet too ignorant.[60]

This comment was indicative of the perceived distinctiveness of race in this period, and the contempt that resulted for Black citizens as a whole. Considering the emancipatory Constitutional amendments that followed the Civil War, Black citizens' perceivably deficient education was the most warranted justification that White Shortridge senators could use to deny Black citizens their privilege to participate in government. This justification served as the basis for Shortridge senators to maintain a significant distinction between White and Black American citizens in terms of their ability to self-govern.

At the next session, the discussion continued in regard to education, and a Black Shortridge student spoke on behalf of his race. The following is the exchange as it was recorded in the school newspaper:

> Senator Heitfield of Idaho (James Myers) in an eloquent and exceedingly able speech defended his race against the accusations that several of the Senators had made at a previous meeting, and replied to their arguments against the bill. His speech was strong and well received, and he was interrupted often by bursts of applause. Senator Lodge then replied to various statements which Senator Heitfield had made, and discussed the equality of man. Senator White also replied to the colored Senator's arguments, stating that if the southern Negroes were on the same level as those in the north he would be in favor of enfranchisement, but not otherwise. Senator DeBoe then arose in support of the bill. In a capable speech he stated

that "the Negro should be given half a chance." Senator Tillman, however, differed with the Ohio legislator, and made a logical speech in which she stated her opinion that if ignorant Negroes could not vote, uneducated Whites should not.[61]

This last comment, made by a female student, seemed to strike a blow at the distinctive American character by highlighting the racist application of an alleged necessary qualification for suffrage. At the next session, the students began to move the focus of the discussion away from Black citizens, as one senator "corrected a mistaken impression which some of the members seemed to have had concerning the bill, that it does not refer only to Negroes only but also whites."[62] Another senator dismissed the support for such a bill as a political maneuver, saying that "the gentlemen in question were supporting the bill with an eye toward obtaining the Negro vote in future races for re-election," while another senator dismissed the previous discussion because the bill had nothing to do with Negro enfranchisement, but dealt specifically with regulating the number of congressional representatives a state should be allowed if it disenfranchised Black citizens.[63]

These exchanges are illuminating for two reasons. First, the bill did not directly deal with Black citizens' rights. It was purely an issue to be discussed in terms of federalism, yet the students almost immediately began to debate the rights of the citizens involved. Second, the students used the same arguments to deny Black citizens the right to vote as they used to deny immigrants the right to citizenship. Even with Black and female students as senators, bringing to the forefront the inequality inherent in the other students' notions of citizenship, the distinctiveness of race, in terms of perceived capabilities to be citizens, prevailed. Black citizens deserved liberty, but they were not part of the distinctive American character that could utilize the privileges of full citizenship and self-government.

Conclusion

The Shortridge students' discussions focused on the nationalities' perceived attributes that made them unfit for American citizenship. These attributes were based on societal constructions of race as nation and were used to justify the groups' perceived capabilities for citizenship. Although some of the Shortridge students held on to Gerstle's conception of civic nationalism, most students embraced the "racialized notions of belonging" associated with racial nationalism, and clung to their distinct American character to rationalize how some groups were unfit for American citizenship.[64]

Regarding the groups discussed in the Shortridge Senate, the students were different from most other schools of this period because they considered and discussed Black citizens, and specifically their citizenship. This phenomenon could possibly be attributed to Donnan's personal devotion to equality and to her advocacy for Black citizens, or to the fact that Black students regularly attended the Shortridge Senate. Regardless of the reason, the discussion of Black citizens was not commonplace in schools. As Burkholder noted, social studies teachers during the Progressive Era "found little cause to celebrate or even consider the culture of American blacks."[65] Black citizens were also unique in these discussions that utilized constructions of race as nation because "African Americans could not be conflated with a single nation—instead they were positioned in, but distinct from, both Americans and Africans."[66] Yet in terms of citizenship, Shortridge students discussed the attributes of Black citizens as if they were immigrants, because of their distinctiveness from the American notion of citizenship. Despite their consideration and discussion of Black citizens, most of the White Shortridge students still thought that the majority of Black citizens were unfit for self-government.

By 1918, students considered Shortridge High School to be "a most cosmopolitan school."[67] In the Shortridge yearbooks from 1915 to 1920, there were articles that discussed the perceivable cosmopolitan aspects of the school. The students who wrote these articles were from England, Germany, Greece, Italy, Japan, the Philippines, Poland, Romania, and Serbia. The articles all discussed life in their respective countries, and most discussed how the students had assimilated into and had come to appreciate American society. These students were considered part of a worldly notion of citizenship that was inclusive of Americans, but was separate from the American notion of citizenship. The Shortridge students viewed these students as part of a community that sought the ideals comprised in civic nationalism and in the American form of self-government.

Since the Black citizens lacked a national association, Shortridge students viewed Black citizens as neither part of the cosmopolitan group nor part of the American notion of citizenship at Shortridge. In consideration of civic nationalist ideals, Black citizens could be discussed in comparable terms to many other groups, but racially they were seen as distinctly different. Black citizens sharply confronted the distinctive American character and notion of citizenship, while other groups had the possibility of contributing to a civic nationalist idea of citizenship and self-government, simply because of their skin color.

The Shortridge Senate held unique value in that it provided a space for students to discuss the ideals of government that were deeply intertwined with the notions of American citizenship. These notions of American citizenship became very complex when coupled with conceptions of race, or of race as nation. Despite the strong influence of Donnan and her brand of civic nationalism, many of the Shortridge students could not break from the popular notions of race, or from the ideology of racial nationalism. This ideology trumped any commitment to civic nationalism and set aside the privileges of self-government for those who were least distinct from White Americans and the American character.

Notes

1. Claude Bowers, *My Life: The Memoirs of Claude Bowers* (New York: Simon and Schuster, 1962); Virginia Cox, *Laura Donnan* [Biographical essay] (Indianapolis: Indiana State Library, 1936); Holman Hamilton and Gayle Thorbrough, eds., *Indianapolis in the Gay Nineties: High School Diaries of Claude G. Bowers* (Indianapolis: Indiana State Library, 1964); and Walter Hendrickson, *The Indiana Years 1903–1941* (Indianapolis: Indiana Historical Society, 1983).
2. *The Annual*, 1926. Catalogued separately LD7501 .I4647 A5, Shortridge High School Collection, 1870–1981, 1995, Indiana State Historical Society.
3. Virginia Cox, *Laura Donnan* [Biographical essay] (Indianapolis: Indiana State Library, 1936), 5.
4. Ibid., 4–5.
5. For a discussion on racial understanding during this era, see the chapter by Thomas Fallace in this volume.
6. Virginia Cox, *Laura Donnan*, 4–5.
7. Claude Bowers, *Indianapolis in the Gay Nineties: High School Diaries of Claude G. Bowers* (Indianapolis: Indiana State Library, 1964). Virginia Cox, *Laura Donnan* [Biographical essay] (Indianapolis: Indiana State Library, 1936). Laura Gaus, *Shortridge High School, 1864–1981: In Retrospect* (Indianapolis: Indiana Historical Society, 1985).
8. Laura Gaus, *Shortridge High School, 1864–1981: In Retrospect* (Indianapolis: Indiana Historical Society, 1985).
9. Editorial Staff, *The Echo*, March 6, 1899.
10. Laura Gaus, *Shortridge High School, 1864–1981: In Retrospect*, 30.
11. Walter Hendrickson, *The Indiana Years 1903–1941* (Indianapolis: Indiana Historical Society, 1983), 131.
12. Laura Gaus, *Shortridge High School, 1864–1981: In Retrospect*, 74.
13. Virginia Cox, *Laura Donnan*, 12.
14. Laura Gaus, *Shortridge High School, 1864–1981: In Retrospect* .
15. Alex Uriebel, "The Making of Citizens: A History of Civic Education in Indianapolis, 1900–1950," PhD dissertation, Indiana University, 1996.
16. Jeffrey Mirel, *Patriotic Pluralism* (Cambridge, MA: Harvard University Press, 2010).
17. Gary Gerstle, *American Crucible*, (Princeton, NJ: Princeton University Press, 2001), 4.

18. Michael Ignatieff, quoted in in Gary Gerstle, *American Crucible* (Princeton, NJ: Princeton University Press, 2001), 45.
19. Gary Gerstle, *American Crucible*, 4.
20. Ibid., 5.
21. Ibid., 59.
22. Rogers Smith, "The 'American Creed' and American Identity: The Limits of Liberal Citizenship in the United States," *The Western Political Quarterly* 41 (June 1988): 233.
23. Gary Gerstle, *American Crucible* (Princeton, NJ: Princeton University Press, 2001); Jeffrey Mirel, *Patriotic Pluralism* (Cambridge, MA: Harvard University Press, 2010); Julie Reuben, "Beyond Politics: Community Civics and the Redefinition of Citizenship in the Progressive Era," *History of Education Quarterly* 37 (1997): 399–420.
24. Julie Reuben, "Beyond Politics," 400–401.
25. Laura Donnan, "The High School and the Citizen," *The Journal of Addresses and Proceedings of the National Education Association Annual Meeting* 28 (1889): 515.
26. Zoë Burkholder, *Color in the Classroom: How American Schools Taught Race, 1900–1954* (New York: Oxford Press, 2011), 16.
27. Ibid., 16.
28. Ibid., 16.
29. Ibid., 35.
30. Laura Donnan, "The High School and the Citizen," 512–520.
31. Rogers Smith, "The 'American Creed' and American Identity: the Limits of Liberal Citizenship in the United States," *The Western Political Quarterly* 41 (June 1988): 233.
32. Senate Minutes, 1901, Bound Volumes, Shortridge High School Collection, 1870–1981, Folder BV 2395, Senate Student Records, Indiana State Historical Society, 81. Senate Minutes, September 19, 1924, Bound Volumes, Shortridge High School Collection, 1870–1981, Folder BV 2392, Senate Student Records, Indiana State Historical Society.
33. Senate Minutes, 1900–1902, Bound Volumes, Shortridge High School Collection, 1870–1981, Folder BV 2395, Senate Student Records, Indiana State Historical Society.
34. Senate Minutes, 1907, Bound Volumes, Shortridge High School Collection, 1870–1981, Folder BV 2390, Senate Student Records, Indiana State Historical Society, 140.
35. Senate Minutes, 1901, Bound Volumes, Shortridge High School Collection, 1870–1981, Folder BV 2395, Senate Student Records, Indiana State Historical Society, 82.
36. Senate Minutes, 1906, Bound Volumes, Shortridge High School Collection, 1870–1981, Folder BV 2390, Senate Student Records, Indiana State Historical Society, 39.
37. Rogers Smith, *Civic Ideals* (New Haven, CT: Yale University Press, 1997), 429.
38. Senate Minutes, September 23, 1923, Bound Volumes, Shortridge High School Collection, 1870–1981, Folder BV 2392, Senate Student Records, Indiana State Historical Society.

39. Ibid.
40. Senate Minutes, 1907, Bound Volumes, Shortridge High School Collection, 1870–1981, Folder BV 2390, Senate Student Records, Indiana State Historical Society, 142.
41. Senate Minutes, 1914, Bound Volumes, Shortridge High School Collection, 1870–1981, Folder BV 2389, Senate Student Records, Indiana State Historical Society, 22.
42. Ibid., 28.
43. Theodore Roosevelt, *Outlook Editorials* (New York: The Outlook Company, 1909), 71–80. The Gentlemen's Agreement (1907) was issued by President Theodore Roosevelt in an effort to restrict the emigration of Japanese laborers from Japan while not rejecting Japanese immigrants that were already present in United States. It was an attempt to appease people who demanded that the government segregate Japanese children in the schools in California.
44. Senate Minutes, 1907, Bound Volumes, Shortridge High School Collection, 1870–1981, Folder BV 2390, Senate Student Records, Indiana State Historical Society, 140.
45. Senate Minutes, 1906, Bound Volumes, Shortridge High School Collection, 1870–1981, Folder BV 2390, Senate Student Records, Indiana State Historical Society, 26–27.
46. Senate Minutes, 1907, Bound Volumes, Shortridge High School Collection, 1870–1981, Folder BV 2390, Senate Student Records, Indiana State Historical Society, 141.
47. Senate Minutes, November 14, 1919, Bound Volumes, Shortridge High School Collection, 1870–1981, Folder BV 2391, Senate Student Records, Indiana State Historical Society.
48. Senate Minutes, October 4, 1910, Bound Volumes, Shortridge High School Collection, 1870–1981, Folder BV 2393, Senate Student Records, Indiana State Historical Society.
49. Senate Minutes, 1915, Bound Volumes, Shortridge High School Collection, 1870–1981, Folder BV 2389, Senate Student Records, Indiana State Historical Society, 131. Senate Minutes, May 14, 1917, Bound Volumes, Shortridge High School Collection, 1870–1981, Folder BV 2389, Senate Student Records, Indiana State Historical Society.
50. Senate Minutes, 1915, Bound Volumes, Shortridge High School Collection, 1870–1981, Folder BV 2389, Senate Student Records, Indiana State Historical Society, 131. Senate Minutes, May 14, 1917, Bound Volumes, Shortridge High School Collection, 1870–1981, Folder BV 2389, Senate Student Records, Indiana State Historical Society.
51. Senate Minutes, 1906–1908, Bound Volumes, Shortridge High School Collection, 1870–1981, Folder BV 2390, Senate Student Records, Indiana State Historical Society.
52. *The Annual*, 1920, Catalogued Separately LD7501 .I4647 A5, Shortridge High School Collection, 1870–1981, 1995, Indiana State Historical Society.
53. Senate Minutes, 1906, Bound Volumes, Shortridge High School Collection, 1870–1981, Folder BV 2390, Senate Student Records, Indiana State Historical Society, 41.
54. Ibid.

55. Senate Minutes, 1902, Bound Volumes, Shortridge High School Collection, 1870–1981, Folder BV 2395, Senate Student Records, Indiana State Historical Society, 97.
56. Ibid.
57. Ibid.
58. Ibid.
59. Ibid.
60. Ibid.
61. Ibid.
62. Ibid.
63. Ibid.
64. Gary Gerstle, *American Crucible* (Princeton, NJ: Princeton University Press, 2001), 127.
65. Zoe Burkholder, *Color in the Classroom: How American Schools Taught Race, 1900–1954* (New York: Oxford Press, 2011), 39.
66. Ibid., 35.
67. *The Annual,* 1918, Catalogued Separately LD7501 .I4647 A5, Shortridge High School Collection, 1870–1981, 1995, Indiana State Historical Society.

Chapter Five
Countering the Master Narrative in US Social Studies: Nannie Helen Burroughs and New Narratives in History Education

Alana D. Murray

In 1909, Nannie Helen Burroughs created the National Training School for Women and Girls in Washington, DC, which was designed to teach African American girls the skills needed to be intellectual contributors to the nation's labor force. Historians of the National Training School have emphasized its conservatism, discipline, and adherence to the industrial Christian model.[1]

A close examination, however, of the "unofficial" curricula of the school, and in particular, of the annual Black history performance, titled *When Truth Gets a Hearing* challenges this view. The pageant, acted by the students, was performed four times between 1916 to 1930, according to extant records found in the Library of Congress. In three crucial respects the Black-centered pageant challenges current historiography. First, a reading of *When Truth Gets a Hearing* subverts traditional underpinnings of the nature of Nannie Helen Burroughs's philosophies of "training" Black girls for their "proper place" in the early twentieth century White-supremacist society.[2] Second, a reading of *When Truth Gets a Hearing* challenges current narratives about how the field of social studies was constructed and reconstructed to incorporate Black history.[3] Finally, the work of Nannie Helen Burroughs also challenges traditional epistemological frameworks of the field of social studies/history education. These interpretations have tended to emphasize the standards of social studies organizations such as the National Council of Social Studies.[4] In contrast, Nannie Helen Burroughs, through her correspondence with Carter G. Woodson and the authoring of *When Truth Gets a Hearing*, reveals a case of how African

American scholars actively sought to reshape social studies, through the creation of an "unofficial" curriculum.[5] In this alternative curriculum, history became a vehicle for uplifting, educating, and inspiring African American girls in the early part of the twentieth century.

Nannie Helen Burroughs's pageant *When Truth Gets a Hearing* demonstrates how African American educators reinterpreted available historical sources to create an alternative Black curriculum that challenged the dominant narrative institutionalized in all schools during the early twentieth century. Throughout the course of this chapter, I will consider the context of the social studies curriculum and its influence on the pageant, give a review of the literature on Nannie Helen Burroughs, and make a textual analysis of the pageant *When Truth Gets a Hearing*.

The Social Studies Canon and African American Responses

The field of social studies developed in the latter half of the nineteenth century. Debates over formal curriculum often reflected different ideological conceptions of the proper role of social studies in a democracy. Initially, in 1893 the National Education Association (NEA) created a standardized curriculum to be taught in the nation's high schools. The Committee of Ten, chaired by Charles Eliot of Harvard University and led by a subcommittee composed of leaders such as Charles Kendall Adams, Woodrow Wilson, and James Harvey, drafted a social studies curriculum that profoundly shaped the social studies field.[6] In their final recommendations, the Committee of Ten suggested a course of study that included a heavy focus on American history, Greek and Roman history, French history, and English history. In 1896, the American Historical Association (AHA) commissioned a group of historians to survey history instruction in the nation's public schools. Embracing social science methods, these historians conducted a comprehensive analysis of how history was being taught in school.[7] In 1916, another group of prominent educators, influenced by the educational philosophy of John Dewey, sought to refine the ideas suggested by the initial Committee of Ten. The group proposed a curriculum that stressed an ideological commitment to civics and democracy.[8] In each of the committees' recommendations, the history sequences placed a heavy value on the accomplishments of Europe.

Although progressive in their embrace of how history should be broadened to include more social history and other types of history, the reformers tended to limit the types of narratives they embraced. The 1893, 1896, and 1916 curricula stressed the narrative of Europe's domination—and by extension, the United States' domination—over the supposedly "inferior" races of Africa, Asia, and Latin America. Moreover, each curriculum stressed a traditional narrative about the United States, which emphasized the founding of our country by a group of intelligent White men. This approach reified the racism that was prevalent in American society.[9]

Although African American historians were interested in larger Progressive Era educational reform, they were more passionate about fighting the rampant Jim Crow endemic in American life. In an attempt to create an intellectual self-defense of Black humanity, African American historians and educators created an alternative Black curriculum. The alternative Black curriculum, as defined below, offered a critique of the normative structure of the dominant historical narrative. The alternative Black curriculum sought to engage with historical scholarship as defined by scholars such as W. E. B. Du Bois and Carter G. Woodson. Recent historiographical inquiry into the development of a historical narrative explored its emergence in the period 1900–1940.[10] These historiographical inquiries tended to focus on the work of Black male scholars. Because of the concentration on the work of the professional Black male historians with degrees from prestigious institutions such as Harvard University, the work of Black women professionals was obscured. One goal of this work is to explore the development of the alternative Black curriculum with a bottom-up historical framework that examines how women without traditional access to knowledge production consumed, as well as generated, new understandings of social studies.[11] The site of school provided Black women teachers, librarians, and administrators with significant latitude about how their students should be taught history.[12]

In generating this curriculum, African American scholars created avenues of response to the more formal meetings conducted by national organizations. Organizations such as the Association for the Study of Negro Life and History (founded in 1915) and the National Association of Colored Women (founded in 1896) formed to discuss how to generate more accurate portrayals of African American history.

From 1890 to 1940, African American scholars created curricula that suggested new narratives for how world history and US history should be taught. W. E. B. Du Bois, Carter G. Woodson, Anna Julia Cooper, and Nannie Helen Burroughs were among many prominent intellectuals who generated new epistemologies about African Americans' contributions to history. As they created frameworks for understanding the African American experience, common elements emerged. The basic principles of the alternative Black curriculum included the following items:

(a) a counterresponse to the existing canon that would stress the importance of African civilizations such as Abyssinia, Nubia, Kush, Mali, and Ghana[13]
(b) a counterresponse to the existing canon that would stress the importance of African American contributions, such as the value

of slave labor in building the key infrastructure of the early United States[14]

(c) a recognition of the roles of Africans and African Americans in shaping the political culture of the United States. African American educators argued that the voices of Harriet Tubman, Frederick Douglass, and other key Black leaders should be studied along with the "Founding Fathers"[15]

(d) a defense of Black labor. For example, scholars wanted to acknowledge the tradition of entrepreneurship in the Black community[16]

(e) a pan-African vision that linked African American struggles with the struggles of people of color from other parts of the world. For example, African American activists stressed the role that the Haitian Revolution played in shaping a Black identity in the Western Hemisphere[17]

(f) a discussion about the impact of race and racism[18]

(g) an inclusion of White allies in the struggle against racism[19]

There is a growing body of work that demonstrates that the basic principles of this revisionist formal curriculum (often created by African American male scholars) in many ways was supplemented and even furthered by an ongoing dialogue with the pedagogical work of African American women school founders, administrators, and teachers.[20] This pedagogical work married the principles of the alternative Black curriculum to the everyday realities of the classroom. For example, the International Council of Women of the Darker Races was created in 1922 for women in education to study the history of the African Diaspora.[21] In this dialogue between Black academics, teachers, and activists, we see a case study of Black women engaging in the types of discussions that created key components of the alternative Black curriculum.

Scholarly Dimensions of the Life and Work of Nannie Helen Burroughs

Nannie Helen Burroughs's *When Truth Gets a Hearing* is a representative example of the alternative Black curriculum in both its content and its form. African American educational leaders Charlotte Hawkins Brown, Anna Julia Cooper, Mary McLeod Bethune, and Nannie Helen Burroughs have been the focus of recent historical investigation, thus adding to the existing scholarship on White women educators. These examples show how African American leaders worked in the shadow of Progressivism while reinterpreting its ideals to meet the urgent needs of African Americans during the post-Reconstruction period.[22]

Scholarship on Nannie Helen Burroughs has focused on two areas. First, a number of scholars have outlined the biographical and social context for her educational philosophy. Opal Easter has authored the most comprehensive biographical review of the life of Nannie Helen Burroughs to date.[23] She outlined Burroughs's roles in the women's auxiliary of the National Baptist Convention (NBC) and the National Association of Colored Women, as well as in the founding of the National Training School for Women and Girls.

Sharon Harley examined the social context of Burroughs's spheres of influence. Harley situated her own research in the class dynamics that influenced Washington, DC, in the early part of the twentieth century.[24] She characterized Nannie Helen Burroughs as an activist for the working class. Burroughs's upbringing influenced her interest in the working class. She was born in Culpeper, Virginia, in 1879. Her mother was determined to provide her with a superior education, so she moved Burroughs to Washington, DC.[25] Nannie Helen Burroughs graduated from the famous segregated DC school, M Street High, in 1896; she hoped to become a teacher of domestic science. It was in her pursuit of a teaching job that Burroughs encountered widespread colorism, and she was unable to find a teaching position.[26] Sharon Harley has argued that it was this experience of interracial discrimination that led Burroughs to advocate for working women's education.[27]

Scholars also have examined Nannie Helen Burroughs's professional work in the field of education, including her instructional leadership at the National Training School for Women and Girls. Karen Johnson compared the work, educational philosophies, and careers of Anna Julia Cooper and Nannie Helen Burroughs.[28] She concluded that Burroughs's work was more practical than Cooper's, given its basis in concepts associated with industrial education. Traki L. Taylor examined the role of Nannie Helen Burroughs in creating a school specifically to develop and uplift the self-esteem of African American girls. Taylor emphasized Burroughs's embrace of domestic education and its potential to uplift the self-esteem of African American girls across the United States, the Caribbean, and Africa.[29] Michelle Reif discussed Nannie Helen Burroughs's founding role in the International Council of Women of the Darker Races, which was created by African American female educational activists after World War I to deepen their understanding of the histories of the countries of China, Egypt, and parts of the Caribbean and Africa.[30] Most recently, Sarah Bair provided an analysis of how Nannie Helen Burroughs implemented a curriculum that emphasized civic education and African American History.[31]

In this chapter, I focus upon a little-known aspect of Nannie Helen Burroughs's role in the development of the alternative Black curriculum, her creation of the historical pageant *When Truth Gets a Hearing*. By focusing on *When Truth Gets a Hearing*, I hope to ascertain how a female author created a narrative that developed and nurtured the identity of African American girls. I argue that it is critical for scholars to explore how Nannie Helen Burroughs analyzed perspectives on womanhood and femininity in *When Truth Gets a Hearing*. Her perspectives on the role of Black women in history added wider scope to the alternative Black curriculum.

Creating a Revisionist Curriculum

When Truth Gets a Hearing is a representative example of the types of pageants that social studies educators and other scholars created in the period between Reconstruction and World War I. In fact, by developing the pageant, Burroughs participated in a historical era in which pageants were in vogue as a form of cultural transmission. Beginning in the early 1900s, pageants became a popular form of expression for communities to express pride in American history.[32] Embracing the popularity of pageants and as a form of race pride, W. E. B. Du Bois penned his own pageant, *The Star of Ethiopia*, which opened in 1913.[33] The extravagantly produced *Star of Ethiopia* played in Philadelphia (1913), New York (1913), Washington, DC, (1915), and in Los Angeles (1925).[34] W. E. B. Du Bois fervently believed that historical pageants served a function in connecting the disciplines of art and history.[35] He also thought that the narrative of the *Star of Ethiopia* directly repudiated movies such as *Birth of a Nation* (1915).[36] He advocated that pageants were essential tools for teaching African Americans about their history.[37] Du Bois argued that pageants also served to connect the histories of the people of the African diaspora. In his pageant, Du Bois connected elements of African history, the Middle Passage, slavery, and Reconstruction into one sweeping narrative.[38]

Staged with approximately 350 actors, *The Star of Ethiopia* occurred on a much grander scale than Burroughs's pageant. However, both of these educators understood the critical role that ritualized ceremonies played in the Black community. Educational researcher Theresa Perry argues that graduations, pageants, and assemblies nurtured the psyches of African American children.[39] She posited that church, school, and community events acted as a "triangulation of influences" that combated doubts about African American students' intellectual skills.[40]

When Truth Gets a Hearing was an attempt by one educator to use a pageant to uplift and educate African American girls. Burroughs developed a pageant that combined an appreciation of past historical triumphs of Africans with contemporary problems that African Americans confronted in the United States. Burroughs embedded religious themes, racial disputes, rich musical traditions, an analysis of labor issues, a critique of lynching, and narratives of ancient and US history in the script. For the purposes of this chapter, I am interested in exploring how Burroughs constructed an alternative Black curriculum in ancient history and US history. In addition, I am interested in how Nannie Helen Burroughs added a significant analysis of the accomplishments of women into the curriculum.

The structure of *When Truth Gets a Hearing* reflected the overriding concern that the scholars and practitioners who worked with African American young people had in creating narratives that challenged the assumed superiority of White culture. *When Truth Gets a Hearing* was designed as a pageant in which a group of African Americans are presented in a court of law, defending their humanity. Burroughs introduced the witnesses as Injustice, Prejudice, Ignorance, and Error. On the other side she had the characters Truth, Law, Peace, Goodwill, Fairplay, Justice, History, and Representatives of the Negro Race and Africa. The structure of Burroughs's pageant allowed African Americans to create a response to the injustices that were prevalent during the time period shortly before World War I. Burroughs selected the pageant as a vehicle to express these images, which demonstrated her intent to engage audiences of students, potential donors, and laypeople.

The pageant's themes were reinforced through Burroughs's reevaluation of content. In the 1916 Report on the Committee on Social Studies of the Commission on the Reorganization of Secondary Schools, members proposed a sequence that included a course titled, "European History to about the 1700's, Including the Discovery and Settling of America." In this curriculum sequence, students were encouraged to learn about the accomplishments of ancient Greeks, the Roman Empire, the Exploration Age, and the rise of England and France as nation-states.[41] This type of course is an exemplar of the importance of European history in secondary schools curricula in the early part of the twentieth century.

In contrast, the section of *When Truth Gets a Hearing* on ancient history challenged traditional notions of how students were taught about the world predating 1500 BC. The section on ancient history begins with Justice declaring, "History, give us the facts about the Negro's contribution to ancient civilization and to the development of the New World."[42] By framing the opening of this section of the pageant with an emphasis on revisionist history, Burroughs provided the reader with a guide to implicit critiques of the traditional narrative that followed.

In the early part of the pageant, Nannie Helen Burroughs constructs a narrative that paralleled accomplishments in Greece and Rome with those of Egypt, Nubia, and Abyssinia (Ethiopia). Burroughs's perspective that Egyptians should be included in the Black racial group in Africa was quite different from that of scholars, who categorized Egyptians as Middle Eastern and Caucasian. She described how Africans created the Sphinx at Giza and the civilization of Meroe and Abyssinia. Burroughs wrote, "Five thousand years before the birth of Christ, Black men are building empires in Africa."[43] By placing the emphasis on the role of race, Burroughs offered an immediate example of how African American scholars were trying to create a link to a past that predated modern Europeans.[44] A critical tenet of the alternative Black curriculum was the acknowledgment of stories of Black leadership in the ancient world. The authors of the alternative Black curriculum wanted to create a narrative that acknowledged the stories of Black leadership in the ancient world.

Another distinctive characteristic of the alternative Black curriculum that was evident in the pageant is the comparison of African civilizations to the mythic European past. In the ancient history section, Burroughs referenced the history of Germany. She directly attacked notions of European superiority when she wrote "In fact, [when] the Anglos were barbarians in northern Germany[,] eating their food out of the skulls of their ancestors and using the bones of their dead for knives and forks, black men were at work building civilization in Africa."[45] This direct attack on European superiority represented an attempt by Burroughs to strengthen her claims that African Americans were equal counterparts to Whites. Although White historians during this period sought to present history in an "objective" fashion, Black scholars and practitioners laid out facts in a defense of African Americans' humanity and freedom.[46]

Another aspect of the alternative Black curriculum evident in Burroughs's work is her attempt to convey that there is a rich tradition of scholarship on the African continent. Since scholars in the nineteenth century had claimed that Blacks lacked civilization, Burroughs connected African Americans to a past that included significant scholarly accomplishments, in order to refute that claim. In the pageant, the character History declares:

> Justice, the best scholars and historians concede, after years of research and investigation, that Ethiopia, or Black men, gave learning to Egypt–Egypt to Greece–Greece to Rome–Rome to Britain–and Britain to the world. This fact, therefore gives the Negro a high place in the intellectual and political history of the world.[47]

By making the argument that Ethiopia and Egypt gave learning to the Greeks, Burroughs attacked the idea that African Americans were intellectually inferior to their White counterparts.

Often the scholarly literature about Burroughs portrays her as a female version of Booker T. Washington, exhorting African American women to a life of labor.⁴⁸ In creating a vision for the National Training School for Women and Girls, which focused on training girls for positions of laundresses and secretaries, Burroughs seemed to remain loyal to Washington's vision. However, in *When Truth Gets a Hearing,* she imparted a more complicated message, which included a passionate defense of Black intellectualism. Burroughs seemed quite aware that Black school leaders needed to communicate a varied message to diverse audiences, who ranged from White philanthropists to the parents of girls who attended her school.

In the US history portion of the pageant, similar themes to those in the section on ancient history begin to emerge in Burroughs's writing. The play was written in subsequent drafts between 1916 and 1921, and clearly the events of the interwar period affected Burroughs's analysis. In the US History section of the play, the focus on African American men's participation in the US military is evident. Burroughs traced how Black men served in the Revolutionary War, the Civil War, Spanish-American War, and World War I. She referenced the death of Crispus Attucks. In the pageant, she reinforced the message that African Americans had been loyal patriots. Burroughs wrote in the shadow of the Red Summer of 1919, when race riots occurred in the summer and fall.⁴⁹ The focus on Black males as citizens and patriots challenged notions of Black men as threats to the White people of the United States.

In addition, Burroughs also examined the contemporary issue of lynching, which was connected to the Red Summer of 1919. During the summer of 1919, Blacks experienced a wave of violence, which included clashes among the races, massacres, and lynching.⁵⁰ By addressing the controversial topic of lynching, Burroughs again demonstrated the subversive tendencies of the alternative Black curriculum. In the section on lynching, Burroughs actively worked to connect racial violence with a lack of enforcement of the Thirteenth, Fourteenth, and Fifteenth Amendments to the United States Consitution. Burroughs, through one of the characters in play named Legislation, explained:

> Justice, I am Legislation. I am here to speak for the enforcement of all laws.
>
> This government has spent millions of dollars for the enforcement of the eighteenth Amendment and not <u>one cent</u> for the enforcement of the 14th and 15th Amendments. It is more important that men have the <u>liberty</u> in America than it is for them to not have liquor.⁵¹

Immediately after discussing issues of legislation, Burroughs referenced the lynching report created by the Commission on Interracial Cooperation. The Commission on Interracial Cooperation was established to investigate the race riots that occurred in the summer of 1919.⁵² By referencing these events in the pageant, Burroughs created a forum for her audience to contemplate the meaning of African American citizenship in the face of racist conditions.

Burroughs also focused on the labor of slaves, which she claimed was a crucial component in the establishment of the United States. Burroughs's character Negro Womanhood stated, "I felled trees, tilled fields, protected homes, nursed the children of another race, made brick, built big houses for others and cabins for myself."[53] In her section on labor, Burroughs explored two key themes. First, Nannie Helen Burroughs sought to combat the stereotype that African Americans lacked a work ethic. One of the central premises of the National Training School for Women and Girls was its emphasis on the role of hard work of women in uplifting the Black community. Nannie Helen Burroughs championed the idea of work during the course of her life.

Second, in the play, she encouraged African Americans to be proud of their work ethic. In fact, with her reliance on references to Christianity, Burroughs clearly wanted to connect the Protestant doctrine to the work that Blacks consistently were required to do throughout the history of the republic.

Negro Womanhood Defined

In the development of a Black historical narrative, Nannie H. Burroughs's work showed similarities with narratives posited by Black male historians such as W. E. B. Du Bois and Carter G. Woodson. Pero Gaglo Dagbovie discussed how Black women served as practical implementers of the alternative Black curriculum.[54] In the case of Nannie H. Burroughs and many other Black women educators, they not only implemented the alternative Black curriculum in their schools, but they also added to key discourses about the history of African Americans in the United States. Much like her male colleagues, Nannie H. Burroughs appeared interested in uplifting and defending the Black race through history. However, Burroughs in her pageant, *"When Truth Gets a Hearing,"* added to the narrative by conceptualizing the role of Black womanhood in US history and world history quite differently than her male colleagues did.

For example, one of the explicit themes both Du Bois and Burroughs considered in their pageants was the impact that Black women had on US history and on ancient history. In the *Star of Ethiopia,* Du Bois idealized the image of a saintly African American woman. He created a character, "The Veiled Woman," who appeared throughout the pageant, symbolizing the dignity and splendor of Black womanhood. He wrote, "At last dimly enhaloed in mysterious light, the Veiled Woman appears, commanding in stature and splendid in garment, her dark face faintly visible, and in her right hand fire, and iron her left."[55]

Clearly evident in this quote is Du Bois's attempt to provide Black women with an exalted status. However, throughout *Star of Ethiopia*, he continued to provide his male characters such as Mansa Musa, Stephen Dorantes, Touissant L'Ouverture, John Brown, and Frederick Douglass with far more agency than women had in the fight against oppression and racism. In Du Bois's framing of Black history, Black womanhood became idealized. As a result, Black women lost their potency as equal advocates to men in promoting freedom in the African American community.

Nannie H. Burroughs conceived of the role of Black women quite differently. She explicitly mentioned the impact of the leadership of the Queen of Sheba and of Candace, Queen of Meroe, in kingdoms in ancient civilization. Although she praised the accomplishments of Black women, Burroughs also mentioned specific moments in history, giving clearer shape to the work of women. More explicitly, she gendered the role of Black labor. In one particular passage, the dynamic became evident. She wrote, "Truth: Justice, this is an ex-slave. Will you let (her) tell about her contribution to the up building of America?"[56]

In the pageant, the character of Ex-Slave delivered a speech about Black women's labor. Burroughs squarely placed the work of Black women on a equal status with the work of Black men. In Burroughs's vision of the alternative Black curriculum, women's agency played a critical role. Instead of idealizing the Black woman, Nannie Burroughs explicitly argued about the concrete contributions of African Americans to the construction of Black nationhood.

One of the unique characteristics of *When Truth Gets a Hearing* is Nannie Helen Burroughs's deliberate inclusion of, and reference to, the role of Black women in history. African American women in the post-Reconstruction era struggled to define themselves in both the private and public sphere. Throughout her pageant, Burroughs seeks to create a narrative that views Black women as significant contributors to their community.[57]

The ancient history section of *When Truth Gets a Hearing* stresses the establishment of the role of Black women as creators in history. Burroughs writes about Candace, Queen of the Meroe civilization. When the Meroe civilization was ruled by a line of "queens," they were also known as a *candace* or *kandake*."[58] With this example, Burroughs tries to establish that women of color have always served as leaders in their communities. Burroughs may have attempted to include a perspective that would highlight the accomplishments of Black women, because she served as a leader in a predominantly African American setting. Burroughs sought to create figures and images that would have supported and uplifted her students.

Indeed, Burroughs subverted common ideologies in which women were relegated to the home. This pageant directly supported the idea that African American girls must serve their world outside of the domestic sphere. Burroughs publicly emphasized the connection between the role of labor and the Black woman, since the National Training School was reliant on outside philanthropists. The use of Candace, however, points to a more subtle message: Black women had royal traits and heritage and could be leaders beyond the narrowly circumscribed roles as domestics that were the focus of much industrial education.

In her section on United States history, Burroughs also extended the alternative Black curriculum (which was often concerned with a defense of African American contributions) to a defense of Black womanhood on the North American continent. Burroughs wrote, "I represent Negro Womanhood. For 250 years I worked in the cornfields, kept the big house like a palace, nursed the children of my master and loved them with a love and tenderness such as the world has never seen and will never see again."[59] Here, Burroughs acknowledges the role over time that labor played in African American women's identity. Again, Burroughs offered a counter-narrative to the role that women in general and Black women in particular were often relegated to in segregated America. She called for Black women's work to be recognized. Burroughs's perspective is complicated, though, by her reliance on the common sentimentality of slave women and their care of White children, which was associated with images of Southern womanhood during that time period.

Conclusion

The pageant has important implications for rethinking the role of Black scholars in the field of social studies. Gloria Ladson-Billings, in *Critical Race Theory: Perspectives in Social Studies,* contends, "The discourse of invisibility is true of every non-European group of people who constitute our nation."[60] Oftentimes in histories of the field of social studies, the work of early Black scholars such as Nannie Helen Burroughs was rendered silent. By examining how these scholars shaped the field of social studies, we can develop key understandings about how narratives can motivate students of color to learn history. In particular, the work of *When Truth Gets a Hearing* demonstrates the development and evolution of a revisionist Black curriculum.

Future research should continue to examine the instructional vision of female African American school founders and principals, in terms of how they created curricula that encouraged active participation by African American students in a racist society. In the social studies classroom, teachers encouraged students to be actively involved in their communities. However, when examining these school founders' visions of citizenship, it would be crucial to discern how individuals trained their students to participate in a society that was inherently structured in ways that discouraged their citizenship. Confronted with the dual nature of oppression, Black women school principals worked to create spaces of safety where African American children defined themselves in the face of harsh racism. Leaders such as Nannie Helen Burroughs recognized the power of history to transform how children understand themselves in society. By writing *When Truth Gets a Hearing*, Nannie Helen Burroughs used history as a source of empowerment and change for the students in her world.

Notes

1. Sarah Bair, "Educating Black Girls in the Early 20th Century: The Pioneering Work of Nannie Helen Burroughs: (1879–1961)," *Theory and Research in Social Education* 36 (Winter 2008): 9–35; Sharon Harley, "Nannie Helen Burroughs: The Black Goddess of Liberty," *The Journal of Negro History* 81 (Winter–Autumn 1996): 62–71.
2. Evelyn Brooks Higginbotham, *Righteous Discontent: The Women's Movement in the Black Baptist Church 1880–1920* (Cambridge, MA: Harvard University Press, 1993).
3. Carter G. Woodson, *The Mis-Education of the Negro* (Trenton, NJ: African World Press, 1990).
4. Gloria Ladson-Billings, ed., *Critical Race Theory: Perspectives on Social Studies: The Profession, Policies and Profession* (Greenwich, CT: Information Age Publishing, 2003).
5. Nannie H. Burroughs papers are voluminous. However for the purposes of this work, I focused specifically on the pageant, *When Truth Gets a Hearing*, Box 47, Papers of Nannie Helen Burroughs, Library of Congress.
6. David Jenness, *Making Sense of Social Studies* (New York: Macmillan Publishing Company, 1990), 67. Ronald W. Evans, *The Social Studies War: What Should We Teach the Children?* (New York: Teachers College Press, 2004). Herbert M. Kliebard, *The Struggle for the American Curriculum* (New York: RoutledgeFalmer, 2004). Thomas Fallace, "Did the Social Studies Really Replace History in American Schools?" *Teachers College Record* 110 (October 2008): 2246.
7. Chara Bohan, "Early Vanguards of Progressive Education: The Committee of Ten, The Committee of Seven and Social Education," *Journal of Curriculum and Instruction* 19 (Fall 2003): 73–94.
8. Jenness, *Making Sense of Social Studies*, 73.
9. Terrie Epstein, *Interpreting National History: Race, Identity, and Pedagogy in Classrooms and Communities* (New York: Routledge, 2008).
10. In each of these texts, authors used terms such as "historical memory" or the "Black history narrative" to describe the narrative that I refer to as the alternative Black curriculum in social studies. Anthony Brown, "Counter-memory

and Race: An Examination of African-American Scholars' Challenges in Early Twentieth Century K-12 Historical Discourse," *The Journal of Negro Education* 79 (Winter 2010): 55–63. Pero Gaglo Dagbovie, "Making Black History Practical and Popular: Carter G. Woodson, the Proto Black Studies Movement, and the Struggle for Black Liberation," *The Western of Journal of Black Studies* 28 (2004): 372–382; and Jeffrey Aaron Snyder, "Race, Nation and Education: Black History During Jim Crow" (PhD dissertation, New York University, 2011).

11. Charles Payne, *I've Got the Light of Freedom: The Organizing Tradition and the Mississippi Freedom Struggle* (Berkeley: University of California Press, 1995), 2. A "bottom-up" approach focuses on the role of "ordinary" individuals and their role in history. In addition, the bottom-up approach focused on the contributions of women to the civil rights movement.
12. Angel David Nieves, "We Are Too Busy Making History...to Write History:" African-American Women, Construction of Nation, and the Built Environment in the New South, 1892–1968," in *We Shall Independent Be: African-American Place Making and the Struggle to Claim Space in the United States,* eds., Angel David Nieves and Leslie M. Alexander (Boulder, CO: The University Press of Colorado, 2008).
13. Woodson, *The Mis-Education of the Negro,* 19; Burroughs, *When Truth Gets a Hearing,* 14.
14. Woodson, *The-Mis-Education of the Negro,* 7; Burroughs, *When Truth Gets a Hearing,* 17.
15. Woodson, *The Mis-Education of the Negro,* 18; Burroughs, *When Truth Gets a Hearing,* 16a.
16. Woodson, *The Mis-Education of the Negro,* 21; Burroughs, *When Truth Gets a Hearing,* 19.
17. Maurice Jackson and Jacqueline Bacon, eds., *African-Americans and the Haitian Revolution: Selected Essays and Historical Documents* (New York: Routledge, 2010).
18. Snyder, *Race, Nation and Education,* 86.
19. Burroughs, *When Truth Gets a Hearing,* 43.
20. Pero Gaglo Dagbovie, "Black Women, Carter G. Woodson, and The Association for the Study of Negro Life and History, 1915–1950," *The Journal of African American History* 88 (Winter 2003): 21–41.
21. Michelle Rief, "Thinking Locally, Acting Globally: The International Agenda of African American Clubwomen, 1880–1940," *The Journal of African American History* 89 (Summer 2004): 214.
22. Alan R. Sadovnick and Susan F. Semel, eds., *Founding Mothers and Others: Women Educational Leaders During the Progressive Era* (New York: Palgrave Macmillan, 2002).
23. Opal Easter, *Nannie Helen Burroughs* (New York: Garland Publishing, 1995).
24. Sharon Harley, "Nannie Helen Burroughs: The Black Goddess of Liberty," *The Journal of Negro History* 81 (Winter–Autumn 1996): 62–71.
25. Easter, *Nannie Helen Burroughs,* 25.
26. Easter, *Nannie Helen Burroughs,* 26.
27. Harley, *Nannie Helen Burroughs: The Black Goddess Liberty,* 64.

28. Karen Johnson, *Uplifting the Women and the Race: The Lives, Educational Philosophies and Social Activism of Anna Julia Cooper and Nannie Helen Burroughs (Studies in African American History and Culture* (New York: Garland Publishing, 2000).
29. Traki Taylor, "'Womanhood Glorified,' Nannie Helen Burroughs and the National Training School for Women and Girls. Inc., 1909–1961," *The Journal of African American History* 87 (Autumn 2002): 390–402.
30. Rief, "Thinking Locally, Acting Globally, 215.
31. Bair, *Educating Black Girls in the Early 20th Century*, 9.
32 David Krasner, *A Beautiful Pageant: African American Theatre, Drama, and Performance in the Harlem Renaissance, 1910–1927.* (New York: Palgrave Macmillan, 2002), 85; Katherine Capshaw Smith, *Children's Literature of the Harlem Renaissance* (Bloomington, IN: Indiana University Press, 2004).
33. W. E. B. Du Bois and Herbert Aptheker. *Creative Writings by W. E. B. Du Bois: A Pageant, Poems, Short Stories, and Playlets* (White Plains, N.Y.: Kraus-Thomson Organization, 1985).
34. Krasner, *A Beautiful Pageant*, 82.
35. Ibid., 81.
36. Krasner, *A Beautiful Pageant*, 85. *Birth of a Nation* (1915) directed by D. W. Griffith is a silent movie that chronicles the arc of two families from the North and South from the Civil War to Reconstruction. The content of *Birth of a Nation* is highly controversial because of its depiction of African Americans and its glorification of the Ku Klux Klan.
37. Krasner, *A Beautiful Pageant*, 81.
38. Ibid., 89.
39. Theresa Perry, "Freedom for Literacy and Literacy for Freedom: The African American Philosophy of Education," in *Young, Gifted, and Black: Promoting High Achievement Among African American Students*. Eds., Theresa Perry, Claude Steele, and Asa Hilliard (Boston: Beacon Press, 2003).
40 Perry, *Young, Gifted, and Black*, 101.
41. Jenness, *Making Sense of Social Studies*, 73.
42. Burroughs, *When Truth Gets a Hearing*, 16.
43. Nannie Helen Burroughs, *When Truth Gets a Hearing*, Box 47, Papers of Nannie Helen Burroughs, Library of Congress.
44. Burroughs, *When Truth Gets a Hearing*, 9.
45. Ibid.
46. Peter Novick, *That Noble Dream: The "Objectivity Question" and the American Historical Profession* (London: Cambridge University, 1987), 14.
47. Burroughs, *When Truth Gets a Hearing*, 14.
48. Harley, *Black Goddess of Liberty*, 67.
49. Leon Litwack, *Trouble in Mind: Black Southerners in the Age of Jim Crow* (New York: Vintage Books: 1998).
50. Leon Litwack, *Trouble in Mind*, 7.
51. Burroughs, *When Truth Gets a Hearing*, 35a.
52. Arthur Raper, "The Tragedy of Lynching," in Robert L. Blaustein and Robert L. Zangrando. eds., *Civil Rights and the American Negro: a Documentary History* (New York: Washington Square Press: 1968).
53. Burroughs, *When Truth Gets a Hearing*, 17.

54. Dagbovie, *Black Women, Carter G. Woodson and the Association for Negro Life and History*, 30.
55. *The Star of Ethiopia*, by W.E.B. Du Bois, directed by Charles Burroughs, New York October 1913; Series 12, W. E. B. Du Bois Papers, University of Massachusetts, Amherst.
56. Burroughs, *When Truth Gets a Hearing*, 17.
57. Stephanie Shaw, *What a Woman Ought to Be and to Do: Black Professional Women During the Jim Crow Era* (Chicago: The University of Chicago Press, 1996).
58. G, Mokhtar., *General History of Africa: Ancient Civilizations of Africa* (Berkeley, CA: Unesco, 1990), 76.
59. Burroughs, *When Truth Gets a Hearing*, 28.
60. Ladson-Billings, *Critical Perspectives in Social Studies*, 4.

Chapter Six

Race in Elementary Geography Textbooks: Examples from South Carolina, 1890–1927

Mindy Spearman

For most of the nineteenth century in the United States, a young learner's first exposure to what we now call social studies came through the field of geography. Geography was—according to United States Commissioner of Education William Torrey Harris (1889–1906)—the most important subject after reading, writing, and mathematics. He lauded the way it gave students a "practical, real knowledge which will be useful later in life."[1] This notion of practicality, coupled with the relative availability of pedagogical resources for teaching geography, made the subject more commonplace in nineteenth-century grammar schools than history was.[2] Moreover, suggestions from the Committee of Ten's Geography Conference in 1894 prompted educators to conceptualize the subject as a broader field than just physical geography; the report suggested that elementary geography include "astronomy, meteorology, zoology, botany, history, commerce, governments, races, religions, etc."[3] Called "home geography" in the primary grades, this curriculum emphasized the use of resources in the local community to teach about the social world, in order to provide a foundation for future scholastic work in history, geography, and the then fledgling field of anthropology.[4] "Social units," focused on subjects like communication, industry, and societal roles, held equal importance with lessons concerning physical geography.[5]

Home geography was in widespread practice during the first few decades of the twentieth century, and the term remained in use, at least occasionally, into the 1960s.[6] The subject of geography, then, seems a reasonable starting point for a beginning exploration of what young students learned about race at the turn of the twentieth century.

Textbooks, which teachers tended to rely upon heavily in American public schools at the turn of the twentieth century, can provide some insight into the curricular content of class work.[7] Textbooks, especially in the nineteenth century, were considered "official organs" that carried with them a sense of authority that influenced discourse(s) about and beyond the text.[8] Historical analyses of geography textbooks have demonstrated prevailing trends in geography education at the time, including the promotion of nationalism and Americanization, the use of geography as a tool to meet societal needs through specialized subdisciplines like commercial geography, the popularity of catechism or recitation as a pedagogical method, the perpetuation of racial and gender stereotypes, and the popularity of hierarchical constructions of cultural development.[9]

Avril M. C. Maddrell, who investigated British geography texts for discussions relating to race and gender, asserts that analyses of geography textbooks can and should be used to investigate cultural norms.[10] He laments the "broader neglect" of studies that analyze the content of geographic textbooks; Maddrell writes that "these texts are a part not only of the geographical and educational arena but also of the wider political and social discourses of the time, either reflecting prevailing or emerging establishment values and ideals, which could be described as hegemonic, or [reflecting] alternative or oppositional/counterhegemonic discourses."[11] In particular, he notes that he found illustrations and pictures in historical textbooks particularly helpful for demonstrating an "encapsulated message."[12] Textbook illustrations, Maddrell suggests, might be analyzed for messages that are not so obvious in prose.

The intent of this study is to examine American elementary geography textbooks[13] for their visual and textual portrayals of race during the late nineteenth and early twentieth century. As Zagumny and Pulsipher explain in their 2008 examination of the portrayals of women in nineteenth-century textbooks, textbooks are a vehicle for passing cultural knowledge to future generations, although they are certainly not the only vehicle. If researchers concentrate on a particular state, rather than on making a national survey of published textbooks, local context(s) can help provide a frame for how and when these books were used with young learners. The context of this study is South Carolina, a state that utilized an official textbook-adoption process that published a mandated list of textbooks that were intended to be used statewide.

Elementary Geography in South Carolina

In nineteenth-century South Carolina, students began to study geography during their first year of school, although they did not use a formal textbook until the third grade.[14] School administrators believed that the inclusion of primary geography work (in first through third grade), which incorporated an amalgam of different subjects, resulted in a more thorough treatment of topics that might otherwise be taught irregularly or completely neglected.[15] Home geography was stressed in the early grades, with the idea that students who learned about their own town or their own state would have a foundation from which to compare and contrast different geographical regions.[16] In particular, teachers were asked to teach four main topics in "the beginning years:" common forms of land and water; plants and animals; how elements of the natural world change according to the four seasons; and stories of races.[17]

Teachers of younger grades were advised to consult Alexis Everett Frye's *The Child and Nature* for pedagogical strategies, while teachers of older grades turned to Charles McMurry's *Special Method in Geography: From the Third through the Eighth Grade*.[18] Both of these texts included discussions about courses of study, suggested supplemental materials, and provided lesson examples. Teachers also received pedagogical guidance through regularly scheduled county teachers' institutes and through optional statewide summer schools for educators. At the four-week-long summer schools for White teachers, attendees could choose from a variety of sessions, one of which routinely focused on elementary geography teaching. Separate summer schools were held for Black teachers; although they did occasionally focus on geography teaching, the Negro summer schools did not have the same variety of choices as the summer schools for White teachers had.[19]

The state of South Carolina had a statewide adoption policy for textbooks at the turn of the twentieth century. Texts were readopted every five years, and use of the approved books only was mandated by the state Board of Education. The policy was a contentious one, occasionally contested by teachers, principals, and administrators.[20] Still, it did represent an attempt, at least, at curricular uniformity. Over the course of 40 years, from 1890 until the late 1920s, when the list of state-adopted textbooks stopped appearing in the annual superintendent reports, the state adopted six different textbook series for geography instruction through grade 5 (two of the texts were adopted simultaneously).

All but one of the texts (the exception was Fairbanks's *Home Geography*) provided a concerted treatment of race. The topic was typically included in an introductory section that listed the races of mankind and their geographic locations, and race was then integrated within the text as particular regions of the world were discussed in detail. Sometimes, as in Frye's geographies, the author gave race special emphasis in the text's preface. Frye stressed the importance of attending to race when teaching geography to young learners and explained that "the word **race** has a deeper meaning than is taught by the size of the cheek bones or the texture of the hair."[21]

Appleton's *Elementary Geography*

Young learners in South Carolina read *Elementary Geography*, a text published by Appleton & Company during the late nineteenth century. Commonly known as Appleton's standard *Elementary Geography*, the text enjoyed popularity in the United States due to the solid reputation of the publisher and repeated editions that remained relatively unchanged for over 25 years. The team of authors who wrote the text designed it for beginners, and they included elements of history, earth science, and "social life," in addition to physical geography.[22] After giving a general introduction to map skills and natural resources, the text introduces the "four conditions of society," which outline a hierarchy of human development.[23] The authors explain that at the top of the hierarchy are "civilized" societies with government, material goods, transportation, and education. Next are "half-civilized" peoples, with minimal agriculture, some education, and some arts. Below the "half-civilized" are "barbarous" peoples, who herd and live in hunts or tents. At the bottom are the warlike "savages," who subsist through hunting and gathering and wear little clothing. This hierarchy mirrors recapitulation theory, a biological proposition influential in the late nineteenth century. Originated by German philosopher Etienne Serress and later popularized by German zoologist Ernst Haeckel, recapitulation theory proposed that animals, over the course of a lifetime, echoed evolutionary changes of their ancestors. Charles Darwin drew from the theory in *The Descent of Man*, where he hypothesized that "civilized races of man will almost certainly exterminate and replace throughout the world the savage races."[24]

Darwin's influence on *Elementary Geography* is understandable, considering the identity of the publisher; D. Appleton and Company published *The Descent of Man* in America during the 1870s and promoted all the science works of Charles Darwin heavily.[25] In *Elementary Geography*, the authors make it clear that "we" belong to the civilized group and most people living in different parts of the world fall within one of the remaining three categories. Although this introductory section makes no explicit connections between the four conditions and race, an illustration accompanying the description indicates otherwise (Figure 6.1).

The remainder of the book is arranged geographically, with sections on the United States and various world regions like "South America" and "Oceania." Within these sections are subheadings detailing the inhabitants of the region, usually containing comparative statements and an

Figure 6.1 "Your Conditions of Society." Illustration from Daniel Appleton, *Elementary Geography* (New York: D. Appleton and Company, 1880), p. 16.

implication of placement within the developmental hierarchy of human conditions. For example, Canadian Indians are not as "troublesome as the Indians of the United States,"[26] and the Japanese are "intelligent and ingenious."[27] Included in the text are a few examples—notably all "Negro" populations—of groups of people who are characterized as having shocking traits, so dehumanizing that it is implied they might not even fall within one of the four societal conditions. When describing a race of "Negroes" in Africa, students are told: "Some even feast on the flesh of their captives. Find on the map where these fierce *cannibals* live. To which grade of society (p. 16) do they belong?"[28] In a discussion on the "black, degraded and repulsive" native Australian population, individuals are characterized as eating "raw flesh, lizards and worms."[29] The authors' placement of Negroes and indigenous Australians at the bottom of the hierarchy once again echoes Charles Darwin. In the *Descent of Man*, Darwin makes a statement that implies that Negroes and Australians are nearer to apes than Caucasians.[30]

Frye's Geographies

In 1895, the state of South Carolina replaced Appleton with a series of geography textbooks written by Alexis Everett Frye. *Primary Geography* and *Elementary Geography,* two very similar editions, seem to have been used interchangeably. Primary teachers were instructed to consult Frye's *The Child and Nature* as an additional resource. Frye's text remained in South Carolina elementary classrooms until 1906 and, notably, summer schools offered a yearly professional development course focusing specifically on strategies for using Frye's textbook in the primary classroom.

Frank Evans, superintendent of the Spartanburg city school system, conducted the sessions. He considered the sessions to be popular among the teachers and believed that they were "particularly suited" for the primary educator.[31] Nationwide, Frye's textbooks were praised for their woodcut illustrations but criticized for focusing heavily on the United States at the expense of international material.[32] The textbook's 25–year publication lifespan may have been due to its expansive illustrations, rather than to the content.[33]

Frye devotes a significant initial portion of *Primary Geography* to a discussion of race. He divides humans into five different races, a characterization which Zagumny has demonstrated was considered "scientifically" accurate in the late nineteenth century and which had been part of geography textbooks since the early eighteenth century.[34] *Primary Geography* uses color words to represent the five racial groups popularized by German anthropologist Johann Friedrich Blumenbach and displays them in an illustration entitled "Homes of the Races" (Figure 6.2). Frye describes the illustration within the text using statements such as, "The red men, or red-brown tribes, are found in many parts of America" and, "In the Old World, the home of the white race is between the lands of the black and yellow races."[35] As shown in Figure 6.2, "the Arab boys are dark, but they belong to the white race."[36]

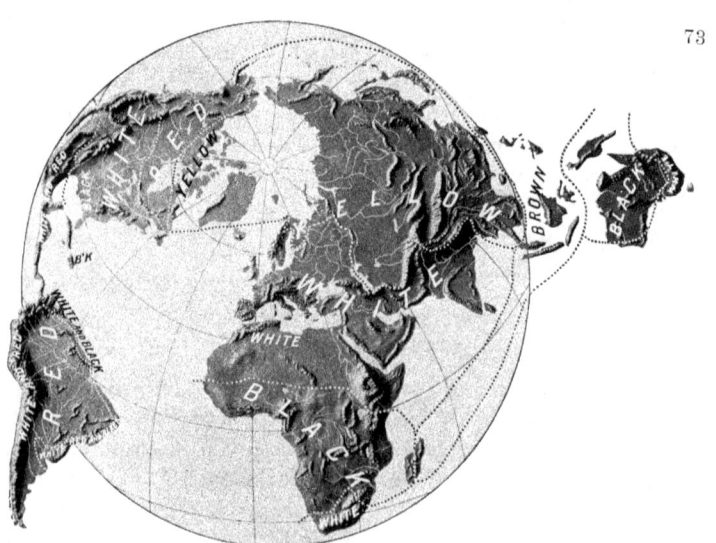

Figure 6.2 "Homes of the Races." Illustration from Alexis Everett Frye, *Primary Geography* (Boston: Ginn & Company, 1894), p. 73, showing the five racial groups.

A portion of the text presents detailed descriptions of peoples, offering storylike descriptions of children from different regions of the world, again emphasizing color words. For example, a section on Japan begins with the statement: "To-day we will visit the homes of the little yellow people who live on the islands east of Asia."[37] Frye emphasizes the otherness of non-White races by using words like "strange" or "odd" within the narratives. A section discussing Arab boys reading from the Koran makes the comment, "listen to the strange words which tell them not to press wine from grapes."[38] While describing the environment of a Black child living near the Congo River, the text asks, "Isn't this a queer place?"[39] Through emphases like these, Frye helps to emphasize to the young reader that the cultural and physical environments of the White race are both preferable and familiar.

Although Frye does not treat the relationship between cultural development, hierarchy, and races, he makes statements characterizing the White race as a civilizing colonizer, which can be found frequently within the text. A discussion about inhabitants of Java reads: "The brown people are called Malays. Most of them live on the large group of islands southeast of Asia. In some places, the Malays have built cities, but the white man rules over most of the brown race. Many of the Malays are savages, like the people in the black tribes of Africa."[40] In a discussion on the inhabitants of Africa, Frye emphasizes that White settlers brought civilizing influences to the southern regions of the continent. While tribes near to the White settlers have improved homes and tools, the remainder of the continent "remains in a wild state."[41]

Redway and Hinman's *Natural Elementary Geography*

The state of South Carolina eliminated the use of Frye's *Elementary Geography* in 1906, although the use of one of Frye's advanced texts continued in the intermediate grades. Redway and Hinman's *Natural Elementary Geography* replaced Frye for five years, until 1911. In the preface, Redway and Hinman explain that the book "points out the great linguistic and racial lines which divide the inhabitants of the earth," although the text focuses on physical geography more strongly than on cultural geography.[42] In fact, the scientific tone of the text was notably different than that of the earlier elementary geography texts.[43]

Redway and Hinman discuss individuals of mixed races, a treatment that the two texts that had previously been adopted in South Carolina did not mention. A section on Mexico, Central America, and the West Indies highlights the intermarrying between Spaniards and native Indians:

> More Indians lived in this part of America than in the northern part, and they were not so savage. Many of the Spanish settlers married Indian women, and their children were half-breeds. Most of the people now are

half-breeds and partly civilized Indians. The Spaniards and a few of the half-breeds own most of the land and are rich and powerful, but the Indians and most of the half-breeds are poor, ignorant, and wretched.[44]

They also devote a short treatment to people of color living in the United States; again, this is a subject completely that was missing in Appleton and was mentioned only in passing in Frye. An illustration contrasts a Black woman and baby in Africa with a Black couple living in the United States (see Figure 6.3). According to the text, people of the "black, or negro race" who have been living in the United States for some time "have learned to speak and dress and live much as the white men do."[45] Still, the text is careful to point out that "the first negroes who were brought to America were

Figure 6.3 African mother and child and Negro couple in the United States. From Jacques Wardlaw Redway and Russell Hinman, *Natural Elementary Geography* (New York: American Book Company, 1897), 13.

ignorant savages, and many of the negroes in Africa are still savages."[46] The textbook also mentions that people of a Yellow race can be found in the United States, and generally "those living here are laundrymen."[47]

As evidenced in Figure 6.3 and in the discussion of half-breeds in Mexico and Central America, *Natural Elementary Geography* stresses the way that various races have become increasingly civilized through contact with Whites, both within the United States and without. Members of the Brown Malay race are described as "savages" yet "generally easy to civilize."[48] Likewise, Japan "has made wonderful progress in civilization" since the country became accessible to outsiders.[49]

Interestingly, Redway and Hinman also present an example of the opposite scenario: that is, Whites becoming uncivilized through contact with another race. The textbook briefly describes how Russian members of the White race are sent to Siberia, to live with "people of the yellow race," as punishment for crimes.[50] This sort of scenario exemplified Social Darwinism, at its peak during the early twentieth century, which suggested that members of the White race could slide down the hierarchal ladder of savagery through contact with other races. Social Darwinists usually cited sexual contact between races as the reason for degeneration of a race; however, such a discussion might be seen as inappropriate for an elementary text. The Siberia example, then, serves much the same purpose, with an alternative scenario.

Maury's *New Elements of Geography* and Fairbanks's *Home Geography*

Although South Carolina school administrators recommended to teachers that they conduct primary geography lessons in the lower elementary grades without the aid of a textbook,[51] the state did adopt a formal home geography text for a five-year span from 1917 to 1922. Fairbanks's *Home Geography*, the longest continually published home geography text, did not include references to race.[52] The book was adopted along with Maury's *New Elements of Geography* (formerly called *Elementary Geography*), which was intended for fourth- and fifth-grade use. Maury's texts, which South Carolina educators used for 11 years, were considered at the time of their initial publication in 1870 a "radical departure from the old methods."[53] Unlike authors of previous texts, Maury wrote in a heavily narrative format, using simple words and stories that were a combination of imagination and fact. Yet by the time the state of South Carolina adopted the texts in 1911, the books were over 40 years old. Although South Carolina adopted a new edition, revisions of the books contained only minor changes.

Maury devoted one of the introductory sections of the text to a discussion about race and the racial groups found within the United States; he explained that the majority of inhabitants are White, some are Black, and a few Red and Yellow. He noted that Brown men, people of a fifth color, are found in other parts of the world and then he provided Blumenbach's "scientific" names for the racial groups: Caucasian (White), Mongolian (Yellow), Negro (Black), Indian (Red), and Malay (Brown). Written below this section, in a font intended to give emphasis, is the explanation: "The white man is found in every continent, and is master of the world."[54]

Perhaps the most arresting feature of *New Elements of Geography* is the direct connection Maury makes between races and cultural development (see Figure 6.4). Using four levels of hierarchy, he writes the following:

> Suppose we go to the home of the red men and see how they live...they have no books and schools of their own. People who live in this way are called **savages**. Now let us go to a country where the people are only a little better than the red savages of our land. We will visit the wandering Arabs. They have no books or schools. Those who live in this way are called **barbarous** people. We will now visit some people who live much better than the Indians and the Arabs...We call people who live like this, the Chinese, **civilized**. In the countries of the white race there are more books, better schools and better governments than anywhere else...people who live as we do are called **enlightened**.[55]

The accompanying illustration recalls that of Appleton (Figure 6.1) and depicts a scene from China as "civilized," an Arabic scene as "barbarous,"

a.

b.

c.

d.

Figure 6.4 a. "Among enlightened people." b. "Civilized life. A Chinese city." c. "Barbarous life. Arabs eating dinner before the tent which is their only home." d. "Savage life. Photograph by Dr. Cook in South America." From Maury, *New Elements of Geography* (New York: American Book Company, 1907), 22.

and a scene with South American Indians as an example of "savages." Although it had been listed as one of the five races in the introduction to the text, the "Negro" race is neither pictured nor described in the discussion of cultural development. Rather, they are left out of the hierarchy completely. However, *New Elements of Geography* contains brief discussions about the inhabitants of different regions of the world in the latter part of the book. In the section about Africa there is a description about the people living there: "Leaving Asia, let us visit Africa, the home of the negro race. Most of the natives belonging to this race and are savages. Many of them used to be constantly fighting and making slaves of one another. European nations are stopping this."[56]

It appears that here Maury places Africans in the "savage" category of cultural development, with special mention of White colonizers. Interestingly, in the section devoted to Australia, the indigenous population is called "degraded savages," a term that stresses that they are below the bottom rung of the cultural development hierarchy.[57]

Brigham and McFarlane's *Essentials of Geography*

The state of South Carolina discontinued the use of Maury's geographical series in 1922, at a point where the books were over 50 years old and were so outmoded that there remained no hope for future revisions.[58] Frank Evans, the Spartanburg city superintendent of schools who taught South Carolina teachers professional development sessions on primary geography, was pleased to discontinue use of Maury's textbook; this was not because of its depictions of race, but rather because its emphasis on rote memorization and recitation was passé in light of the popularity of McMurry's project method.[59] In their *Essentials of Geography,* published in 1920, Brigham and McFarlane blended a variety of subjects—geography, history, economics, and government—in a way that garnered praise.[60] An advertisement for the textbook in a South Carolina educational periodical touted the way the textbook was "fully up-to-date" with maps and illustrations that better reflected the state of the country after World War I.[61] Teachers must have found the current illustrations and maps an appealing feature after spending over a decade with Maury's 1870 texts.

Essentials of Geography was the first geography text in South Carolina to utilize photographs as illustrations. Four anonymous photographs of men are used to illustrate four different races (Figure 6.5). The text details these four photographs:

> As the people of the world are divided into large groups, or **races**, and the races are named by the color of their skin, the Indians are called the **red**

race. Most of the people of Europe and of North America, as well as many people in other parts of the world, belong to the **white** race... early in our history, also, negroes, or people of the **black** race, were brought here from Africa as laborers. There are now many negroes in different parts of the country, especially in the South. People from Japan, in Asia, who belong to the **yellow** race, also came to our country. They are not now allowed to come so freely as they once were.[62]

Mention of a Brown, "Malay" race is missing from *Essentials of Geography*. Rather, inhabitants of India, Persia, and Arabia are categorized as "belong[ing] to dark-skinned branches of the white race."[63]

Figure 6.5 a. "Indian, or red man." b. "White man." c. "Black man." d. "Yellow man." From Brigham and McFarlane, *Essentials of Geography*, (New York: American Book Company, 1920) 88–89.

Figure 6.6 "Native with boomerang." Illustration from Brigham and McFarlane, *Essentials of Geography* (New York: American Book Company, 1920), 249.

Nowhere in the text do Brigham and McFarlane mention a hierarchy of races, although the word "savage" is used several times in the text: to describe South American natives prior to Spanish invasion, and to describe most of the natives of Africa. Members of the "yellow or Mongolian race" are generally characterized positively, as "a small but active and courageous people."[64] Australian natives are listed as being Black men, and their use of the boomerang as a weapon is portrayed as a cultural object that is mildly interesting. Moreover, for the first time in South Carolinian elementary geography texts, students were presented with an illustration of an indigenous Australian man (Figure 6.6).

In *Essentials of Geography*, White colonizers are depicted as improving the living conditions of the colonized. In a discussion about Mexico, a paragraph recounts White settlers coming to the area, with the implied consequence of Mexico setting up a government "like that of the United States." Yet, after independence, the book notes, "their president often rules the country as he pleases."[65] Likewise, the book notes that White Europeans coming to Africa have made "much progress" by taking "possession of a large part of Africa" and "trying to develop their territory."[66] South Africa is characterized as the most successful area of the continent, "because its climate is healthful and also because it has many white settlers."[67]

Nationalism, Subjugation, and Colonization

The rhetoric of most geographical texts, particularly those published during the early twentieth century, supported the burgeoning American empire. An emphasis on "we versus them" is prominent throughout the texts that South Carolina elementary children used for nearly 40 years. First-person pronouns like "we" and "our" are used in discussions of both the White race and "enlightened" civilizations. Non-White races outside of the United States are exoticized and othered through the use of descriptors like "strange," "queer," and "odd." White American children, these schoolbooks claimed, should be proud of the development of their nation; thus, the discourse of Social Darwinism served to support nationalism in these elementary geography textbooks.

Woven within this theme of Social Darwinism was a thread of American exceptionalism. African Americans and American Indians living within the United States are shown, through both illustrations and prose, as having become more like Whites and, consequently, increasingly civilized. Zagumny, who sampled nineteenth-century geography textbooks from a variety of grade levels for elements of class, religion, gender, and race, suggests that it was a desire to create a "homogeneous national identity"[68] that fostered these sorts of representations. "To become American was to forget the geographies and cultures of the Old World," explains Neil Smith, "or else to bleach them into categorical nationalisms, which themselves, somehow, reflected and reaffirmed U.S. exceptionalism."[69] This "invention of ethnicity"[70] explained how the residence of non-Whites in the United States could be cited as evidence to support American hegemony. By positing that people of non-White races who had been somewhat enculturated into an American identity had somehow progressed beyond people of non-White races in other parts of the globe, textbook authors affirmed American superiority.

In particular, American children were informed that they were better off than those living in Africa, a continent which was characterized by Frye, in particular, as a "dark" and "foreboding" place.[71] The Black race was routinely characterized as the least desirable racial group, appearing lowest in the cultural development hierarchy. This characterization of "Negroes" as the ultimate savages was popularized by nineteenth-century geo-historian Arnold Guyot, whose writings elevate the White race to the top of the racial hierarchy, characterize the Yellow race as "half-civilized," and ask the question, "where have we seen barbarism reign triumphant, if not in Africa and Australia?"[72] Guyot's own *Elementary Geography* textbook was the first large-format geography textbook to be widely distributed and, consequently, it influenced many of its successors.[73] Ruth Miller Elson notes that this placement of "Negroes" on the bottom rung of the ladder is typical of nineteenth-century textbooks.[74] She further suggests that nationalism is tied to this hierarchy; the American Indian, she explains, must "have qualities superior to other savages because he was the original occupant of the American continent."[75] The subjugation of the Black race in elementary geography books, furthermore, helped to delegitimatize claims of inequitable treatment post-Reconstruction.

It should be noted that in the case of both Frye and Maury, the Black race does not appear in the hierarchy of cultural development at all. Rather, in both of these examples, American Indians are placed at the bottom of the ladder. Characterized with culturally deviant practices like cannibalism and the consumption of uncooked flesh, "Negroes" are portrayed as almost sub-human. Indigenous Australians, in particular, are portrayed as animal-like; no illustrations of Aboriginal Australians, their culture, or their environment appear in any of the South Carolina readers until Brigham and McFarlane's *Essentials of Geography* was adopted by the state in the 1920s. Indigenous Australians are typically characterized as a dwindling population of little no relevance to America—a people with whom contact is quite undesirable.

With the exception of Aboriginal Australians, populations of non-White races are portrayed as being helped by White colonization. Regions of Africa and Southeast Asia, for example, are described as having been at least marginally improved under White rule. "The natives are being kept in order by foreign powers, and many of them are learning how to labor," Brigham and McFarlane state in *Essentials of Geography*, "...but it is not easy for some of the natives to learn to work."[76] Notably, colonization attempts by these "foreign powers" are not painted with as much success as the colonization of non-Whites within the American domestic context. Moreover, the textbooks describe areas of the world under direct control of the United States as progressing at a rapid rate, even if they have significant non-White populations. In Puerto Rico (described as "three-fifths white and two-fifths negro"), "a modern educational system is being developed, and roadways, including railroads, are being constructed, with telegraph and telephone lines."[77] American protectorates in Southeast Asia are described in similar ways, and some of the texts stress that immigration is limited in these areas.

Nowhere in these texts is any form of resistance by the colonized described at all. Furthermore, colonization is generally constructed as a peaceful, nonviolent process. Only one of the texts even hints otherwise; in *Essentials of Geography*, the authors acknowledge that when White European settlers encountered Native Americans "many cruel deeds were done on both sides."[78] Although assimilation of non-White races is generally implied to be desirable, Redway and Hinman's description of "half-breeds" in Central America demonstrates the undesirability of interracial mixing. The texts also stress the importance of holding and maintaining power; Brigham and McFarlane's example from Mexico warns of what might happen if a White colonizer returns power back to the colonized.

These geography texts were adopted and distributed to all elementary students in South Carolina at both White and Black schools. At the turn of the twentieth century, the state of South Carolina had a large Black scholastic population; in fact, the number of Black students enrolled in the public school system was higher than the number of White children. The state Department of Education promoted the textbooks' use, and both White and Black teachers received professional development relating to the content and the use of these books. Black teachers, in professional development sessions taught by White administrators, heard the rhetoric of Social Darwinism. A White University of South Carolina education professor, William H. Hand, after completing a geography-themed professional development session for Black teachers in South Carolina in 1900, stated that his participants "are able to see the mistakes of their race; they are ready to profit by experience; they are able to see their opportunities and are willing to improve them ... they stand for justice and harmony between the races."[79] Although one cannot assume that all teachers listened and that these books were constantly in use classrooms—especially in under-resourced Black schools, which often failed to receive even provisional materials—the power of textbooks to convey discourses that might help shape reality is documented; thus, the content of these early geographies serves as a sobering testament to American attitudes about imperialism and how these beliefs were conveyed to young learners at the turn of the twentieth century.

Notes

1. Annual Reports of the Department of the Interior for the Fiscal Year Ended June 30, 1897 (Washington: Government Printing Office, 1889), 1482.
2. Anne-Lise Halvorsen, "The Origins and Rise of Elementary Social Studies Education, 1884 to 1941" (PhD dissertation, University of Michigan, 2006).
3. National Education Association, *Report of the Committee of Ten on Secondary School Studies: with the Reports of the Conferences Arranged by the Committee* (New York: *American Book Company, 1894*), 204–205.
4. Keith C. Barton, "Home Geography and the Development of Elementary Social Education, 1890–1930," *Theory and Research in Social Education* 37, no. 4 (2009).
5. Richard Ellwood Dodge and Clara Barbara Kirchwey, *The Teaching of Geography in Elementary Schools* (Chicago: Rand McNally & Company, 1913), 30.
6. Barton, "Home Geography," 508.

7. Ian Michael, "Textbooks as History: the Work of the Colloquium," *Paradigm: Journal of the Textbook Colloquium*, 25 (1998), http://www.open.ac.uk/Arts/TEXTCOLL/paper1.html
8. Lisa L. Zagumny and Lydia Mihelič Pulsipher, "The Races and Conditions of Men:" Women in Nineteenth-Century Geography School Texts in the United States," *Gender, Place and Culture* 15, no. 4 (2008), 414.
9. Karen M. Trifonoff, "Geographic Education and Elementary Geography Texts, 1850–1900," *Research in Geographic Education* 3, no. 2 (2001); Zachary A. Moore, "Evolution of Geography in the United States Public School Curriculum: An Analysis of the Influence of Societal Movements and Historical Events" (PhD dissertation, Texas State University San Marcos, 2008), [available online at https://digital.library.txstate.edu/handle/10877/3095]; Penny S. Arnold, "A Description of a Content Analysis of Elementary Geography from 1789 to 1897 Textbooks" (PhD dissertation, University of Akron, 1991); Jack Vazzana, "A Visual History of the Role of Stereotypes in Geography Textbooks from 1880 to 1910" (PhD dissertation, University of Pittsburgh, 1994); Lisa Lynn Zagumny, "The Social Construction of Identity in Nineteenth Century Geography Schoolbooks" (PhD dissertation, The University of Tennessee, Knoxville, 2003), [available online at http://sunzi.lib.hku.hk/ER/detail/hkul/2984591]
10. Avril M. C. Maddrell, "Discourses of Race and Gender and the Comparative Methods in Geography School Texts, 1830–1918," *Environment and Planning D: Society and Space* 16 (1998).
11. Maddrell, "Discourses of Race and Gender," 81.
12. Ibid., 100.
13. During the late nineteenth and early twentieth century, the term "elementary" was generally used to refer to all grades before high school (through seventh or eighth grade, depending upon the state). The term "primary" often referred to first through third grades (sometimes including kindergarten). For the purposes of this chapter, I concentrate on geography work for the grades typically found in a contemporary elementary school (first through fifth grades).
14. South Carolina State Department of Education, *Twenty-Third Annual Report of the State Superintendent of Education of the State of South Carolina* (Columbia: James H. Woodrow, 1891), 30.
15. South Carolina State Department of Education, *Twenty-Third Annual Report*, 31.
16. William Knox Tate, *Teachers' Manual for the Elementary Schools of South Carolina* (Columbia: The State Company Printers, 1911).
17. South Carolina State Department of Education, *Thirty-First Annual Report of the State Superintendent of Education of the State of South Carolina* (Columbia: The Bryan Printing Company, 1900), 85.
18. South Carolina State Department of Education, *Thirty-Second Annual Report of the State Superintendent of Education of the State of South Carolina* (Columbia: The Bryan Printing Company, 1901).
19. For example, see South Carolina State Department of Education, *Thirty-Second Annual Report*, 109.
20. For examples, see South Carolina State Department of Education, *Forty-Second Annual Report of the State Superintendent of Education of the State*

of South Carolina (Columbia: Gonzales and Bryan Printers, 1910), 26–27; also Frank Evans, "Uniform Textbooks," *South Carolina Education* 3, no. 4 (1922).
21. Alexis Everett Frye, *Primary Geography* (Boston: Ginn & Company, 1894), iii. Emphasis in the original.
22. Daniel Appleton, *Elementary Geography* (New York: D. Appleton and Company, 1880), 2.
23. Appleton, *Elementary Geography*, 16–17.
24. Darwin, Charles. *The Descent of Man, and Selection in Relation to Sex* (New York: D. Appleton and Company, 1971), 193.
25. Valentine, James W. "The Early American Printings of Darwin's *Descent of Man*...," *Archives of Natural History* 24, no. 2 (1997).
26. Appleton, *Elementary Geography*, 58.
27. Ibid., 91.
28. Ibid., 82.
29. Ibid., 94.
30. Darwin, *The Descent of Man*, 193.
31. South Carolina State Department of Education, *Thirty-Fourth Annual Report of the State Superintendent of Education of the State of South Carolina* (Columbia: The Bryan Printing Company, 1902), 64.
32. Hugh Robert Mill, "Geographic Literature of the Month," *The Geographical Journal* 5, no. 2 (1895); "Book Notices," *Journal of the American Geographical Society of New York* 27, no. 1 (1895).
33. Charles Redway Dryer, "A Century of Geographic Education in the United States," *Annals of the Association of American Geographers* 14, no. 3 (1924) 125.
34. Zagumny, "Social Construction."
35. Frye, *Primary Geography*, 73.
36. Ibid., 67.
37. Ibid., 57.
38. Ibid., 67.
39. Ibid., 55.
40. Ibid., 60.
41. Ibid., 56.
42. Jacques Wardlaw Redway and Russell Hinman, *Natural Elementary Geography* (New York: American Book Company, 1897), 3.
43. Charles Dryer, "Century of Geographic Education."
44. Redway and Hinman, *Natural Elementary Geography*, 69.
45. Ibid., 13.
46. Ibid., 13.
47. Ibid., 14.
48. Ibid., 114.
49. Ibid., 117.
50. Ibid., 114.
51. Frank Evans, "The Teaching of Primary Geography," *South Carolina Education* 2, no. 8 (1921).
52. Keith Barton, "Home Geography," 501. See Barton for a more detailed discussion of Fairbanks's text. Harold Fairbanks, *Home Geography for Primary Grades*, (Boston: Educational Publishing Company, 1903).

53. Charles Lee Lewis, *Matthew Fontaine Maury: The Pathfinder of the Seas* (Annapolis, MD: The United States Naval Institute, 1927), 211. Mathew Maury, *New Elements of Geography* (New York: American Book Company, 1907).
54. Maury, *New Elements of Geography*, 18.
55. Ibid., 18. Emphasis in the original.
56. Ibid., 96.
57. Ibid., 101.
58. Dryer, "Century of Geographic Education."
59. Evans, "Teaching of Primary Geography," 1921.
60. Dryer,"Century of Geographic Education." Albert Brigham and Charles McFarlane, *Essentials of Geography* (New York: American Book Company, 1920).
61. "Revised Edition of Brigham and McFarlane's *Essentials of Geography*," *South Carolina Education* 2, no.1 (1920), 2.
62. Brigham and McFarlane, *Essentials of Geography*, 88–89. Emphasis in the original.
63. Ibid., 218.
64. Ibid., 232.
65. Ibid., 161.
66. Ibid., 240.
67. Ibid., 245.
68. Zagumny, "Social Identity."
69. Neil Smith, *American Empire: Roosevelt's Geographer and the Prelude to Globalization* (Berkeley and Los Angeles, CA: University of California Press, 2003), 21.
70. Ibid.
71. Michael McCarthy, *Dark Continent: Africa as Seen by Americans* (Westport, CT: Greenwood Press, 1983), 127.
72. Arnold H. Guyot, *The Earth and Man: Lectures on Comparative Physical Geography in Its Relation to the History of Mankind* (Boston, New York, 1863), 170.
73. Charles Carpenter, *History of American Schoolbooks* (Philadelphia: University of Pennsylvania Press, 1963), 260.
74. Ruth Miller Elson, *Guardians of Tradition: American Schoolbooks of the Nineteenth Century* (Lincoln: University of Nebraska Press, 1964).
75. Ibid., 71.
76. Brigham and McFarlane, *Essentials of Geography*, 374.
77. Ibid., 192.
78. Ibid., 88.
79. South Carolina State Department of Education, *Thirty-Second Annual Report*, 112.

Chapter Seven

Atlanta's Desegregation-Era Social Studies Curriculum: An Examination of Georgia History Textbooks

Chara Haeussler Bohan and Patricia Randolph

In the context of the desegregation of Atlanta Public Schools (APS), we sought to explore issues of race and the social studies curriculum during the 1970s and 1980s in Atlanta, Georgia. In the Southeast region of the United States, Atlanta is one of the largest cities. In 1973, the tenure of Dr. Alonzo Crim, the first African American APS superintendent of schools, began and a 15-year court battle over school desegregation in the city schools came to a conclusion. Issues of race were of central concern during this time period. We wondered how the social studies curriculum and textbooks reflected the context of the times with respect to race. Were there changes in the way social studies was taught and learned within the context of the desegregation of schools? As an extension of prior research,[1] in which we searched through archival materials, conducted interviews with students, teachers, and administrators, and examined court records, we extended the investigation into the social studies curriculum by initiating a new examination of the Georgia history textbooks that were used in the state's classrooms. The textbooks reveal a story of resistance and limited progressive change in the social studies curriculum.

Setting the Stage: The History and Impact of the National and State Social Studies Curricula

The recent history of the social studies curriculum and textbooks in Georgia is a reflection of the post–Civil War South. Indeed, vice-president of the Confederacy and Georgia native Alexander H. Stephens wrote a history of the United States for schools in the 1870s reflecting his desire for the Southern narrative to be preserved in the battle for memory between North and South. Subsequent Southern authors followed suit, in a response that aimed to counteract the Northern monopoly of the publishing industry. As Joseph Moreau recounts, state textbook adoption developed as a means to keep profits in the South and create teacherproof materials, although state adoption was not an easy sell, as local control of education had a long history throughout the country.[2] The United Daughters of the Confederacy (UDC) played an important role in preserving the Southern perspective in history, as Mildred Lewis Rutherford, principal of a female academy in Athens, Georgia, was the UDC historian and leading textbook critic in the early part of the twentieth century.[3] Miss Millie, as she was known, led a formidable campaign to monitor textbooks and keep books out of Southern schools in which Lincoln was glorified and Jefferson Davis was vilified, the South was portrayed as traitor or rebel, and/or the slaveholder was depicted as cruel and unjust to slaves.

Carter G. Woodson worked to change the White-dominated social studies curriculum with the introduction of Negro History Week. Although he favored integration of the Black narrative into United States history, he knew that establishing a separate history was a starting point. In several Black schools, a separate Black History course was often taught. In Atlanta in the 1930s, at Booker T. Washington High School, the all-Black school, students could not graduate without passing the celebrated Black History class. Separate history for Blacks and Whites led to the publication of "mint julep" editions of textbooks, all-White books for the Southern market, and more diverse editions for other parts of the country.[4]

Joseph Moreau argues that the civil rights movement ended the ideological grip that conservative Southern Whites held on educational publishers.[5] Sputnik also helped provide an impetus for funding, as did the Elementary and Secondary Education Act of 1965, which earmarked $400 million to schools and libraries for purchasing multiracial and multiethnic books. Congress also assisted by passing the Ethnic Heritage Act of 1972, which provided more money to stimulate greater awareness of cultural variety in the curriculum. John Hope Franklin's eighth-grade history textbook, *Land of the Free,* was ground-breaking in changing the content of social studies textbooks.[6]

In the post-Sputnik era, the federal government poured considerable money into education. Indeed, Urban and Wagoner report that the most significant consequence of Sputnik was not the space race or the attention to academic studies, but "the impetus it gave to federal financing of public education."[7] By the late 1960s, social studies education was a beneficiary of federal funding. Hundreds of new social studies programs flowered throughout the country. MACOS (Man: A Course of Study), was perhaps the most well-known of the many inquiry-based social studies curricula that resulted.

When Dr. Crim became APS superintendent of schools, there were more than one hundred "new social studies" curricula developed nationwide.[8] One of the most well-known of the "new social studies" curricula was MACOS, and Atlanta education administrators considered the curriculum for their social studies courses. MACOS was based on the theories of Jerome S. Bruner.[9] Bruner created a "spiral curriculum," and MACOS focused on what made human beings human.[10] The curriculum did not emphasize specific social studies content, but emphasized the process of the discovery and as such, fostered inquiry-based knowledge.

The MACOS curriculum included the study of different cultures and helped students broadly understand the human condition. Bruner (1996) believed that "learning and thinking are always situated in a cultural setting and always dependent upon the utilization of cultural resources."[11] MACOS afforded students the opportunity to experience a more culturally relevant social studies curriculum. The curriculum did not have a Eurocentric emphasis, but purposely examined non-Western cultures. MACOS encouraged students to ask questions, discuss alternatives, and reach conclusions based upon evidence and argument. One of the units of study, for example, focused on the practices of the Netsilik Inuit, whose cultural customs were markedly different from those of most Western cultures.

Many local educators viewed MACOS materials as inherently controversial.[12] The curriculum fostered a questioning of life and morality that many conservatives found unacceptable. Historically, Georgia had always had a large conservative Baptist population, as 1 in 5 Georgians was Southern Baptist in 1970.[13] Most Georgia conservatives ardently opposed the MACOS curriculum. Although the MACOS curriculum gained negative attention in the local newspapers, it also enjoyed some limited support from the Atlanta community.[14] Ultimately, the conservative local opposition squelched the possibility of adopting MACOS. MACOS represented an opportunity to implement an innovative curriculum that promoted a broad examination of culture, one that might have been more relevant for Atlanta's African American students. Instead, as one Northside High School graduate from the mid-1970s noted, most of her social studies classes comprised the traditional narrative of dead White men.[15] Ron Evans's 2011 examination of inquiry learning in social studies provides a complex analysis of the strengths and flaws of inquiry projects, and suggests that educators were for the most part left out of the conversation and development of them.[16] Such omission, Evans believes, is rooted in arrogance and antieducation attitudes. Inquiry learning was also flawed because it made assumptions about student motivation and readiness and ignored the contexts of culture and social class that have exerted power in schools.[17]

By the early 1970s, new social studies projects had grown in popularity, but many critics had arisen, as well. For example, Edwin Fenton authored a textbook series that also promoted an inquiry approach in social studies education.[18] Fenton, although a respected academic from Carnegie Institute of Technology, nonetheless became a target of criticism. The Georgia State Board of Education banned Fenton's 1972 textbook on American history.[19] Clearly, the new social studies movement had many opponents in Georgia. Thus, prevailing resistance to an innovative curriculum such as MACOS, with its broad examinations of culture that might have been more relevant to APS's African American students, prevented significant changes in social studies education in Atlanta.

Georgia History Teacher Guides

In addition to the controversy over MACOS and other new social studies curricula in 1975, eighth-grade Georgia History was an important concern in the APS social studies curriculum. Here again, evidence demonstrates that resistance existed to employing critical pedagogies and to expanding the curriculum beyond the traditional American historical narrative. In 1983, the eighth-grade social studies curriculum included two principal areas of study: geography and cultural history. A common teacher's guide was given to all eighth-grade Georgia History teachers in 1983 to "bring about a degree of standardization in the teaching of Georgia History in the Atlanta Public Schools and to assist in creating a learning experience that is meaningful, exciting, and rewarding."[20] It is interesting that the guide used words like "meaningful, exciting, and rewarding" and suggested that if teachers followed the guide, their "creativity will be stimulated" and "they will motivate students to master the study of Georgia History."[21] Although, the 1983 *Georgia History Teacher's Guide* was intended to create a "rewarding learning experience," the objectives set forth typically fostered lower-order thinking skills. The teacher's guide suggested that students would be able to identify, recognize, or know part or all of the objectives. In addition, the "Suggested Evaluation Procedures"[22] also asked low-level questions and even suggested certain evaluations for better students compared to weaker students.

Many of the "suggested evaluation procedures" were aimed at lower-order thinking skills and not at critical thinking. Jonathan Kozol is a prominent education critic who has observed and described the prevalence of rote memorization, mindless drills, and scripted curricula in urban classrooms.[23] He pointed out that a disproportionate number of minority students filled special education classrooms. In many Georgia classrooms, activities were implemented that were no different from the educational practices Kozol detailed nationwide. In fact, the NAACP filed suit in 1984 against 13 Georgia school districts for discriminating against Blacks, because it assigned them to special education classes before testing and evaluating the students.[24] True-false questions and map tests, as suggested in the APS guide, often require simple recall, rather than complex analysis. The *Georgia History Guide,* like many social studies curricula, emphasized factual content over higher-level thinking processes.

Culture and diversity were emphasized as major areas of concentration in the eighth-grade Georgia History curriculum, which was important. In the 116 pages of instructional topics, approximately 25 pages (22 percent) specifically addressed culture and diversity,[25] but out of 7 units and 30 chapters, only about 6 chapters (20 percent) emphasized the African American impact on the history of Georgia, and their focus was largely on slavery. Four chapters touched on the Native American (Indian) impact on the history of Georgia.[26] No evidence in the teacher's guide, however, indicated that culture and diversity were taught beyond the basics of introducing American Indians to the students and the early impact of slavery on the state of Georgia. The recollections of several APS students suggest that many social studies teachers did not address culture and diversity in their social studies classes.[27] When Norman Thomas, an African American social studies teacher and the Georgia Parent Teacher Association's first Black president (1985), was moved to teach in a newly integrated APS school in 1970 and began to teach a unit on Black history, he recalled that the White students were permitted to stay at home.[28] He was grateful that he did not lose his teaching job, but he remained steadfast in his commitment to teach African American culture and history. Clearly, it took many years before the APS social studies curriculum reflected the culture and history of its student population.

Given the predominantly African American student population of APS by the early 1970s, the need for a social studies curriculum that included the contributions of African Americans and of other ethnicities should have been more obvious. However, most of the content in the social studies teacher's guide placed a distinct emphasis on the European impact on the history of Georgia and was not culturally relevant to the majority of students. Culturally relevant pedagogy, according to Ladson-Billings, empowers students intellectually, socially, and emotionally, by using cultural referents to impart knowledge, skills, and attitudes.[29] Geneva Gay notes that using cultural knowledge, prior experiences, and frames of reference for ethnically diverse students makes learning more relevant and effective for students.[30] Many APS students could not relate to the experiences of the past, because they could not see themselves in the past or view themselves as positive contributors to history. D. S. Grant states that many Black students in Georgia "believed school administrators and teachers held high-handed disregard for their beliefs and traditions."[31] Given the desegregation battle in APS and the prolonged local struggle for educational equality that African American parents and students fought for, the curriculum guide's lack of emphasis on critical thinking skills and on diverse ethnic groups is salient to the study of the desegregation era social studies curriculum.

Growth of the Standards Movement in the Early 1980s

National and local newspaper headlines in 1984 and 1985 reemphasized the importance of lower-order thinking skills that was evident in the 1983 APS teacher's guide for eighth-grade Georgia History. In particular, the newspapers depicted geography as one of the weakest areas of school-age children's knowledge. Not only did these reports of US students' lack of geographical knowledge stress a need for teaching basic content, but they also emphasized the need for standardized testing. In October of 1984, the *Atlanta Journal* featured an article that revealed that "99 percent (of a group of incoming freshman at St. Mary-of-the-Woods College) could not pick out Vietnam [on a map], 75 percent couldn't find Moscow, more than 50 percent missed Chicago, and about 9 percent couldn't even locate Mexico."[32] The article stressed the deficiencies of US students compared to students in other countries, and reiterated the need for more geography courses at the pre-college level and more testing. The tradition of questioning and inquiry promoted by MACOS in the 1970s had lost stature in favor of standards and testing, even in the local social studies curriculum.

In fact, by the 1980s, APS began to develop some in-depth social studies cocurricular programs to provide students with a variety of real-world learning opportunities outside of the classroom. These curricular shifts reflected a stronger emphasis on providing learning opportunities in social studies that had more cultural relevance for the APS student body. Nonetheless, the textbooks remained a dominant aspect of teaching and learning social studies in many classrooms, instead of opportunities offered by the cocurriculum.

Atlanta Public Schools' Eighth-Grade Social Studies Textbooks

In 1977, authors of an article reviewing textbooks commented, "Merely acknowledging a problem does not remove it. And guidelines without timetables and procedures for enforcement and monitoring will not remove bias from textbooks."[33]

In order to extend our investigation of race and the social studies curriculum, we examined four social studies textbooks selected for the Atlanta Public Schools, which were used in classrooms in the 1970s and 1980s. All four textbooks were adopted in Georgia History eighth-grade classrooms during this time period. The four textbooks were: *Georgia: History and Government* by Albert B. Saye; *The Georgia History Book* by Lawrence R. Hepburn; *A Panorama of Georgia* by Louis DeVorsey, Jr., Marion Rice, Elmer Williams, and Bonnie London; and *Georgia in American Society* by W. B. Wingo, S. M. Terry, and R. Bussler. Each textbook depicts the culture, politics, history, economy, and symbols of the state of Georgia throughout its pages.

As we attempted to evaluate the complexities associated with race in the social studies curriculum in Atlanta Public Schools from 1970 to 1990, these textbooks helped to reveal a more complete picture. We found several common themes in the textbooks, but here we emphasize five that occurred repeatedly in the social studies curriculum for the time period under investigation:

1. American Indians are written out of Georgia's history after the Trail of Tears.
2. From the early days of slavery through the twentieth century, Blacks are depicted as contributors to society and culture mainly through physical labor.
3. Martin Luther King, Jr., is seen as the most prominent Black person to contribute to Georgia's history.
4. The Confederacy is a way of life and lives on through the history of Georgia as it promotes White dominance over all other ethnicities.
5. White culture is portrayed as the American way, and those who are not part of White culture are portrayed as having had less of an impact on the history of Georgia than Whites have had.

American Indians Removed from Georgia's History after the Trail of Tears

Several patterns are evident with respect to the portrayal of American Indians in the Georgia history textbooks we studied. These patterns include discussion of Indian life only in the beginning of the text, portrayal of Whites as conquerors and Native Americans as primitive, and lengthy descriptions that focus on Indian removal. For example, *Georgia: History and Government* by Saye displays in a portrait on page 19, "a tribe of the Creek Indians" with an interpreter in native headdress and clothing meeting with James Oglethorpe and his men, who are dressed in full uniform from head to boots. The textbook author later discusses the removal by 1840 of the American Indian population, which had coexisted with the Caucasian population since the early 1700s. Shortly thereafter, the reader learns that by 1840 all Native Americans or "Indians" had been forced out of Georgia by the Indian Removal Act.

The perspective that all American Indians were removed from Georgia stands in sharp contrast with the contemporary perspective offered by the Georgia Tribe of Eastern Cherokee (a state-recognized, but not federally recognized tribe), who note on their website that "The story that ALL Cherokees were removed in 1838 is a myth... even though it was a horrible event and many thousands of Cherokee died."[34] According to the Tribe of Eastern Cherokee, in the early 1800s some Cherokee Indians hid in the north Georgia mountains, and several mixed-blood Cherokee remained in the state. The textbook author provides a second picture of the "Red" people on the Trail of Tears as they are forced off their Georgia land. In this book, colors are used to designate racial categories.

Much like *Georgia: History and Government* by Albert Saye, *The Georgia History Book* also focuses on Native American life only in the beginning of the book's narrative. In contrast to the aforementioned text, Lawrence Hepburn, the author of *The Georgia History Book,* depicts Native American civilization as highly complex. Unit one is largely dedicated to sharing evidence found on how "25,000 years ago Asian people migrated from Siberia to Alaska..." and "how these people developed four *traditions.*"[35] The author provides considerable information to facilitate understanding of the Georgia Indians' ways of life. Detailed pictures are included to show "Pre-colonial sites" like Rock Eagle and replicas of what an Indian village might have looked like, based on evidence uncovered by archaeologists.[36] Not only does this textbook provide more literature and pictures to support the description of early settlements in Georgia, the author also gives evidence of the complex and highly structured ways of life the early American Indians had.

The comprehensive narrative provides indication of "complex trading systems, high artistic levels, social organization, and even a highly organized religious system"[37] among the four traditions of Indian tribes who were the early inhabitants of Georgia. Although the portrayal does not emphasize primitive characteristics, the Native American culture is still viewed as foreign and ultimately problematic for the European settlers. The author describes how conflict developed between the natives and Europeans once they arrived. "Each tribe had its own economy, government, religion, and family patterns... differing greatly from those of the Europeans... as a result, a conflict of ideas soon developed between the Indians and the whites."[38] This portrait is very different from the picture given in Saye's textbook, which gives a sparse description of the lives of the native peoples and of the reasons that conflicts might have taken place between the American Indians and early colonists. Through pictures and details in the literature, Hepburn paints a clearer picture of what took place across the Georgia lands in the 1600s and 1700s, and how the land developed from an area once controlled by American Indians to a land controlled by Whites. In the next unit, the author describes the arrival of the Europeans and how and why they inhabited Georgia lands.

In the first three units where European relations with natives are characterized, the units are labeled as "The Indian Problem." The author further details White culture and dominance in developing government and land, viewing it not only as an individual settlement, but also as part of what came to be the United States. White dominance and power are described through details describing war with England, the tremendous shift in the landscape of Georgia's racial makeup from American Indians to mostly Whites, and the forced introduction of Blacks.[39] Instead of describing the contributions of American Indians, the author emphasizes in great detail their removal and quickly decreasing numbers, and expresses the events as "*The Indian Problem 'Solved.'*"[40] Hepburn's historical perspective sharply contrasts with the accounts of some of the Georgia native tribes of events surrounding the Trail of Tears. Even more curious is the fact that, according to Hepburn, the American Indian problem was "solved," and native peoples are not mentioned after the Trail of Tears.[41]

A Panorama of Georgia, by L. DeVorsey et al., provides even more evidence to support our view that the prevailing theme in the APS social studies curriculum of the time is that American Indians were written out of Georgia's history after the Trail of Tears. The story begins with "Natives and Explorers" and includes a drawing of Hernando de Soto on the very first page. De Soto is dressed in military armor, and holds his sword at the ready. He possesses a serious demeanor, one of power and honor, much like the depiction of numerous White men portrayed on most pages of the textbook.[42] The de Soto image sets the tone for the rest of Georgia's history, and the book unfolds much the same way as the other textbooks.

Native Americans grace the early pages and very quickly encounter Europeans. The book states, "It was not until 1540 that an explorer reached the land we now know as Georgia."[43] It is interesting to note that the natives in Georgia arrived "around 8,000 years ago"[44] according to archaeologists; Black people arrived shortly after the first Europeans, but the history detailed in the narrative is the White man's story.

In part, the emphasis on White history is due to the existence of written records, which occupy an important aspect of European culture. Written records preserve accounts of who, what, when, and where, and can be passed down through the generations without alteration. Oral traditions were more common among native people and Africans, thus making research and recorded history more difficult to construct, especially when oral traditions were lost. The way textbooks organize, display, and provide historical accounts makes it appear that one culture has been more influential; this attitude resonates and affects how people view their world, who creates their world, and who and what is important in that world.

Most portraits of American Indians and of African Americans are recreations based on descriptions written by Whites or are portraits taken by White men and preserved. Native descriptions of culture and history in early Georgia appear in the early pages of *A Panorama of Georgia*, but their presence abruptly stops shortly after the War of 1812. The history of the natives in Georgia, who occupied the Georgia lands for thousands of years, much longer than any other ethnic group, has the least coverage and the fewest recorded contributions to Georgia's history in *A Panorama of Georgia*.[45]

The fourth textbook, by W. Bruce Wingo, Steven M. Tenny, and Ron Bussler, *Georgia in American Society*, demonstrates the lack of Native American representation seen in other Georgia history books. Once the geography of Georgia is established, and the reader understands why people would want to settle in the Georgia area, the authors discuss the people who first inhabited Georgia. In "The Indians Came First," Chapter Two, Native American contributions to Georgia history are described.[46] Remarkably, a picture of a current-day "young Indian" is displayed, with her face barely visible as she looks down to make an arrowhead.[47] The textbook does not provide pictures that give individual personality to the American Indians, as no names are offered, nor are natives portrayed occupying high government positions. Most pictures display the traditional native culture, in sharp contrast with the more modern depictions of White contributions to Georgia's history.

The textbook quickly moves into the arrival of the Europeans after a very brief overview of the native culture. Immediately, European culture is depicted as the dominant culture. For example, the textbook uses "primitive"[48] to describe much of the Native American culture and "dominated"[49] to describe the presence of the European culture in what became the state of Georgia. Each of the visuals provided supports this perspective. For example, native culture is portrayed with "primitive" characteristics: people wearing little clothing, makeshift shelters, simple weapons made by hand (bow and arrow, knives, carved utensils), elaborate religious structures to worship many gods, and very tight-knit communities that provide only the basic necessities for life.[50]

In contrast to the American Indians, the textbook authors depict the Europeans with visual evidence of dominance. The Europeans are described with words like, "explorers, conquerors, scholars, wealthy,"[51] which sets their way of life apart from that of the American Indians and places Europeans in a higher position. The traditional way of life displayed by natives makes their culture seem less intelligent or less advanced, and ultimately less American. The Europeans' "desire to learn and create" sets the tone for the rest of the textbook.[52] The idea of expanding and spreading knowledge is the dominant way Europeans are portrayed in *Georgia in American Society*.

In *Georgia in American Society,* the description of the Indian Removal divides the American Indians into those who adopted the White culture and those who refused.[53] The number of pictures that the textbook displays of important American Indians, as well as of important Blacks, is very small, and the pictures of natives or Blacks in which their names and accomplishments are displayed is even smaller. To be exact, three pictures of American Indians with individual identities are found in *Georgia in American Society:* Mary Musgrove; Tomochichi, Chief of the Yamacraw Indians; and Chief Vann. These are the only pictures in the textbook that provide an individual personality to American Indians. Although the picture of Chief Vann is labeled, in the photo Vann has adopted White culture and wears a suit. He does not wear native clothing, and he seems to be posing for the picture as most White men would. The American Indians are not mentioned again after page 136, as it seems they are completely written out of Georgia history.

The portrayal of Native American culture in all four of the Georgia history textbooks gives readers the incorrect impression that natives no longer exist in the state at all. Such impressions contribute to young people's misconception that Native American culture only existed a long time ago and is not part of contemporary society. All four of the textbooks portray American Indian culture as primitive or foreign, and one that ultimately disappeared.

Blacks Contributed to Georgia History Primarily through Physical Labor

Each Georgia history textbook used in the Atlanta Public Schools in the 1970s and 1980s characterized African American contributions by showing imagery of Blacks, from early slavery through the twentieth century, who contributed to society primarily through physical labor. According to Juanita Roderick, who conducted a 1970 study, such images reinforce stereotypical negative images of Blacks:

> A review of literature and research on minority groups in textbooks revealed that the textbook, a principal teaching source, appears to have a major role in projecting images of minority groups…, however, adult Negroes in textbooks are slighted in the respect that they are most often pictured in occupational uniform, they are not named and they are not given speaking roles. Spanish-Americans, Orientals, European immigrants, and Indians are not treated as extensively as Negroes, and when they are considered, they appear to be cast in stereotype[d] occupations and living quarters.[54]

The *Georgia: History and Government* textbook by Albert Saye has few images of Black people or other diverse racial and ethnic groups. "The Old South" unit begins on page 94, as does the depiction of Blacks as physical laborers. For example, the reader is able to view a picture labeled "Slaves at Work." This picture shows Blacks picking cotton in a large field as they are being watched by an overseer on a horse.[55] Saye notes, the "Indians were all gone," and "99.9 percent of Blacks in Georgia were slaves."[56] The text emphasizes the physical labor of Blacks and justifies the visual representations via statistics.

Not until much later in the textbook (Unit Ten) does the reader first encounter African Americans who appear as individuals, or as people who participate in non-labor-intensive roles in society. For example, on page 170, Booker T. Washington's portrait shows him wearing a suit. The portrait of Washington appears next to a portrait of Henry W. Grady, and it is placed chronologically after the Civil War.[57] Before the Civil War, the textbook does not show any persons of color in a portrait by themselves or with a given name, but only shows them as persons worthy of low socioeconomic and labor-intensive ways of life.

The textbook authors convey the sense that few Black people are well known or have made considerable contributions to the state of Georgia outside of physical labor and low-wage jobs. The representation of political leadership, visually and via text, is so limited that it appears to be token. Furthermore, there are no photographs of ordinary African Americans engaged in roles such as lawyer, doctor, nurse, teacher, scientist, newspaper reporter, policeman or woman, retail salesperson, or even in higher-paid physical jobs. The textbook makes it appear that Blacks such as "Daniel A. Payne, a free Black educator, in the 1830s"[58] from Charleston, South Carolina, did not exist, nor was it true that any "Black men and women played critical roles in skilled occupations"[59] in the South.

Hepburn's *The Georgia History Book* paints the same portrait of Black people as *Georgia: History and Government* does. However, Hepburn's book is unique and noteworthy because the author provides many primary-source documents throughout the text. For example, Hepburn includes the Laws of the Creek Nation, the Cherokee Syllabary, an 1829 memorial for John Ross from representatives of the Cherokee Nation of Indians, and US President Andrew Jackson's reply.[60] Unit Two begins with the dominant presence of the Europeans in Georgia, and halfway through the unit, the author introduces the "Black People in Georgia."[61] Interestingly, Hepburn describes all encounters separately, and provides firsthand accounts of these encounters through artifacts and oral histories. The natives occupied "Georgia" lands at the time the Europeans arrived, and "Blacks did not come by choice.... They were brought as slaves to work for White settlers. Slavery lasted until 1865."[62] Other sections titled, "Background on Slavery," "Slavery in British America," and "A Slave's Account" describe the Black experience in early Georgia. The only visual representation is a "diagram of a slave ship...called a slaver," which "killed thousands of Africans before they reached America."[63] Like the visual representations of American Indians, visual representations of Black people of prominent stature in the early 1600s through late 1800s, which might show pride, dignity, grace, or importance do not exist in the book. The number of visuals provided to show labor-intensive, low socioeconomic jobs outnumbers those of people of prominent stature for both American Indians and African Americans throughout the textbook.

The Georgia History Book, despite the inclusion of primary-source documents that reflect a range of historical perspectives, paints a mostly negative characterization of Blacks. "The Slavery Issue" is described in detail, but many positive contributions of African Americans are neglected.[64] Thus, readers remain unaware of Black contributions to Georgia's early history and focus solely on their socially constructed subordinate positions to White people. Not until halfway through the textbook are contributions of Black culture illuminated. In a section labeled "Change at the Turn of the Century," Blacks still are not pictured in a positive light, but are shown in largely menial positions. For example, a picture on page 149 shows a group of Black women in a sewing class at Atlanta University.[65] On page 157, a picture of "A Chain Gang" shows a Black man in prison attire with chains around his legs. Such depictions place African Americans at the bottom tiers of society.[66]

These images make it hard for Black students to find pride in their heritage. These negative images are reflected throughout the textbook. During the author's account of the Depression, Blacks continue to be portrayed in pictures that show them in low-income, labor-intensive jobs; for example "Chopping Cotton on Rented Land."[67] Even when poor White people are shown sitting in their overcrowded apartment revealing that "eight families shared one bathroom,"[68] the poorest Whites still occupy a higher social strata than Blacks.

Positive images of Blacks, beyond token political positions that appear at the end of the textbook, reveal portraits of physical ability, as demonstrated by a picture of Hank Aaron hitting his 715th home run, "breaking Babe Ruth's long-standing record...in Atlanta-Fulton County Stadium, April 8, 1974."[69] Although Aaron's accomplishment is certainly noteworthy, such a depiction contributes to the notion that the only respect Blacks receive in history is through physical accomplishments; indeed, they are portrayed in the majority of textbooks engaging in physical or labor intensive work as their primary contribution to Georgia's state history.

Louis DeVorsey, Jr., Marion J. Rice, Elmer Williams, and Bonnie London begin their history of Blacks in *A Panorama of Georgia* similarly to the other texts, with a discussion of slavery and its impact on the history of Georgia. Pictures appear of Black people as slaves picking cotton by hand or working a field to grow crops. The African origins of Black people are mentioned, but no depictions of Africans in Africa are provided to portray a Black in a position of power and dignity, in comparison to the pictures provided of European explorers. Even when descriptions of post–Civil War era Blacks or free Black men are provided, illustrations are not included. There were free Black men who fought in the Union Army during the Civil War and who worked as abolitionists to help free many slaves in Georgia, but these images are not shown.

In the section, "A Changing Georgia" as in other textbooks, a picture of Dr. Martin Luther King, Jr., appears.[70] The photograph prepares the reader for the changes that will take place during this period. As the reader turns the page to begin the section, a picture of a "moonshine still in the Georgia low country about 1880,"[71] appears. In the photograph, a Black man dressed in old, torn work clothes stands next to a shed and moonshine jugs. Once again, the lower social status of Black people is depicted. The hope of positive representation through the image of Dr. King was taken away by displaying an image of a moonshine still with a Black man located next to it. Samantha King argues, "The criminalization and pathologization of Black masculinity is so deeply inscribed and so utterly pervasive as to make...all Black men, always already potential criminals."[72]

Georgia in American Society by W. B. Wingo, S. M. Terry, and R. Bussler also does not give much visual representation to emphasize or minimize the portrayal of Blacks in Georgia's history. Most of the textbook is dedicated to memorializing the White history of Georgia and the White man's contributions. There are no pictures displaying the early history of Blacks, but the authors do provide minimal representation via text and photographic images of contributions at the turn of the century.

Martin Luther King, Jr., as the Most Prominent African American in Georgia's History

Images and text about Martin Luther King, Jr., tend to dominate all four Georgia history textbooks, giving the impression he is the only accomplished Black Georgian. Albert Saye, author of *Georgia: History and Government* starts to represent Blacks as more prominent contributors to Georgia's history in the last unit of the text. This unit allows the reader to encounter African Americans in pictures that represent them as individuals and not as groups of people. Saye does not show any persons of color in a portrait by themselves or with a given name before the Civil War. Most group pictures of Black people depict how African Americans have made progress in a world of adversity and inequality by portraying civil rights leaders such as Martin Luther King, Jr. (p. 219), Andrew Young (p. 239), and Senator Leroy Johnson (p. 239).[73] No pictures or examples of Georgians of color who have generated positive public awareness for something other than political leadership are presented. The sparse existence of the visuals makes them seem like tokens. The textbook could have easily depicted a well-accomplished Black, such as Benjamin Banneker, as one of the many people who made a significant impact on history. As noted in another book, Banneker "published six almanacs, for the years 1792 to 1797, in twenty-eight editions, printed in Baltimore, Philadelphia, Petersburg, Richmond, Wilmington, and Trenton."[74]

The Georgia History Book emphasizes the prevailing theme that Martin Luther King, Jr., was the most prominent Black person to contribute to Georgia's history. Immediately, Hepburn emphasizes this idea as it displays King as the lone portrait of an African American among the ten visuals on the cover. The repeated imagery of Martin Luther King, Jr., contributes to the impression that possibly no other people of color besides King have contributed in an important way to the history of Georgia. On page 196, Dr. King is shown "on the steps of his boyhood home in Atlanta."[75] A picture of another prominent Black Georgian, Andrew Young, appears on page 198 in book that totals 207 pages. The caption on the picture reads, "After serving in the US Congress and as US Ambassador to the United Nations, Andrew Young became mayor of Atlanta in 1982."[76] This caption provides evidence that Black people held prominent positions in Georgia's society, but this acknowledgment comes at the very end of the textbook. Many history teachers have difficulty completing the curriculum, and often contemporary history is neglected or rushed at the end of the semester, thus leaving little time to discuss the content at the end of textbook.

A Panorama of Georgia opens its section "A Changing Georgia" with a portrait of Dr. Martin Luther King, Jr.[77] There is no text, caption, or words to describe the meaning of the prominent and dominating larger-than-life visual. King was and is the symbol of the contributions of Black people to Georgia's history. No other visuals come close to crediting other prominent Black people in this textbook. *A Panorama of Georgia* also expounds upon King's contributions.

The first picture of a prominent Black person in *Georgia in American Society* is of Booker T. Washington, and the caption notes that he "began Tuskegee Institute to teach young Blacks a trade."[78] Along with Booker T. Washington's contributions, purposefully setting the history of Blacks apart from White history, the textbook also mentions W. E. B. Du Bois, but does not provide an image, and after briefly mentioning these two leaders, the textbook dismisses Black history quickly, and immediately returns to the familiar narrative of White history. No other ethnic groups are recognized as important until page 246, when Dr. Martin Luther King, Jr., is noted for contributions to Georgia's history for two reasons: "his impact on the social and political change that has occurred in the state," and the fact that he was a native son, "King was born in Georgia in 1929."[79] *Georgia in American Society* dedicates three pages to the contributions of Dr. Martin Luther King, Jr. After the textbook addresses Dr. King as the most prominent Black figure in the state's history, the only other picture that appears of someone who is not White in Georgia is of Andrew Young, mayor of Atlanta from 1982–1990 and ambassador to the United Nations. Mayor Young appears in a picture on page 271 with a brief caption, but there is no reference to him in the narrative content. Thus, readers of the four Georgia history textbooks likely are given the impression that King is the most prominent, if not the only, African American contributor to Georgia history.

The Confederacy Is a Way of Life and It Lives on through the History of Georgia

All four of the textbooks reviewed in this research, including *Georgia: History and Government,* extend the idea that the Confederacy is a way of life that lives on through the history of Georgia and all four promote White dominance over all other ethnicities. The first noticeable symbol recognizing the Confederacy and White dominance is displayed on the front cover of *Georgia: History and Government*—the old Georgia state flag. The flag is set apart from the rest of the textbook cover. The flag is small, but beams with bright blue and red. On the right side of the flag is the familiar cross of the Confederacy, commonly known as the rebel flag, and to its left, on about one-quarter of the rectangular space, is the state seal. Unlike *Georgia: History and Government, The Georgia History Book* does not display the Confederacy as a way of life or show the Whites as the dominant culture, but the textbook emphasizes the events leading up to the Civil War, events during the Civil War, prominent figures of the Civil War, and the impact to Georgia after the Civil War. The discussion of the Civil War stands in sharp contrast to other events addressed in *The Georgia History Book*.

A Panorama of Georgia does not have the symbols of the Confederacy on the front cover and does not immediately draw unwarranted attention to it. The cover includes pictures that depict the economy of Georgia: tourism, textiles, timber, shipping, manufacturing, and sports, but the pictures the authors choose to represent these areas are dominated by people with disposable income who engage in golf, horseback riding on Georgia's coast, rafting, and other leisure activities. The back cover has a picture of the United States flag flying above the state flag. Both are proudly displayed on a flagpole. The Confederate rebel flag symbol, which was part of the 1980s state flag, is thus on the back cover. This symbol of the Confederacy was a prominent component of the state flag into the early twenty-first century.

The idea that Confederacy is an undying way of life and that White dominance reigns is evident in *Georgia in American Society*, as the cover is boldly decorated with the Georgia flag, displaying the stars and bars of the Confederacy alongside the state seal. Several Confederate heroes are pictured, such as Robert E. Lee, Jefferson Davis, and prominent Georgians Alexander H. Stephens (vice president of the Confederacy), Howell Cobb (president of the Convention to create the Confederate government) and Thomas R. R. Cobb (author of the Confederate Constitution). There are two of portraits of Abraham Lincoln and three of Robert E. Lee. In the section of the book about the Reconstruction era, carpetbaggers and scalawags are depicted with the caption noting that they "...became rich and powerful in many Southern states under the Republican governments."[80] The Klu Klux Klan is depicted, as is a Black Confederate soldier who was disenfranchised after the Civil War. Several of the other textbooks include descriptions of Southern Civil War heroes, the Lost Cause, and Civil War depictions in books and movies, such as *Gone with the Wind*. The cover overtly illustrates dedication to the South and the Southern way of life. Thus, all four Georgia history textbooks establish and focus on the Civil War and on the Confederacy. In the South, in many respects, the Civil War is not only part of the past but lives on in the present.

White Culture as the American Way

A final common theme we found in all four textbooks was the idea that White culture equates to American culture. Although *Georgia: History and Government* describes the "varied" makeup of Georgia's people, the "White" people are described from the top of page 20 to the bottom of page 21; the "Red" and "Black" people share page 22.[81] Throughout the first 93 pages and first three units, the textbook displays only one picture of a person from Georgia's "varied" makeup. This characterization of White culture as the American way does not shift at any point to show change over time in the racial makeup of the state or in racial representation in Georgia's politics, government, economy, education, or leisure. However, this textbook does display the oppressive nature of existence that people of color have experienced in Georgia. According to the authors, only a handful of Black people or Native Americans are well known or have made considerable contributions to the state. Few representations in this text show groups of African American or Native American people in prominent roles.

Other ethnic groups do receive "honorable mentions." For example, in *Georgia: History and Government,* a picture of a Cambodian girl appears on page 201. The girl's family is compared to "the settlers of 1733, they came looking for a new start in life, a new opportunity."[82] The text paints these modern-day settlers in a subordinate position to White people. A herolike status is attributed to these immigrants in the section, "A Chance for a Better Life" as they settle in Georgia "on charity," and "learn English while older family members find jobs."[83] Thus, these immigrant groups are portrayed as part of the American success narrative.

All four of the textbooks' depictions provide a Eurocentric perspective. For example, many pictures of prominent White men, such as Joseph S. Pemberton, Joe Frank Harris, Franklin D. Roosevelt, and Jimmy Carter, appear in pictures throughout the text and display their prominence in Georgia's history and in national history. These men are shown as dignified, honorable, reputable, and of high social class, unlike most of the small number of pictures displayed of American Indians, Blacks, or people of other ethnicities.

Even White women do not appear until the latter third of the texts. Margaret Mitchell and Martha Berry are two White women who are portrayed. The text adjacent to their photographs reads, "The period between the two World Wars was one in which Georgia women played an increasing number of roles."[84] Apparently, women's contributions in Georgia only became important during the early twentieth century. A few prominent Black women are portrayed in the last third of the book. Charlayne Hunter, one of the first two African American students admitted to the University of Georgia, is seen in a photograph, obviously taken from a distance, as she walks the campus.[85] Her face is barely visible, unlike the faces of the White women who appeared in previous pages. Ms. Hunter does not appear in the photo alone, but surrounded by a crowd of people. The reader then encounters the second photo of a prominent Black woman, two pages later, as the authors present a section on "Civil Rights in Georgia." A photo of Coretta Scott King is labeled as, "President of the Martin Luther King, Jr. Center."[86] This photograph of Coretta Scott King is the only photograph of a solitary Black woman appearing in the entire 301 pages of *A Panorama of Georgia*; it is the only picture of a Black woman that offers individual personality to Black women. The depiction of Coretta Scott King is more than likely due to the representation in all Georgia history textbooks to of Dr. Martin Luther King, Jr.'s role as the most recognized Black individual in Georgia's history.

After reviewing these four textbooks, several questions arise. Did very few Black people contribute to Georgia's history? Did Native Americans cease to exist in Georgia? Did only a few Blacks and women contribute to the state history? Were most contributions to Georgia's history made by White men? Other ethnic groups appear in the later history of Georgia, as the reader is introduced to pictures of Asians coming to Georgia because of the economy, and to information about the impact of businesses locating in Georgia in the twentieth century. These textbooks seem to recognize the contributions of other ethnic groups only in very recent history. The authors provide a picture of Asian men at "Macon's Cherry Blossom Festival."[87] No names or other identification of the men are offered, nor do the authors give an explanation as to why these men are in Georgia at the festival. The lack of characterization is also true for a picture of Asian men surrounding "Atlanta Mayor Andrew Young and City Council President Arrington during a trip overseas."[88] With both pictures, the authors do not explain who the Asian men are or what their contributions to society are.

In *A Panorama of Georgia,* the authors describe what Georgia has to offer at length, and suggest that it is a result of the dedication and hard work of White men. The textbook shows in its final pages how the White man's contributions to and implementations of government, the economy, and politics have made Georgia a "desirable" place for living, working, and doing business. "It is easy to see why Georgia is seen as a desirable location for new business."[89] Because the books took little interest in what other ethnic groups offer to the history of Georgia, the reader is left with questions about why the White history of Georgia is the most recognized and personalized.

Conclusion

The four eighth-grade Georgia history textbooks reviewed in this chapter are just a snapshot of how race was portrayed in social studies education during the desegregation era. Common themes emerged in each textbook, including the following ideas:

1. American Indians are written out of Georgia's history after the Trail of Tears.
2. Blacks are contributors of mainly physical labor depicted from early slavery through the twentieth century.
3. Martin Luther King, Jr., is seen as the most prominent Black person to contribute to Georgia's history.
4. The Confederacy is a way of life and it lives on through the history of Georgia as it promotes White dominance over all other ethnicities.
5. White culture is portrayed as the American way, and those who are not part of White culture have had less impact on the history of Georgia.

All four textbooks support the common concept that traditional history curriculum means White history, because White history is the primary narrative that is described. One need only to contrast the stories of Georgia history in the four textbooks with a nontraditional curriculum or non-Western curriculum such as MACOS to become aware of the impact of race on social studies textbooks. Inquiry-based learning curricula such as MACOS offered opportunities to learn about less familiar, non-Western cultures. However, several factors, including political opposition, led to the demise of MACOS and other new social studies curricula. In order to keep the White culture in power, however, the White narrative must be prominent in the history taught in public schools; it must be common across boundaries, and it must have common themes across centuries and history. In the words of B. Fields:

> Nothing handed down from the past could keep race alive if we did not constantly reinvent and re-ritualize it to fit our own terrain. If race lives on today, it can do so only because we continue to create and recreate it in our social life, continue to verify it, and thus continue to need a social vocabulary that will allow us to make sense, not of what our ancestors did then, but what we choose to do now.[90]

The question of how race featured in the eighth-grade Georgia History curriculum cannot be simply or singularly answered. Context, teacher, student, and textbook all mattered and affected the kinds of learning that occurred in the classroom. Nonetheless, the narrative and the photographs in the Georgia history textbooks clearly favor a dominant Southern White perspective, with Martin Luther King, Jr., included to demonstrate a recently improved, more inclusive society. The overriding historical story in Georgia, however, does not included non-Whites in prominent positions prior to the civil rights era. The glimpse that is offered from the archival materials, the interviews with students and teachers, and the four textbooks reveals missed opportunities for inquiry-based curricula in favor of traditional, familiar narratives of European progress and success.

Notes

1. C. H. Bohan and P. Randolph, "The Social Studies Curriculum in Atlanta Public Schools During the Desegregation Era," *Theory and Research in Social Education* 37, no. 4 (2009): 543–569.
2. J. Moreau, *Schoolbook Nation: Conflicts over American History Textbooks from the Civil War to the Present* (Ann Arbor: University of Michigan Press, 2003), 69–70.
3. J. Zimmerman, *Whose America: Culture Wars in the Public Schools* (Cambridge, MA: Harvard University Press, 2002), 36–39.
4. J. Zimmerman, *Whose America*, 4, 127; J. Moreau, *Schoolbook Nation,* 306.
5. J. Moreau, *Schoolbook Nation,* 264–70.
6. J. W. Caughey, J. H. Franklin, and E. R. May, *Land of the Free* (New York: Benziger Brothers, 1966).
7. W. J. Urban and J. L. Wagoner, Jr., *American Education: A History* (New York: McGraw-Hill, 2004).
8. B. S. Stern, *The New Social Studies* (Charlotte, NC: Information Age Publishing, 2009).
9. Jerome S. Bruner is a prominent American psychologist who has made significant contributions to cognitive learning theory during the mid-twentieth through early twenty-first centuries. Bruner earned his doctoral degree at Harvard University and went on to teach at Harvard, Oxford, and New York University. He is the author of more than a dozen books in the field of education, psychology, and learning theory.
10. J. S. Bruner, Toward a Theory of Instruction (Cambridge, MA: Belknap Press, 1966). J. S. Bruner, *In Search of Mind: Essays in Autobiography* (New York: Harper & Row, 1983). J. S. Bruner, *The Culture of Education* (Boston: Harvard University Press, 1996).
11. J. S. Bruner, *The Culture of Education* (Boston: Harvard University Press, 1996).
12. G. T. Lappan, "The MACOS Materials: How Success Can Go Awry. In "Reflecting on Sputnik: Linking the Past, Present, and Future Educational Reform," Symposium conducted by the Center for Science, Mathematics and Engineering Education. http://www.nas.edu/sputnik/lappan3.htm, October 1997.
13. C. Quinn, "Baptist Population Plummets in Georgia," *The Atlanta Journal Constitution.* http://www.ajc.com/metro/content/metro/stories/2008/05/15/decline_0515.html, May 15, 2008.
14. J. J. Kilpatrick, "A Teacher's View of MACOS," *The Atlanta Constitution,* 4A, April 24, 1975.

15. S. Smith, "An Oral History Interview with Susan Smith, Northside High School graduate/Interviewer Chara Haeussler Bohan," Georgia State University, College of Education, Atlanta, GA, May 11, 2007.
16. R. W. Evans, *The Hope for American School Reform: The Cold War Pursuit of Inquiry Learning in Social Studies* (New York: Palgrave Macmillan, 2011), 82.
17. R. W. Evans, *The Hope for American School Reform*, 215.
18. F. Shaftel, "Review of The New Social Studies," *Teachers College Record*, 69 No. 7 (1968): 618. Edwin Fention, *The New Social Studies* (New York: Holt, Rinehart and Winston, 1967).
19. "Georgia history textbooks." In *The New Georgia Encyclopedia*. www.georgiaencyclopedia.org/nge/Article.jsp?id=n-859 (n.d.).
20. Atlanta Public Schools. *Georgia History Teacher's Guide: Eighth grade*. Social Science Papers, Atlanta Public School Archives, Atlanta, GA (1983).
21. Ibid., ii.
22. Atlanta Public Schools. *Georgia History Teacher's Guide: Eighth grade*. Social Science Papers, Atlanta Public School Archives, Atlanta, GA, section on "Suggested Evaluation Procedures," (1983), 10.
23. J. Kozol, *Savage Inequalities: Children in America's Schools* (New York: Crown Publishers, Inc, 1991); J. Kozol. *The Shame of the Nation: The Restoration of Apartheid Schooling in America* (New York: Crown Publishers, 2005).
24. D. S. Grant, *The Way It Was in the South: The Black Experience in Georgia* (Athens: The University of Georgia Press, 1993).
25. Atlanta Public Schools. *Georgia History Teacher's Guide: Eighth grade*. Social Science Papers, Atlanta Public School Archives, Atlanta, GA (1983), iii–iv.
26. Ibid.
27. J. Doe, An Oral History interview with Jane Doe, Henry W. Grady High School graduate by Chara Haeussler Bohan. Georgia State University, College of Education, Atlanta, GA, February 13, 2008. S. Smith, an oral history interview with Susan Smith, Northside High School graduate by Chara Haeussler Bohan. Georgia State University, College of Education, Atlanta, GA, May 11, 2007.
28. N. Thomas, An Oral History interview with Dr. Norman Thomas, Atlanta Public Schools Social Studies Teacher, 1966–1973, and Community Relations Coordinator under Dr. Alonzo Crim, 1973–1988 by Interviewer Patricia Randolph. Georgia State University, College of Education, Atlanta, GA, January 15, 2009.
29. G. Ladson-Billings, *The Dreamkeepers: Successful Teachers of African American Children* (San Francisco: Jossey-Bass, 1994).
30. Geneva Gay, *Culturally Responsive Teaching* (New York: Teachers College Press, 2000).
31. D. S. Grant, 530.
32. United Press International, "Students Need to Learn Geography, Teachers Say," *The Atlanta Journal*, 5B, October 29, 1984.
33. G. E. Britton and M. C. Lumpkin, "Subliminal Bias in Textbooks," *The Reading Teacher*, 31, no. 1 (October, 1977): 40–45.
34. "Georgia Tribe of Eastern Cherokee," copyright 2003–2010, http://www.georgiatribeofeasterncherokee.com

35. Lawrence R. Hepburn, *The Georgia History Book* (Athens, GA: Institute of Government, University of Georgia, 1982), 9.
36. Ibid., 11.
37. Ibid., 9–12.
38. Ibid., 13.
39. Ibid., 41–144.
40. Ibid., 76–86.
41. Ibid., 86.
42. L. DeVorsey, Jr., M. J. Rice, E. Williams, and B. London, *A Panorama of Georgia* (Marceline, MO: Walsworth Publishing, 1987), 19.
43. Ibid., 25.
44. Ibid., 22.
45. Ibid., 22–35, 49–63.
46. W. B. Wingo, S. M. Terry, and R. Bussler, *Georgia in American Society* (Stone Mountain, GA: Linton Day Publishing, 1987), 19–33.
47. Ibid., 20.
48. Ibid., 30.
49. Ibid., 38.
50. Ibid., 19–33.
51. Ibid., 36–39.
52. Ibid., 38.
53. Ibid., 126–135.
54. J. Roderick, "Improving College and University Teaching," *Teaching Goals and Strategy*, 18, no. 2, (Spring 1970): 129–132.
55. Albert B. Saye, *Georgia: History and Government* (Austin, Texas: Steck-Vaughn Company, 1982), 94.
56. Ibid., 95.
57. Ibid., 170.
58. B. E. Powers, Jr., *Black Charlestonians: A Social History, 1822–1885*, From Black Charleston Photographic Collection, College of Charleston Library (Fayetteville, NC: The University of Arkansas Press, 1994), 72b.
59. B. E. Powers, Jr., *Black Charlestonians: A Social History, 1822–1885*, 106.
60. Lawrence R. Hepburn, *The Georgia History Book*, 77–83.
61. Ibid., 37.
62. Ibid., 37.
63. Ibid., 39.
64. Ibid., 37–40.
65. Ibid., 149.
66. Ibid., 157.
67. Ibid., 173.
68. Ibid., 172.
69. Ibid., 205.
70. L. DeVorsey, Jr., M. J. Rice, E. Williams, and B. London, *A Panorama of Georgia*, 195.
71. Ibid., 202.
72. S. King, "How To Be Good: The NFL, Corporate Philanthropy, and The Racialization of Generosity." In *Race, Identity, and Representation in Education*, ed. C. McCarthy, et al. (New York: Routledge, 2005), 273–286.

73. Albert B. Saye, *Georgia: History and Government*, 219, 239.
74. S. Kaplan and E. N. Kaplan, *The Black Presence in the Era of the American Revolution* (Amherst, MA: The University of Massachusetts Press, 1989), 137.
75. Lawrence R. Hepburn, *The Georgia History Book*, 196.
76. Ibid., 198.
77. L. DeVorsey, Jr., M. J. Rice, E. Williams, and B. London, *A Panorama of Georgia*, 195.
78. W. B. Wingo, S. M. Terry, and R. Bussler, *Georgia in American Society*, 215.
79. Ibid., 246.
80. Ibid., 177.
81. Albert B. Saye, *Georgia: History and Government*, 20–22.
82. Lawrence R. Hepburn, *The Georgia History Book*, 201.
83. Ibid.
84. L. DeVorsey, Jr., M. J. Rice, E. Williams, and B. London, *A Panorama of Georgia*, 204.
85. Ibid., 216.
86. Ibid., 218.
87. Ibid., 248.
88. Ibid., 300.
89. Ibid., 250.
90. B. Fields, "Slavery, Race, and Ideology in the United States of America," *New Left Review* (May/June, 1990), 118.

Chapter Eight

Placing Social Justice at the Center of Standards-Based Reform: Race and Social Studies at McDonogh #35 Senior High, New Orleans, 1980–2000

Erica DeCuir

Louisiana educational policies produced two overlapping yet distinct forces that complicated social studies teaching and learning in the years 1980–2000: the standards-based reform (SBR) context that stressed classical European history, national heritage, and basic facts; and the policy framework of prescriptive curriculum guidelines and high-stakes testing. How does a social studies program committed to multiculturalism, social justice, and project-based learning coexist within such an environment? Remarkably, at the same time Louisiana enforced standards-based reform through policy directives, a historically Black high school in New Orleans embraced a contrary position on the purposes and practices of social studies education. McDonogh #35 Senior High School was founded upon the principles of cultural excellence, community service, social justice, and Black cultural appreciation. These principles were rooted in the school's early history and were formally sustained through the social studies program that emerged during the years 1980–2000.

For Louisiana public schools, the period 1980–2000 was marked by racial resegregation and intense school accountability reform. Race relations, which had violently exploded during the civil rights movement, were still tenuous, because of Louisiana's persistence in defying court-ordered desegregation mandates.[1] By the 1990s, Black students comprised almost half of the public school population in Louisiana and over 90 percent of students in New Orleans.[2] The majority of these students attended impoverished and racially segregated schools because of school redistricting and financing schemes, White flight to suburban areas, and the large Black middle-class enrollment in private and parochial schools. Louisiana's low student achievement levels on national norm-referenced tests prompted school accountability reform. According to a 1986 comparative testing study of National Assessment of Education Programs (NAEP) scores, Louisiana's average reading scores for its eleventh-graders were the lowest among all Southern states participating in the study and were well below the national average.[3] In response, Louisiana state officials developed the Louisiana Educational Assessment Program (LEAP) as a policy for school accountability via standards-based curriculum and assessment. Prior to SBR, social studies teaching in Louisiana emphasized social and civic responsibility; it was similar to the Hampton model advanced by Thomas Jesse Jones.[4] American history and Louisiana history typified course offerings, and teacher training institutes prioritized the role of education in increasing "efficiency in all of the activities of life."[5] The rise of SBR lead to social studies programs that were less functional and more grounded in classical European curriculum and pedagogy. High-stakes testing accompanied curriculum standards that embraced an Anglo-American political and cultural identity while neglecting local, community, and state matters of racial inequality and social justice.

McDonogh #35's efforts for a progressive, multicultural social studies program coincided with Louisiana's systematization of centralized curriculum standards and high-stakes testing in social studies. How did McDonogh #35 develop its social studies program in scope and emphasis? How did the themes of social justice and Black cultural appreciation emerge within curriculum and instruction? What role did teachers, students, and community leaders play in designing social studies curricula? How was McDonogh #35 able to sustain its program within the larger context of SBR in Louisiana? This historical analysis examines the scope and organization of McDonogh #35's social studies curricula, teachers' instructional practice, extracurricular programs, and innovative educational initiatives. I will also evaluate how the school's social studies program endured within the larger framework of state-mandated, standardized curriculum and assessment. The social studies program of McDonogh #35 can serve as a model for other social studies programs committed to social justice while being challenged by the policy mandate for SBR in schools around the country.

Early History

The inscription in the 1967 yearbook of McDonogh #35 recognizes the school as a beacon of cultural appreciation and academic excellence that prepared students for their roles in fashioning the Great Society in

America.[6] Surely, the yearbook dedication reflects the progressive thinking of 1960s counterculture, but its spirited words are also emblematic of the school's founding principles of educating Black youth in academic and cultural excellence for service to their community. In 1917, McDonogh #35 was established as the first public high school for Black children in Louisiana. Its inauguration can be attributed to the vision and diligence of Black business and civic leaders, who petitioned the Orleans Parish School Board to convert an unused White elementary school to a secondary facility for Black children.[7] Between 1914 and 1917, Black leaders repeatedly petitioned the school board for a high school to remedy Blacks' unequal access to secondary education in Louisiana. Initially the school board refused, but it soon yielded to pressure from the White community to maintain a fully segregated, dual school system for the two races. A small contingent of Black physicians, teachers, lawyers, and clergyman was needed to sustain a self-contained Black community.

School financing was obtained from the estate of John McDonogh, a former slave owner who willed much of his multimillion-dollar estate to the Orleans Parish Schools and to the advancement of free education for the city's poor. McDonogh #35 was among dozens of schools financed through the McDonogh fund, and the high school was named in honor of John McDonogh as the thirty-fifth educational facility erected through his substantial donation.[8]

Although the school board originally purposed McDonogh #35 to maintain segregation in New Orleans, the Black faculty and community had different intentions for the new high school. Its first principal, Lionel Hoffman, identified the school's mission as one that served the educational needs of Blacks while meeting the larger needs of the community.[9] The school opened with a small and highly educated Black faculty, then considered the New Orleans creole elite. The faculty developed a college preparatory curriculum that included upper-level courses in the natural sciences, foreign languages, and humanities. Curricula were supplemented by vocational training in the professional trades of printing, plumbing, and woodworking. From 1924 to 1931, McDonogh #35 also offered a two-year Normal Training Course, a teacher preparation program that trained teachers for service in Black schools throughout the country. McDonogh #35's early educational programming was similar to that of other Black high schools in the South, many of which developed teacher training programs and college preparatory curriculum in the early twentieth century.[10] Black high schools shouldered the responsibility for Black professional training in teacher education and other fields, because most Southern postsecondary institutions were reserved for Whites only.[11]

High school enrollments during the period 1890–1930 increased substantially throughout the country and within Louisiana as well.[12] However, as historian James Anderson notes, Southern Blacks were excluded from the revolution in public secondary education that characterized the nation.[13] Southern school boards were slow to erect public high schools for Blacks, but escalating Black rural migration to Southern cities intensified pressure on urban areas to create opportunities for secondary education. When McDonogh #35 was founded in New Orleans in 1917, Blacks of secondary school age constituted 44 percent of Louisiana's total secondary school-age population. Soon after McDonogh #35 opened as the only public high school for Blacks, students seeking educational opportunities traveled across the state of Louisiana to attend. School enrollment escalated from 143 in 1918 to 2,182 in 1931, and as its popularity rose, a distinctive ethos of progressive social change through cultural excellence emerged as well. A summary of the 1931 school year demonstrates the rise in academic standards and competition in student admissions:

> The standards for the normal and college preparatory students were raised. In order to remain in the normal preparatory course, not only was a student compelled to maintain a general average of eighty-five, but he must at no time fall below eighty-five in English, and must maintain this average in at least sixty percent of his subjects.[14]

Students embodied the spirit of competition, particularly in their school participation, leadership, and extracurricular activities. By the 1940s, students had created over 20 clubs, which included French, tennis, library, and journalism. Students also developed plays, newsletters, musical performances, debates, and art exhibitions, which defined the social calendar for the local Black community. These community events promoted Black cultural appreciation and challenged prevailing stereotypes of Black intellectual and cultural inferiority.[15]

Another strong element conveyed in the school ethos was the campaign for social justice. This element was cultivated through teachers like James F. Browne, a teacher in the early 1920s who was fired by the school board for proclaiming the equality of the races in his newspaper, *The New Orleans Bulletin*.[16] In 1923, the school board convened a special session to discuss the "outrageous claim" and requested that Browne retract his statement. Mr. Browne refused, and his teacher contract was terminated as a result. Mr. Browne's termination did not deter Mr. Belfield C. Spriggins, an art instructor active in grassroots political organization during the 1930s. He worked tirelessly in the campaign for Black voting rights and was once arrested for urging fellow citizens to register to vote.[17]

In 1944, in response to escalating tensions in World War II, the school faculty developed an elective course entitled "War and War Problems" to critically examine the impact of World War II on the school, its community, and Black people at large.[18] And in 1965, teachers encouraged students to participate in the civil rights debate that dominated discussions in both the local community and the country. A caption reading "Students learn democracy in action" is found in the 1965 yearbook, just under a picture of students and teachers engaged in political debate at a school event.[19]

As early as 1965, the school required students to perform community service. The project was first organized as the "Good Citizens Project;" students chose a specific community organization to support in service, leadership, or donation.[20] The school soon required student participation in community service as a graduation requirement. Community leaders reciprocated with service to the school, as evidenced by the prominent visitors who spoke at school assemblies. For example, the 1965 calendar year featured presentations by Dr. Herald Hunt, Eliot Professor of Education at Harvard University, and a coteaching lesson with the schools' English teacher and Mr. Katz of the *Times Picayune*. Historically Black Colleges and Universities (HBCUs) also maintained a constant presence on campus, relaying the expectations and qualifications for college admittance as they recruited from the large pool of student candidates. The cooperation between McDonogh #35 and civic and political leaders solidified its role as the center of academic and Black cultural excellence in the community.

By the 1980s, McDonogh #35 garnered an impressive reputation for college preparatory curriculum, student leadership, and community service. As the school no longer existed within a repressive, segregated society, its focus turned toward intensifying its academic prowess and bestowed honors. The school eliminated its vocational curriculum in favor of gifted and advanced placement courses. In 1992, outstanding student achievement scores earned the school national recognition as a Blue Ribbon recipient by the United States Secretary of Education.[21] Student extracurricular activities such as tennis, drama, and society clubs were replaced by the Future Business Leaders of America, Louisiana Engineers, Mu Alpha Theta National Honor Society, Mathematics Honor Society, and Varsity Quiz Bowl. The school's founding principles of Black cultural appreciation and social justice became formally embedded within the school's social studies program through course offerings, curriculum and instruction, and extracurricular activities. The social studies program that defined the period from 1980–2000 embodied the school's social justice philosophy, which not only withstood the pressures of SBR in Louisiana, but affirmed the school's role as a leader in community building through political activism.

Standards-Based Reform (SBR) Comes to Louisiana

Ronald Reagan's 1980 presidential election was the impetus for a national reform agenda that promoted standards-based curriculum and assessment in the classical liberal tradition. Soon after taking office, the Reagan administration organized the National Commission on Excellence in Education to study the country's public educational system and propose recommendations for school reform. The commission issued its *Nation at Risk* report in 1983 and announced deficiencies in school curriculum that threatened the nation's ability to produce a competitive workforce.[22] The commission found the secondary school curriculum to be "diluted and diffused" to the point that curricula no longer had a central purpose.[23] It made 38 recommendations to reform schools through aggressive policy making, standardized curriculum, and rigorous assessments. The 1983 *Nation at Risk* report popularized core values of a standards movement, which had been gaining ground in local governments since desegregation. In the late 1970s, Florida, Mississippi, and Louisiana were among several states that enacted laws to raise academic standards in schools through a prescribed curriculum and annual assessments.[24] A year after the *Nation at Risk* report surfaced, the Education Commission of the States (ECS) convened a national conference with state policy makers to discuss implementation of *Nation at Risk* recommendations through SBR.[25] Preference for a common national history reverberated in *Nation at Risk* recommendations and characterized the nature of social studies education within the standards movement.

The popular works of Diane Ravitch and Chester Finn further refined the position of social studies programs.[26] Both were decisive critics of process-oriented social education and favored classical history to enrich students' core content knowledge in the humanities. Ravitch wrote, "there is increasing reason to fear that history is losing its integrity and identity as a field of study within the umbrella called the social studies."[27] She continued that history has "value as a generator of individual and social intelligence" and should exist as an independent study with teachers trained in subject matter, as opposed to method.[28] Increasingly, rigorous subject matter embracing classical European and Anglo-American history replaced broad, issues-centered social studies programs as SBR policies advanced throughout the nation. Louisiana's curriculum developers looked to national models to develop their social studies standards,[29] which all but eliminated curricular topics that were local or multicultural in nature.

Louisiana state officials acted swiftly in response to *Nation at Risk* by standardizing a high school course of study and increasing graduation requirements in 1984.[30] In 1986, the state legislature passed Act 146, creating the Louisiana Educational Assessment Program (LEAP), the state's high-stakes testing program that requires a successful score on content-area-standardized exams for student promotion and graduation from high school. The LEAP exit exam in social studies, implemented through the years 1988–1999, reflected content and skills from three specific social studies courses: United States History, Civics, and Free Enterprise. United States History was weighted heavily in the test items; it represented about 44 percent of the test, followed by social studies skills (24 percent), Civics (17 percent), and Free Enterprise (15 percent).[31] Test items required students to recall facts or understand generalizations found in curriculum guidelines that were also aligned to specific page numbers within state-issued textbooks. Prescriptive curriculum guides narrowed social studies curriculum to what Ronald Evans dubbed "an inert laundry list of topics and dates" that detailed national political events and figures.[32] State-issued textbooks organized social studies concepts through a historical and theoretical lens, ignoring local social issues and Black perspectives on history and society. Aside from some mention of popular Black leaders and inventors, textbooks failed to examine the Black experience as uniquely different from the larger narrative of Anglo-American national history. The exclusion of local history, particularly the absence of local struggles for racial equality, is especially disturbing for New Orleans as the site of *Plessy vs. Ferguson*, Ruby Bridges and the first desegregation of an elementary school, and the 1811 Slave Revolt—the largest slave uprising in United States history. Lecture, memorization, and recitation were encouraged as instructional practices to prepare students for recall questions featured on high-stakes tests. The pressure for successful passing scores on the high school exit exam prompted social studies programs to concentrate more heavily on the mandated curriculum while limiting curricular topics of local or multicultural basis. Louisiana's transition to SBR centralized curriculum, instruction, and assessment firmly under state control. However, McDonogh #35's social studies program intensified its commitment to social justice, local issues, and interdisciplinary curriculum at precisely the same time SBR advanced throughout the state.

Crafting a Social Studies Program at McDonogh #35 (1980–2000)

The McDonogh #35 social studies program contrasted distinctly with state curriculum standards and the LEAP social studies test. Pedagogy and practice were not limited by a unitary curriculum or method; rather, the acquisition of knowledge was as important as its application. Skills development, or the utilization of course content to impart decision making, critical thinking, and comparative understanding, was an important feature of the social studies program. In addition, student and community experiences were not de-emphasized in the social studies program; instead, the curriculum was supplemented by community-based educational initiatives such as the Spring Arts Festival and Students at the Center. The McDonogh #35 social studies program was a reflection of the school's history and culture, but teachers provided the impetus and ideology to sustain its integrity.

Content and Organization

The McDonogh #35 social studies program featured a broad array of autonomous course offerings in the social studies: Civics, World History, United States History, Free Enterprise, Afro-American Studies (later changed to Black Studies), Sociology, and Psychology. The behavioral sciences were offered as electives in the program, but the Black Studies course was a mandatory requirement for graduation. The courses were organized in a liberal arts format, and there were interdisciplinary connections through content embedded within the curriculum, instruction, and extracurricular activities. The 1986 yearbook described the goals as follows:

> The Social Studies Department is designed to prepare the student to become a contributing member of the American political system. The department helps the student to understand the foundation and function of our history and government.[33]

An important note is the expansiveness of the social studies program, far beyond the limited focus of LEAP curriculum guidelines. Study in the behavioral sciences indicated that multiple critical perspectives of American government and society could be examined alongside chronological lists of facts and figures emphasized in the United History, Civics, and Free Enterprise guidelines. The importance of social studies courses was manifested in the graduation requirements for the school. Students were required to successfully complete five social studies courses in order to graduate: World History, American History, Free Enterprise, Civics, and Black Studies. The Black Studies course was an outgrowth of a "special period" for the senior class created by the first principal of McDonogh #35, Lionel Hoffman. He designed this class to impart specific and critical knowledge of society and of the role of Black people within it.[34] The Black Studies course was reserved for seniors, and the course was assigned to teachers within the social studies and literature department on a rotating basis each year.

Curriculum and Instruction

Over half of McDonogh #35 school faculty held advanced degrees, and teachers averaged 23 years of classroom experience.[35] About 85 percent of teachers were Black, which was reflective of the school's early history and of teacher demographics in New Orleans public schools as a whole.[36] Teachers possessed the pedagogical expertise and training to construct innovative strategies to support higher level learning. State curriculum guidelines were consulted in the core social studies courses, but teachers generally retained a degree of professional autonomy to develop lessons that supported their own teaching philosophy. It was common for curriculum topics to change yearly as teachers rotated their course assignments, and this constant rotation allowed for diverse and varied content within the social studies program. In United States History, World History, Black Studies, and Civics courses, most of the curricular aims drew upon historical events to explain current circumstances and social structures. Other issues that were of local or student concern also found their way into the classroom through teacher contributions. Students in the 1986 class remarked that teachers "take time to talk to us about subjects unrelated to the curriculum courses. This [teacher input] is what is so unique about this environment."[37]

The social studies department formed a committee to make suggestions for textbook adoption, and individual teachers utilized their own resources to supplement textbooks. Teachers created syllabi very similar to those at the collegiate level, which included multiple texts, such as general social science textbooks, historical novels, anthologies, and guides for writing. A syllabus from the 1996 Black Studies course shows an emphasis on primary documents and historical narratives depicting Black culture and experiences in early Louisiana history and in American history.[38] The required books included Frederick Douglass's *Narrative of the Life of Frederick Douglass*, Alice Walker's *In Search of Our Mother's Gardens: Womanist Prose*; Ivan Van Sertima's *They Came Before Columbus;* and Gwen Midlo Hall's *Africans in Colonial Louisiana*.[39] A curriculum focus in the 1993 civics course examined the words "We the people" in the *United States Constitution* as a frame for understanding the contents of the historical document, as well as the position of African Americans within it.[40] One of the assignments for this curriculum topic was to investigate the deliberations surrounding the three-fifths compromise and to debate its fairness. Another assignment directed students to watch video excerpts of the civil rights movement documentary *Eyes on the Prize* and to discuss limitations in the Bill of Rights.

Instructional methods varied according to each teacher and ranged from lecture and primary document analysis to problem-based and small-group learning. A dominant instructional practice was the use of social studies projects that targeted skills development such as historical thinking, critical analysis, and positionality. By doing projects similar to the ones developed in the New Social Studies of the 1960s, students produced portfolios and projects that added depth and meaning to academic content. In the core social studies courses, students' projects emphasized positionality—weaving together textual and contextual sources to explain, interpret, and critique historical developments. In the behavioral sciences, students' projects explored the multiple layers found in psychological or sociological phenomena.

Veteran teacher Richard Grey remembered these social studies projects as a fundamental instructional practice within the program. He attributed the regularity of social studies projects to the spirit of rivalry and competition that came to define the school culture in its early years:

> The projects made great demands upon students' time, but they did not object because they were trying to stand at the top of the ladder or as near to the top as possible. The projects were heavily involved, but they [the students] had a choice of what topic they would research and how they wanted to collect and organize their data. They had to show historical accuracy, construct a sound argument, and make it presentable on a posterboard.[41]

Other teachers indicated that the social studies projects allowed students to realize the interconnectedness of past events and current society, and to interject their own personal narratives into the study of history and culture. Avril Hunt, a retired social studies teacher, recalled how he assisted students in developing their social studies projects.[42] The projects were made at the end of an instructional sequence that included in-depth reading, writing, and critical discourse. The projects gave students the opportunity to research a particular interest from the curriculum focus. First, students developed their interests into a research topic and explained the historical significance of the topic. Second, they arrived at a problem or tension in the historical record they wanted to address. Finally, they presented ideas that clarified a historical perspective or detailed a solution that involved the democratic process. Students competed in routine social studies fairs, where they presented their projects to school faculty for scoring.

The curriculum and instruction in the McDonogh #35 social studies program emphasized the development of critical skills. The popularity of social studies projects reflects a departure from the narrow, fact-heavy curriculum prescribed by the LEAP test and its accompanying curriculum guidelines. Teachers crafted their curricula through a multicultural lens in which readings, assignments, and instructional materials were selected to examine Black history and cultural appreciation comparable to the larger Anglo-American narrative of history.

Extracurricular Activities

The social studies program sponsored activities, clubs, and assemblies that continued the dedication to community service and to Black cultural appreciation established by the school's early founders. By the 1980s, the yearly "Good Citizen's Project," created in 1965, had evolved into an extensive community service initiative that required each student to volunteer a number of community service hours throughout the year. The Key Club took charge of this endeavor as a student club sponsored by the social studies department. The Key Club also led yearly drives to raise funds for national social service agencies assisting families and children of the working poor.

Student assemblies that highlighted Black history, music, dance, and art were sponsored by all departments in the school, but the social studies department worked specifically to invite speakers and create plays that celebrated Black history and culture. Jerome Smith, a community activist and local New Orleans civil rights historian, was invited to the school on numerous occasions to share his story as a young activist in the civil rights movement. He explained the historical context as well as the modern-day challenges of working in the rural parishes of Louisiana. Other assemblies included the annual Kwanzaa celebration, New Orleans jazz and dance performances, and student plays based on popular slave narratives. Often, student assemblies were organized in cooperation with the drama, music, and dance clubs to enhance the visual and emotional representations evoked in the assemblies.[43]

In 1995, teacher Jim Randels led an interdisciplinary committee of students, faculty, and community members to establish the annual Spring Arts Festival. Each year the planning committee selected a festival theme for classroom teachers to address in their curriculum goals and assignments. Teachers, local artists, scholars, and writers were invited to lead student workshops in the arts. The 1998 festival theme was "Rites of Passage and Family Values: Linking Our African Past to the American Present and Future."[44] On the festival day, classes were not in session; students attended workshops to learn about the festival theme from different artistic perspectives. Workshops were complemented by an African marketplace, exhibits, and special guest performances.

The extracurricular activities organized by the social studies faculty served to strengthen the relationship between McDonogh #35 and the Black community. Community service initiatives through the Key Club provided thousands of volunteers to serve in local organizations. Invited community guests raised student awareness of local social justice issues, which continued long after the civil rights movement. The Spring Arts Festivals galvanized not only students and teachers around a central theme, but also embraced parents, community leaders, and local artists in the school's efforts. Contrary to the emphasis on Anglo-American history and culture evoked in SBR, the extracurricular activities at McDonogh #35 sustained both social justice and community service as important legacies of the school's founders.

Placing Social Justice and Students at the Center (1996–2000)

As Louisiana strengthened its accountability policy at the turn of the century, McDonogh #35 teachers and students took greater steps to integrate student experiences and social justice within curriculum, pedagogy, and assessment. In 1997 a student-teacher collaborative founded Students at the Center (SAC), a progressive educational model inspired by Freirean theory.[45] The SAC model purported to: embrace student experiences, culture, and history as curricular frameworks; utilize critical pedagogy and discourse as learning paradigms; and engage students in civic participation and social justice. Popularized in social studies courses, SAC philosophy posited that students' experiences provide relevant connections to academic content through which analytical thinking and progressive social change are fostered.

The first SAC classes developed a series of literary works documenting the history of Black resistance and activism in New Orleans. Beginning with maroon colonies and slave revolts in antebellum Louisiana, students traced the stories of local lesser-known Black leaders of the Jim Crow era and of the civil rights movement. In capturing their stories, students commented through their writings on the persistence of racial inequality and the need for continued political action to eliminate oppression. A host of themes later emerged: war and the effects on youth, teen violence, media stereotypes, juvenile justice, and educational policy. SAC students worked extensively within the community to identify local issues and to find ways to solve them through reading, writing, and activism.

SAC classes were often coordinated with community activists and local historians to forge a link between earlier Black struggles for racial equality and the complexities of modern-day political activism. During the 1998–1999 school year, Kalamu ya Salaam, a New Orleans poet and local radio personality, trained students in video and radio production to create media that advances a social commentary. The local radio station provided guest lecturers and technical consultants to develop students' ability to conduct interviews, document folk traditions, and compose news stories. After technical training in audio recording and mixing, students created short, one- to two-minute pieces for broadcast. Three SAC student filmmakers later collaborated with a local nonprofit domestic violence agency to create a video on masculinity and violence that was used as an educational piece at local high schools and colleges. These students also created a piece on rape among teenagers, which they screened at community and city events.

SAC students also supported community initiatives to raise awareness of racial injustice that occurred in the city. In the year 2000, students began volunteering in an archaeological dig of the Treme neighborhood in New Orleans to investigate incidents of environmental racism. Students first completed reading, writing, and interviews of residents in order to understand the history and experiences of the Treme neighborhood. Second, they read scholarly work concerning anthropology, archaeology, and environmental racism to enrich their understanding of the academic disciplines and the interplay of race and class. Students detailed their findings in prose, poetry, and media, which supported larger research projects in the Treme area conducted by local environmental agencies and the University of New Orleans.

The SAC program at McDonogh #35 was later modeled in other New Orleans public high schools, with McDonogh #35 students serving as peer writing coaches. Because SAC's curriculum aims were derived from student and community experiences, pedagogy and assessment directly affected local efforts for social justice and racial equality. Students engaged in political activism through volunteering, writing, video production, and public appearances. The SAC program represented a strong commitment to progressive social change through direct community action. Instead of viewing social studies through a historical and theoretical lens found in SBR, the SAC program drew from historical and theoretical frameworks to examine modern-day social problems facing the local Black community. SAC teacher and cofounder Jim Randels correctly remarked, "Optimum learning occurs when the immediate concerns of community and family are addressed in academic course content."[46]

McDonogh #35, Social Studies, and SBR in Louisiana

Students and teachers at McDonogh #35 were able to craft a unique social studies program that embedded their founding principles of Black cultural appreciation, community service, and social justice. Instead of narrowing their social studies program to align to SBR and the LEAP test, the social studies program expanded to include Black studies and the behavioral sciences. Teachers incorporated project-based learning in which students were encouraged to critically analyze course content, practice argumentation and debate, and develop their own perspectives on historical figures and events. The SAC program coordinated student investigation and political activism to expose racial injustice and promote progressive social change.

How was the high school able to sustain its social studies program within the larger context of SBR and high-stakes testing in Louisiana? A possible explanation can be found in the record of academic excellence within the school. McDonogh #35 had long established academic rigor as the first public high school for Blacks in Louisiana. Students were carefully selected through a competitive admissions process that evaluated academic grades, standardized test scores, and scores on the school's entrance exam. High expectations of teaching and learning reinforced academic success through advanced course work and innovative instructional practice. During the period 1980–2000, McDonogh #35 students had the highest LEAP test scores and American College Testing (ACT) test scores of any Black high school in the city.[47]

The enduring relationship between McDonogh #35 and local leaders also may have shielded the school from the pressures of SBR. The school's active alumni were among the city's leading professionals, and the school enjoyed a favorable relationship with the local educational leadership. Sidney J. Barthelemy, New Orleans mayor during the late 1980s, wrote in the 1986 yearbook, "McDonogh #35 has upheld its commitment to the education of our Black youth and many of our civic and business leaders have emerged from the ranks of its graduates."[48] Dr. Everett J. Williams, then superintendent of New Orleans Public Schools, concurred by noting "McDonogh #35 Senior High School has always been a symbol of excellence and accomplishment. Its graduates have influenced the decision-making process in virtually every aspect of society, not only in this community but throughout the country."[49] Dr. Williams had served as an assistant principal at McDonogh #35 during the late 1960s. Finally, the school maintained a stable student body, faculty, and administration throughout the period 1980–2000, unlike other New Orleans public schools that were affected by White flight and economic divestment. McDonogh #35 had a citywide attendance zone and was relatively unaffected by the instability many other schools faced as neighborhoods changed both racially and economically. Because it was a selective high school, disruptive students could be easily expelled to their neighborhood school for not meeting expectations of conduct or performance.

Intraracial demographics distinguished McDonogh #35 from other predominantly Black schools in New Orleans during the rise of SBR. The

Orleans Parish School District, where Black students constituted 92 percent of the student enrollment, was ranked as the state's lowest-performing school district in LEAP test scores in 1999.[50] State assessments represented the heart of Louisiana's accountability system, and poor tests scores resulted in strict state oversight of curriculum and instruction. State educational leaders regularly intervened in local schools to assure compliance with curriculum guidelines, textbooks, and resources. Because the LEAP social studies exit exam affected students' graduation, parents and students also placed pressure on Black high schools to adhere to the prescribed state standards by "teaching to the test."

Social studies researcher S. G. Grant examined this phenomenon in a national study, and found that high-stakes testing narrowed social studies curriculum and instruction to items emphasized on the test.[51] Grant identified two types of social studies teaching in the high-stakes environment: defensive teaching and ambitious teaching. Defensive teaching responds to demands of standardized tests with a narrowed curriculum and textbook-centered methods. This type of instructional practice discourages classroom teaching about the diversity of human experience, history, culture, and environment within American society.[52] Even in cases where major Black historical figures are featured in state curriculum, they may only represent a fraction of test items. Low-performing schools may forgo teaching about Black historical figures, because the content is not considered vital to students' achievement scores. The "unrelenting pressure for high test scores" also reduces authentic assessment in classrooms, such as portfolios and project-based learning.[53] These alternative assessments emphasize process and application of subject matter, which expands students' power to interject their own experiences into the classroom. In contrast to defensive teaching, ambitious teaching seeks to apply curriculum standards to real-world contexts where students' experiences are valued. Ambitious teachers create opportunities for powerful teaching and learning by forging meaningful connections between state standards and progressive instructional practice. McDonogh #35's distinguishing characteristics granted the school the professional autonomy to develop ambitious teaching in its social studies program and to escape much of the strict state oversight and defensive teaching that affected other Black public high schools in New Orleans.

Conclusion

The dedication to Black cultural excellence created in McDonogh #35's early history also provides some explanation of the uniqueness of the social studies program developed in the years 1980–2000. Early founders and school leaders took care to establish a school faculty who were experienced, highly educated, and socially conscious, who held high expectations for student conduct and learning. School faculty assured students that academic and cultural excellence were not only necessary to their own success, but served a larger purpose—to improve the quality of life for their community and city. As one student noted in the 1986 yearbook, "the assemblage of these particular teachers was indeed wise and well-planned, for without their constant persistence where would we be?"[54] School administration exercised strong will to hire teachers that believed in the mission of the school and the level of high expectations for its students, and by doing so they nurtured academic and cultural excellence for thousands of Black Louisianans in a place that was unrivaled by any other public Black high school in the state's history.

McDonogh #35's history of cultural excellence is similar to that of other segregated Black schools in the early twentieth century, some of which were profiled in the works of Mary Gibson Hundley and Thelma Cayne Tilford-Weathers.[55] In a comprehensive review of successful segregated Black schools, Vanessa Siddle Walker outlines five common themes that created high standards of teaching and learning, long before the arrival of SBR: exemplary teachers, exemplary curriculum and extracurricular activities, and exemplary parental support and school leadership.[56] Perhaps most prominent in Walker's review is the concept of shared responsibility among the school, parents, and community to promote high expectations for student performance along multiple measures of academic achievement. In keeping with this line of research, this historical analysis of McDonogh #35's social studies program demonstrates how a majority-Black school was able to establish high academic achievement, Black cultural excellence, and social justice within a segregated school system. This narrative also traces the school's incredible resilience, despite the influence of desegregation, standards-based reform, and high-stakes testing on Black schools in the late twentieth century. A small yet influential body of research portrays successful Black schools and their commitment to cultural excellence, despite the pressures of standardized testing.[57] McDonogh #35 and its enduring commitment to a progressive and multicultural social studies program not only deepens our understanding of successful Black schools, but also contributes to a critical dialogue concerning social studies education within the context of standard-based reform.

Notes

1. Liva Baker, *The Second Battle of New Orleans: The Hundred Year Struggle to Integrate the Schools* (New York: HarperCollins, 1996).

2. Louisiana Department of Education, "2000–2001 Louisiana District Accountability Report Card: Orleans Parish," Released Report (Louisiana Department of Education: Baton Rouge, LA, 2002).
3. Southern Regional Education Board, "Measuring Student Achievement: Comparable Test Results for Participating SREB States, the Region, and the Nation. A Report of the Southern Regional Education Board/National Assessment of Educational Progress 1986 Program with Arkansas, Florida, Louisiana, North Carolina, South Carolina, Tennessee, Virginia, West Virginia (Atlanta, GA, 1986)." Retrieved from ERIC, EBSCOhost on March 15, 2011, http://www.eric.ed.gov/contentdelivery/servlet/ERICServlet?accno=ED292863
4. William Alexander, *State Leadership in Improving Instruction: A Study of the Leadership Service Function of State Education Departments, with Special Reference to Louisiana, Tennessee, and Virginia* (New York: AMS Press, 1972).
5. Ibid., 17.
6. *McDonogh #35 Senior High School 1967 Yearbook*, May 1967, McDonogh #35 yearbook collection, New Orleans Public Library.
7. Donald Devore and Joseph Logsdon, *Crescent City Schools: Public Education in New Orleans 1841–1991* (The Center for Louisiana Studies, University of Southwestern Louisiana, 1991), 189–191.
8. Ibid., 191.
9. Ibid., 193–194.
10. James D. Anderson, *The Education of Blacks in the South 1860–1935* (Chapel Hill: The University of North Carolina Press, 1988), 199.
11. Adam Faircloth, *A Class of Their Own: Black Teachers in the Segregated South* (Cambridge, MA: The Belknap Press of Harvard University Press, 2007), 138–139.
12. David Angus and Jeffrey Mirel, *The Failed Promise of the American High School 1890–1935* (New York: Teachers College Press, 1999), 53.
13. James D. Anderson, *The Education of Blacks in the South 1860–1935*, 186.
14. *McDonogh #35 Senior High School 1931 Yearbook*, April 1931, McDonogh #35 yearbook collection, New Orleans Public Library, 15.
15. *McDonogh #35 Senior High School 1944 Yearbook*, May 1944, McDonogh #35 yearbook collection, New Orleans Public Library, 29.
16. Students at the Center, *The Long Ride: A Collection of Student Writings for the New Orleans Civil Rights Park* (New Orleans: SAC Press), 2007, 113.
17 *McDonogh #35 Senior High School 1986 Yearbook*, May 1986, McDonogh #35 yearbook collection, New Orleans Public Library, 10.
18. *McDonogh #35 Senior High School 1944 Yearbook*, 22.
19. *McDonogh #35 Senior High School 1965 Yearbook*, May 1965, McDonogh #35 yearbook collection, New Orleans Public Library, 68.
20. *McDonogh #35 Senior High School 1965 Yearbook*, 82.
21. Blue Ribbon Archives. "Blue Ribbon Schools Program: Schools recognized 1982–1983 through 1999–2002." Last modified September 9, 2009. http://www2.ed.gov/programs/nclbbrs/archives.html
22. National Commission on Excellence in Education, *Nation at Risk: The Imperative for Educational Reform. An Open Letter to the American People. A Report to the Nation and the Secretary of Education* (Washington, DC: U.S. Government Printing Office, 1983).

23. Ibid., 10.
24. Jan Schechter, "Issues of Competency and Accountability. The Proceedings of an Invitational Symposium," Austin, Texas, May 13–14, 1981. Washington DC: National Institute of Education. Retrieved from EBSCOhost on January 14, 2012.
25. Chris Pipho, "States Warm to Excellence Movement," *The Phi Delta Kappan* 65 no. 8 (April 1984): 516–517.
26. Chester Finn and Diane Ravitch, *Against Mediocrity* (New York: Holmes & Meier, 1984).
27. Diane Ravitch, *The Schools We Deserve: Reflections on the Educational Crises of Our Times* (New York: Basic Books, 1985), 115.
28. Ibid., 130–131.
29. Sandra Finley, "The Progress of Education in Louisiana," Southwest Educational Development Laboratory (Austin, Texas, May 1, 1999). Washington, DC: Office of Educational Research and Improvement. Retrieved from ERIC, EBSCOhost on February 12, 2012, http://www.eric.ed.gov/contentdelivery/servlet/ERICServlet?accno=ED431235
30. Dan Loupe, "New Standards Are Too Tough, Educators Say," *The Times Picayune*, March 4, 1984, 15.
31. Louisiana Department of Education, *Instructional Strategies Guide: Grade 11, Social Studies. Louisiana Educational Assessment Program, 1989*. Retrieved from ERIC Database ED313299.
32. Ronald Evans, "Thoughts on Redirecting a Runaway Train: A Critique of the Standards Movement," *Theory and Research in Social Education* 14 (Spring 2001): 330–339.
33. *McDonogh #35 Senior High School 1986 Yearbook*, 25.
34. Donald Devore and Joseph Logsdon, *Crescent City Schools*, 194.
35. Personal papers of veteran teacher Jim Randels (hereafter referred as Randels papers).
36. Louisiana Department of Education, "Summary of Reported Personnel/Salaries as of October 2008: Planning, Analysis, and Information Resources Database." Accessed on August 9, 2010. http://www.doe.state.la.us/lde/pair/1089.html.
37. *McDonogh #35 Senior High School 1986 Yearbook*, 18.
38. Jim Randels, McDonogh #35 teacher, "Black Studies Syllabi," e-mail attachment to Erica DeCuir, August 17, 2010.
39. Ibid.
40. Jaceta Quillens, McDonogh #35 student, "Civics Syllabi," personal documents to Erica DeCuir, August 21, 2010.
41. Author's personal interview with retired teacher Richard Grey, New Orleans, Louisiana, August 28, 2010.
42. Author's personal interview with retired teacher Avril Hunt, New Orleans, Louisiana, August 28, 2010.
43. Jim Randels, McDonogh #35 teacher, "Spring Arts Festival," e-mail attachment to Erica DeCuir, August 17, 2010.
44. Ibid.
45. Paolo Friere, *Pedagogy of the Oppressed* (New York: Continuum International, 1970).

46. Personal interview with McDonogh #35 teacher Jim Randels, New Orleans, Louisiana. August 15, 2010.
47. Louisiana Department of Education, "2000–2001 Louisiana District Accountability Report Card: Orleans Parish," Released Report (Louisiana Department of Education: Baton Rouge, LA, 2002).
48. *McDonogh #35 Senior High School 1986 Yearbook*, 7.
49. Ibid.
50. Louisiana Department of Education, "2000–2001 Louisiana District Accountability Report Card: Orleans Parish," Released Report (Louisiana Department of Education: Baton Rouge, LA, 2002).
51. S. G. Grant, "High-Stakes Testing: How Are Social Studies Teachers Responding?" *Social Education* 71 (2007): 250–254.
52. Asa Hilliard, *The Hidden Consequence of a National Curriculum* (Washington, DC: American Educational Research Association, 1995).
53. Sheila Bernard and Sarah Mondale, "A Nation at Risk?" In *School: The Story of American Public Education*, ed. Sarah Mondale (Boston: Beacon Press, 2001), 180.
54. *McDonogh #35 Senior High School 1986 Yearbook*, 22.
55. Mary Gibson Hundley, *The Dunbar Story 1870–1955* (New York: Vantage Press, 1965). Thelma Tilford-Weathers, *A History of Louisville Central High School, 1882–1982*, 2nd ed. (Kentucky: Central High School Alumni Association, 1996).
56. Vanessa Siddle Walker, "Valued Segregated Schools for African-American Children in the South, 1935–1969: A Review of Common Themes and Characteristics," *Review of Educational Research* 70, no. 3 (Autumn 2000): 253–285.
57. Jerome E. Morris, "A 'Communally Bonded' School for African American Students, Families, and a Community," *The Phi Delta Kappan* 84, no. 3 (November 2002): 230–234; Norma Dabney and Mary Hoover, *Successful Black & Minority Schools: Classic Models* (California: Julian Richards Associates, 1990); Mary Eleanor Rhodes Hoover, "The Nairobi Day School: An African American Independent School, 1966–1984," *The Journal of Negro Education* 61, no. 2 (Spring 1992): 201–210.

Chapter Nine
Black History, Multicultural Education, and Racial Desegregation in Dayton, Ohio

Joseph Watras

Multicultural Education replaced Black History in many social studies curriculums. To some extent, they had different aims. While Black Studies sought to highlight the contributions that African Americans had made to American society, Multicultural Education promised to reduce the prejudices that children might harbor against other racial or ethnic groups. The experiences in Dayton, Ohio, offer a way to compare certain aspects of these different programs. Dayton's curriculum specialists designed Black History to aid racial desegregation in the late 1960s. In later years, Multicultural Education became a substitute for integration.

The research in this chapter explains this assessment. The opening section describes the conditions in Dayton that led to the adoption of a Black Studies curriculum for the city's middle schools. The second part explains how the curriculum supervisor for Dayton City Schools created materials and demonstrated teaching methods for Black Studies. The third section considers some reasons that educators gave to advance Multicultural Education and some criticisms other educators made of it. The conclusion contrasts the differences between the aims of Black History in Dayton and the aims of Multicultural Education. Although the comparison cannot evaluate the effectiveness of either model, it suggests that Black History has strengths that Multicultural Education seems to lack.

The Social Conditions in Dayton

The city of Dayton and its schools had endured racial segregation for many years. Education began to change in 1968 when the Dayton Board of Education hired a new superintendent, Wayne Carle. One reform that Carle instituted early in his career in Dayton was to designate a social studies teacher to serve as the district's resource teacher in Negro history. The hope was that this program would reduce prejudice among White and Black students by teaching them about the positive contributions of African Americans. In this way, Black history might serve as a necessary step in the movement toward the end of racial separation.

Dayton was fortunate to have one of the most successful large-city school desegregation plans in the country. It began on September 2, 1976. The chief of the US Justice Department's Civil Rights Division and stories in the *New York Times* congratulated Dayton on the success of the cross-district busing plan. Local papers told the reaction of African American teachers who faced classes of White and Black students for the first time. They claimed that it was wonderful.[1]

The addition of Black History to the public school curriculum may not have helped Dayton enjoy a successful program of school desegregation. The national mood had changed from defiant resistance to racial desegregation to acceptance. In 1976, several other cities, such as Dallas, Texas, and Flint, Michigan, undertook similar plans and experienced similar success. The results vindicated a report the US Civil Rights Commission had issued in August 1976, which concluded that desegregation works. Although the report acknowledged that problems remained in those districts that had successfully desegregated their schools, it added that positive and forceful leadership and careful planning could bring about smooth implementation of court-ordered reforms.[2]

Dayton's officials utilized the factors the US Civil Rights Commission had named. Although the conservative public school board members had argued repeatedly and strongly against cross-district busing, they joined their liberal opponents to repeat that the courts should decide this issue. In 1975, a lone mentally deranged gunman shot and killed Charles Glatt, a consultant from Ohio State University, while Glatt sat in his office working on the desegregation plan. Fearing increased violence, the candidates running for election to the school board agreed to avoid any direct or confrontational speeches. Before the day of implementation, local church leaders held prayer vigils. The city's African American mayor appeared on television, asking for peaceful cooperation with a lawful order, and the police warned of increased surveillance.

Another factor aiding success was that the desegregation plan was simple. The city was small, and its shape was square. In 1960, a population of about 260,000 residents lived within its 50 square miles. Furthermore, the Great Miami River geographically divided the city from north to south. The river separated the races, and the Board of Education had spread the schools throughout the neighborhoods, placing schools with Black students on opposite sides of the river from schools with White students. The placement of Dayton's schools meant that desegregation could occur by pairing a school on one side of the river with another school on the opposite side and exchanging some students between the pair of schools. This pairing is what the Master of the Court overseeing the case did.[3]

Ironically, Dayton's officials had made the court master's job easier, because they had ensured that the schools remained racially segregated, even after the Ohio General Assembly adopted a resolution in 1887 stating that regulations about education had to apply to all children, regardless of race or color. Their strategy had been simple. Neighborhoods followed patterns of racial segregation, and the officials had designed the schools to serve specific neighborhoods.[4]

Residential housing in Dayton followed severe patterns of racial segregation. For example, in 1988, Douglas Massey studied the housing patterns in Dayton and its suburbs and found it to be the third most racially segregated place among the 50 largest metropolitan areas in the United States. According to Massey's findings, the only metropolitan areas with higher levels of racial segregation than Dayton were Cleveland, Ohio, and Chicago, Illinois.[5]

According to Davison Douglas, this strategy of neighborhood schools distinguished Northern school segregation from Southern school segregation. Southern legislatures mandated segregation, but the legislatures in Northern states enacted laws prohibiting the exclusion of Black students from public schools. In response, Northern school administrators assigned children to separate schools according to the neighborhoods in which they resided. Because people of one race tended to live in a neighborhood, residential attendance zones and the so-called neighborhood schools made the schools racially segregated. In 1973, the US Supreme Court decided in *Keyes v. Denver School District* that such actions by Northern school officials constituted segregation by law. This meant the school districts had to repair the damage the officials caused.[6]

For years, officials in the Dayton public schools denied that they had segregated the schools. Pressure to change increased on September 1, 1966, when a tumult arose on the West Side of Dayton. Crowds of angry residents formed after a group of White men riding in a car shot an African American man as he stood in front of his apartment. Within a short period, National Guard soldiers quelled the disturbance. In an effort to reduce the threat of violence, Dayton's mayor created an ad hoc citizens committee and asked a prominent local African American politician, C. J. McLin, to head the study group. The final report criticized all aspects of city life. The municipal dumps were in Black neighborhoods.

The West Side residents endured inadequate sanitation services and police brutality. The report did not mention school desegregation, but it listed 22 recommendations about education. These included increasing attention to Black history, organizing in-service workshops to help teachers work with African American children, and hiring more African American administrators.[7]

At the same time, the Ohio State Advisory Committee to the US Commission on Civil Rights asked the Dayton Committee on Civil Rights to study the issue. In April 1967, the Dayton Committee issued its report, *A Call to Action*. According to this report, segregated housing caused racially segregated schools. Nonetheless, the report saw promise with the inception of Head Start programs and Dayton's recruitment of teachers from Historically Black Colleges and Universities (HBCUs). The report recommended hiring quality teachers for schools serving low-income families, constructing an educational park to bring about racial desegregation, developing alternative ways to educate dropouts, opening school buildings for after-school use, employing more school counselors, and creating a community-wide review board for the schools.[8]

In August 1967, a few months after the reports appeared about the shooting, the Dayton Board of Education issued a statement promising five reforms. The first was to seek racially integrated housing within school attendance zones. The second was to select teachers on merit alone. The third was to seek curriculum materials that portrayed the contributions of various ethnic groups. The fourth was to encourage dialogue among different groups, and the fifth was to engage all the agencies that might facilitate these reforms.[9]

On the one hand, the board's 1967 statement may have illustrated the members' reluctance to act. On the other hand, it was a cautious statement promising such innovations as the introduction of Black History. Further, the Dayton school board moved toward reform as the members hired a new superintendent. When Wayne Carle attended his first board meeting in June 1968, he met 30 White college students spending the summer in the city who were sponsored by a church federation to work in projects that would try to reduce racial problems. They demanded a Black principal for a local high school and more Black History in the schools.[10]

In November 1968, five months after Carle took office as Dayton's school superintendent, the US Department of Health, Education, and Welfare issued a warning about the distribution of students and the assignment of teachers. According to the letter, 85 percent of the Black high school students in Dayton attended three of the ten high schools in the city. Further, about 85 percent of the African American elementary students attended 20 out of the 53 elementary schools. To make matters worse, the district assigned Black teachers to schools with more than 90 percent African American enrollment.[11]

Almost immediately, the superintendent and the Board of Education entered a binding agreement to desegregate the teachers within two years, and the board adopted a resolution on August 22, 1969, to promote faculty desegregation through voluntary methods. The Dayton Classroom Teachers Association, the union at that time, agreed to the policy. Members of the union joined with administrators to form a task force to solve the problems related to desegregation.[12]

The main problem was that older teachers were apprehensive about moving to new buildings. The administration solved the difficulties in several ways. They changed the organization of elementary schools, which had been from kindergarten to grade 8, and opened six middle schools in 1971. In addition, the administration offered incentives for teachers to shift schools. It offered teachers opportunities to move in groups. The administration gave teachers release time to visit the new schools before they moved and promised that they could return to the former school after a year, if necessary. Officials took pride in the fact that out of the 600 teachers who transferred, the administration only forced about 90 to move and, after one year, only 20 requested to return to their former schools.

Because Southern school districts removed Black teachers and principals in the 1960s, the US Department of Health, Education, and Welfare warned school districts that any decline in Black personnel during desegregation would raise questions.[13] Dayton avoided any such problems. The district did not release or demote Black teachers or principals, although several had to move to new buildings to bring about faculty desegregation in 1971.

The establishment of middle schools offered advantages beyond making faculty desegregation easier. The new middle schools would use innovative curriculums. These changes allowed the introduction of Black History.[14]

Black History in Dayton's Schools

In some cities, Black Studies became a series of anti-White exercises. An example of such an experience took place in the racially diverse district of Sausalito, California. A Black Studies committee introduced members of the Black Panther Party into the elementary schools. The new teachers advocated Black militancy to the point where White parents complained to the district superintendent that their children experienced racial discrimination.[15]

In Dayton, the curriculum of Black Studies did not cause such problems. An important reason that Dayton avoided this difficulty was that the person who led the effort believed that Black History was a vehicle for racial integration.

Dayton schools included Black Studies in the curriculum when the superintendent, Wayne Carle, and the Board of Education adopted middle schools. With the new configuration of grades, the Dayton schools had the opportunity to introduce Black History as a required course for all middle school students. A group of teachers at Roth High School had pushed for this innovation. Among those teachers was Margaret Peters, an African American woman who the district had assigned to the school in 1963 as a social studies teacher. Peters had joined with other African American faculty and administrators to push the district to require all middle school children to take a course in Black History. Although those teachers wanted Black history to appear in other courses, they wanted a separate required course as well to ensure that the students had the chance to learn the material.[16]

As noted above, this topic had appeared whenever people spoke about the city's problems and the disturbance on the West Side. Accordingly, soon after arriving in Dayton, Superintendent Carle convened a citywide meeting to consider the need for Black History. He engaged a speaker for the citywide meeting, but the speaker could not appear. Carle asked Ms. Peters to lead the discussion. After the citywide meeting, Carle appointed her as the resource teacher for Black History for the Dayton Public Schools.

In its weekly newsletter, *Schooldays,* the Dayton schools announced Ms. Peters's appointment as the first full-time resource teacher in Negro History. The newsletter listed her first project as providing a monthly bulletin to inform teachers and administrators about developments in the field. These bulletins included announcements of plans of the Dayton newspapers to carry a serialization of a history of African Americans entitled *Before the Mayflower* by Lerone Bennett, Jr. In addition, the newspaper sponsored an essay contest on the topic. Ms. Peters advertised the contest in her bulletin.[17]

From her appointment in 1968 until 1975, a period of about seven years, Ms. Peters was the only resource teacher for Black History in the school district. She held the position of curriculum supervisor, and she obtained a supervisor's certificate from the Ohio State Department of Education. The appointment required her to travel to the 36 buildings in the district to help teachers incorporate Black History into their classes. At that time, total enrollment in Dayton schools was about 55,000 pupils.

Ms. Peters fulfilled her duties in three ways. First, she wrote a text entitled *Striving to Overcome, Negro Achievers* to accompany or supplement American history texts. Second, she offered workshops for Dayton teachers, in which she discussed lesson plans and ways to approach Black History. Third, she provided demonstrations of how to teach Black History.

Striving to Overcome was 24 pages in length. The biography of each person filled a single page and appeared with a small pencil drawing of the person's face. A few of the subjects were widely known. These included Frederick Douglass, Ida Wells, and W. E. B. Du Bois. Booker T. Washington did not appear. The book included other lesser-known African American heroes, such as Tack Sission, who fought in the War of Independence, and Charles Spaulding, who presided over the North Carolina Mutual Life Insurance Co., which was the largest African American business in 1952.

According to the foreword of *Striving to Overcome*, the Dayton Board of Education considered the booklet to be part of "the district's effort to provide information about the history of the Negro." The hope was that such information would help free young Americans from the burden of prejudice. The foreword added that there was a need for such material because many textbooks omitted or distorted facts about African Americans.[18]

Ms. Peters's booklet, *Striving to Overcome,* was such a success that the Johnson Publishing Company reprinted it in 1970 as *The Ebony Book of Black Achievement.* Although the Ebony version was 90 pages long, it carried the same 21 biographies. It was designed and illustrated by Cecil L. Ferguson; the drawings of the heroes were larger and more elaborate. The book's foreword notes that the author chose 21 outstanding Black men and women to illustrate the richness and diversity of the Black heritage. The foreword added that Ms. Peters's aim was to remedy omissions and correct distortions about the contributions and tribulations of Black people. The Johnson Publishing Company released a second edition in 1974.[19]

According to Ms. Peters, teachers and students found the text easy to use. The biographies were short and clearly written. The pictures accompanying the written sections made the text more accessible. More important, Ms. Peters emphasized in her book and in her classes that many African Americans had lived as free people. She showed how they served the United States as soldiers, scientists, and intellectuals, even though they had to overcome many obstacles.

Ms. Peters believed that she accomplished two goals by approaching Black History as a means to discuss the strengths and the contributions of African Americans. First, she overcame the resistance that many African American teachers had to the idea of Black History—namely, that they did not want to discuss slavery. Ms. Peters agreed that the continued association of African Americans with slavery contributed to racist feelings, because it cast African Americans as coming from an inferior background. Accordingly, she sought to present the accomplishments of free Black people. Second, a positive approach to Black history prepared the way for better relations between the racial groups. Such lessons taught White students that Black people made important contributions to society, and they gave Black students reasons to be proud of their heritage.

Although Ms. Peters disliked discussions of slavery, she entitled her master's thesis in history at the University of Dayton in 1972 "The Malê Insurrection: An Investigation of Sources." It appears strange that someone who avoided discussions of slavery chose to investigate a slave revolt for her thesis; however, Ms. Peters believed the topic offered an opportunity for her to show that the White owners' attitudes toward the slaves came from the owners' fears, not from the actions of the slaves. To her, this finding was important, because she believed racism derived from false ideas people had about other groups. She found reasons for teaching the positive accomplishments of African Americans to White students in her investigations of an event far from Dayton.

The second and third way that Ms. Peters spread Black History through the district was through workshops and demonstrations of effective lessons that she conducted as part of the district's curriculum department. Ms. Peters incorporated an interesting feature in the workshops. She had a White man conduct some of the lessons to show that African Americans did not have to teach Black History. Ms. Peters felt that no group could claim sole ownership of Black History, because it was an opportunity to teach history in the best and most inclusive way possible.

Public education changed in Dayton in 1973. Carle left Dayton when a newly elected conservative majority on the school board began to reverse the innovations he had introduced. The board's main effort was to stop any effort to introduce cross-district busing for racial balance within the district or to bring about wider plans for metropolitan desegregation. Black History remained in the schools, even though Ms. Peters stepped down from being the district's resource teacher in 1975 to become the Black History teacher at Colonel White High School. She continued in this position until 1993.

Although several people asked Ms. Peters to apply for an administrative position within the district, she replied that she wanted to work with the students. In making the change, Ms. Peters did not feel she was deserting the effort to advance Black History in the Dayton schools. The programs were well established, she said, and teachers were introducing the information to their classes.

One problem that remained was the lack of good instructional materials. Accordingly, as a high school teacher, Ms. Peters continued to publish materials for the instruction of Black history. For example, in 1992, she collected materials that the *Dayton Daily News* published as a booklet entitled *In Celebration of Black History Month*. The aim was to provide a collection of readings and activities for students to learn about the international contributions of African Americans. The activities included groups of pictures of famous African Americans with lists of names. Students had to match the faces with the names. Crossword puzzles required the students to fill in the names that corresponded to the clues. For example, the clue for number 1 Across was the physician-surgeon who discovered a vaccination against smallpox. One of the readings described a local Dayton museum, the Dunbar House. This museum was the former home of the poet, Paul Lawrence Dunbar.[20]

After her retirement, Ms. Peters published books about African Americans in Dayton. For example, a hardcover pictorial history entitled *Dayton's African American Heritage* appeared in 1995. This nearly 200-page book was a project of the National Afro-American Museum and Cultural Center. Several prominent Dayton companies contributed funds to support its publication.

Multicultural Education as an Alternative

When Peters returned to the classroom, the Ohio Board of Education tried to help public schools introduce Multicultural Education into the curriculum. For example, in 1974, the board produced a guide, *Providing K-12 Multi-Cultural Curricular Experience*, for districts to use as a resource while officials phased out old texts and bought new ones. This guide was a list of facts about events and short descriptions of famous members of minority groups.

The Ohio multicultural curriculum guide treated ethnic and racial groups as separate and fixed entities. The popular texts that introduced multicultural education to the nation did the same. For example, in 1974, James Banks published *Teaching Strategies for Ethnic Studies*. Banks claimed his text would illustrate how to teach about ethnic groups using a comparative perspective. According to Banks, the problem with existing programs was that they focused on particular ethnic groups in isolation. He wanted teachers to enable students to recognize how all the ethnic groups shared some characteristics and differed in others.[21]

Banks wrote that the purpose of Ethnic Studies should be to teach students to solve problems of poverty, deteriorating cities, and ethnic conflict. Thus, he asked that students learn to use the scientific method, to understand the facts about the situations different ethnic groups faced, to use concepts from the social sciences to structure their knowledge about ethnic groups, and to draw generalizations from their studies. From these activities, Banks hoped the students could develop theories to explain such concepts as cultural behavior and use what they learned to make decisions about ethnic issues.[22]

Banks did not make a plea in the text for racial integration, but he included sections on discrimination and racial problems. In part, this arrangement fit his purpose of teaching children to think critically. At the same time, he presented the various ethnic groups as if they existed separately. He added that groups tended to conflict with each other because the members remained partial to their own particular orientations.[23]

In subsequent years, other curriculum specialists retained Banks's view of multicultural education. For example, in 2004, Geneva Gay traced the development of multicultural education from the US Supreme Court decision in *Brown v. Board of Education*. Noting that the justices did not address curriculum matters, Gay suggested that the justices seemed to believe that desegregating schools would repair the psychological attitudes of African Americans. She added that desegregation did not help African Americans achieve school success, because they had to travel to White schools where teachers used the same instructional methods they used with White children. Gay added that concern for curriculum arose in the 1960s, when African American scholars sought to include Black history in social studies texts. The hope was that accurate and positive portrayals of African Americans would help children improve their self-concepts. After other groups, such as Mexican Americans, undertook the same effort, the scholars wrote curriculums that showed the students how each group had struggled against oppression. Finally, multicultural educators moved to creating culturally sensitive methods of instruction.[24]

According to Gay, in these efforts, the multicultural educators sought "to genuinely integrate educational programs, procedures, and practices with the ethnic, racial, cultural, and social diversity that characterizes U.S. society."[25] Gay's statement revealed the same bias that Banks expressed in 1974. That is, Gay made integration appear as an effort to match school programs to a society made up of different and separate ethnic groups; she did not define integration as expressing an ideal that brought together people from those different racial or ethnic groups.

Because multicultural education presented culture as a fixed set of customs, some educational philosophers contended that it presented a distorted view of human development. For example, Maxine Greene claimed that people should think of multiculturalism and pluralism in concrete terms, not as abstract definitions of society. She claimed that a community took shape when diverse people spoke as who they are, not what they are. Greene contended that plurality was the condition of human action. That is, classrooms, streets, or flowers appeared differently to different people, even though people shared the same human traits. The reality of the objects in the world arose out of the total of those appearances. For

Greene, this meant that people had to engage in dialogue, exchanging their views, if they wanted to learn about the world.[26]

Greene acknowledged that racism prevented people from learning from some groups, but she worried that multiculturalism could lead people to think that each group had its own sense of truth. In such a situation, relativism implied that people could learn only to tolerate each other. Criticizing the stereotypes linked to multiculturalism, Greene argued that when people saw another person as representative of a culture such as Hispanic, African American, or European American, they presumed an objective reality called *culture* that the person could represent. Greene contended that cultures were not homogeneous and fixed. For example, she noted that Bigger Thomas, in Richard Wright's novel *Native Son,* stood for a different character than Miss Celie, represented in Alice Walker's novel, *The Color Purple,* even though both were African Americans. The point was that teachers could not know the student sitting in a class by knowing his or her cultural affiliation.[27]

Greene went on to suggest that a person's cultural background might shape his or her identity, but it could not determine it. For example, although people should honor the differences among cultures, Greene pointed out that different people within each group had unique aspects, tastes, and affections. The ways to recognize this multitude of differences was to encourage students in classrooms to tell their own stories in ways that reached toward the common or shared sense of values. Her hope was that students from different backgrounds might build bridges among themselves and seek to create community.[28]

Some educators did not find problems with the views of Banks and Gay. For example, Christopher M. Span and Rana Dyer-Barr claimed that Multicultural Education could turn desegregation, which they defined as mixing pupils of different races in the same building, into integration, which they defined as efforts to overcome educational disadvantages and to encourage positive interracial relationships. They claimed the shift occurred because Multicultural Education empowered students with the tools to pursue social justice, and it informed all students about the different customs and cultures various groups held.[29] Multicultural Education could be a substitute for racial desegregation, despite the assertion that Span and Dyer-Barr made that Multicultural Education increased integration. The events in Dayton area Catholic schools illustrate this point.

Shortly after the civil disturbance in 1966, members of several parishes in Dayton sought to bring about racial integration of the Catholic schools. These activists included avowed religious women, lay people, and teachers in the Catholic schools. With the permission of the superintendent of the Dayton area Catholic schools, they formed a committee, made a study, and submitted recommendations to reorganize the Catholic schools. The problem was that each parish and its elementary school served a specific neighborhood. To overcome the residential segregation in Dayton, the proposal divided the city into six sections. In each section, the students attending Catholic elementary schools within that section would attend the same parish school for the first two years and move to another for the next two years, and so forth. The hope was to mix all students in the Catholic schools within each section and thereby reduce racial segregation.[30]

In 1970, after the archdiocesan school board reviewed the proposal, the members agreed with the statement of the problem, but they disapproved the recommendations. For example, the school board was unwilling to separate children from their parish priests. In Catholicism, the parish and the priest cooperate in religious formation. Attending school in the same parish where the family worshiped was supposed to strengthen the child's religious understanding. Nonetheless, the school board approved setting up some magnet schools among the Catholic schools so that racial integration could take place. Unfortunately, the archdiocese could not create these schools, because enrollment in Dayton's Catholic schools dropped precipitously in the 1970s, as it did across the nation.[31]

In 1977, after the racial integration of Dayton's Catholic schools appeared impossible, the superintendent of Dayton area Catholic schools presented a paper to the Ohio Catholic Education Association. In that paper, he made some suggestions the schools might enact to recruit African American students and teachers. Acknowledging that these efforts might be inadequate, he recommended that schools introduce Multicultural Education to reduce racism among the students and faculty. While the superintendent's recommendation to introduce Multicultural Education was praiseworthy, he substituted a curriculum reform for actual change. In fairness, though, the superintendent reminded his listeners to stress in schools the Gospel values that would make racial integration a desirable goal.[32]

Conclusion

Ten years after the public schools in Dayton began cross-district busing, public support for the program remained high; however, public approval of busing fell along racial lines. When the local newspaper surveyed parents in 1986, about 67 percent of the Black parents approved of the busing plan, while only 15 percent of White parents agreed. In 2001, the approval rating of racial desegregation that required busing fell among all parents. Answering an identical newspaper survey, about 53 percent of the Black parents felt that desegregation should end and about 84 percent of White parents thought it should end in Dayton.[33]

In 2001, Dayton was the last city in Ohio with court-ordered desegregation. On April 15, 2002, representatives of the Dayton Board of Education, the Ohio State Department of Education, and the local chapter of the NAACP signed an agreement to end busing for racial balance. When newspaper reporters asked for comments, the participants said that the era for litigated desegregation had ended; the academic achievement of Black students did not increase with desegregation; and the threat of attending schools outside familiar neighborhoods caused White families to move to suburban communities.[34]

These complaints about the desegregation of Dayton's schools suggest that people held shallow views of the benefits of the racial desegregation of schools. None of the criticisms spoke about the schools' failure to reinforce a racially integrated society. This result may be because people tend to think of the aims of education in narrow utilitarian ways. Most attempts to strengthen the educational achievement of children from low-income homes schools rely on a conception of education as a means to advance economically. While schools should help a student obtain the skills to earn a living, schools should do much more than raise a particular student's social status. As Maxine Greene suggests, schools should help students think about the type of human beings they could become. Ms. Peters's approach to Black History was a step in this process. Her lessons told stories about notable African Americans from the past who overcame obstacles and made important contributions to the common good. The books included similar accounts about living people, and the lessons asked about the students themselves. Unfortunately, the remarks people made when Dayton schools ended the program of desegregation suggest that they did not value what Black History and the racial desegregation of schools tried to accomplish.

Notes

1. "Pottinger: Calm Here Helps Others," *Dayton Daily News,* September 15, 1976.
2. U.S. Civil Rights Commission, *Fulfilling the Letter and Spirit of the Law: Desegregation of the Nation's Public Schools* (Washington, DC: U.S. Government Printing Office, 1976), 152.
3. John Finger, Jr. "Report of the Master for the Southern District Court of Ohio, 15 March 1975." *Brinkman v. Gilligan* papers, retrieved from the Dayton office of the NAACP, Dayton, Ohio.
4. Frederick McGinnis, *The Education of Negroes in Ohio* (Blancester, Ohio: Curless Printing Co., 1962).

5. Douglas S. Massey and Nancy A. Denton, "Suburbanization and Segregation in U.S. Metropolitan Areas," *The American Journal of Sociology* 94 (November 1988): 592–626.
6. Davison M. Douglas, *Jim Crow Moves North: The Battle over Northern School Desegregation, 1865–1954* (New York: Cambridge University Press, 2005).
7. Mayor's Ad Hoc Riot Study Committee, "Preliminary Report" (unpublished, 1966).
8. Dayton Committee on Civil Rights, *A Call to Action* (Dayton, OH: Dayton Committee on Civil Rights, 1967), accessed from Dayton, Ohio, NAACP branch office.
9. Board of Education of City School District of Dayton, Ohio, *Minutes*, Public Board Meeting of 10 August 1967, (Dayton, OH: Board of Education), 414–417.
10. Jim Lashley, "Carle's Debut on the Board," *Dayton Daily News*, June 14, 1968.
11. Lloyd R. Henderson, Letter to Wayne Carle, March 17, 1969, accessed from Dayton, Ohio NAACP branch office.
12. Dayton Public Schools, "Task Force on Staff Desegregation," vols. 1–3 (Dayton, OH: Dayton Board of Education, 1970).
13. Gary Orfield, *The Reconstruction in Southern Education: The Schools and the 1964 U.S. Civil Rights Act* (New York: John Wiley and Sons, 1969), 106–107.
14. Board of Education of City School District of Dayton, Ohio, "Resolution Establishing Middle School Sites" (Dayton, OH: Board of Education, March 4, 1971).
15. David Kirp, *Just Schools: The Idea of Racial Equality in American Education* (Berkeley: University of California Press, 1982), 195–210.
16. This information and many of the subsequent points about Ms. Peters and her work come from an interview the author had with her on December 21, 2010.
17. "Resource Teacher Begins," *Schooldays in the Dayton Public Schools*, November 10, 1968, obtained from Margaret Peters.
18. Margaret Peters, *Striving to Overcome, Negro Achievers* (Dayton, OH: Dayton Board of Education and Dayton Daily News, 1969).
19. Margaret Peters, *The Ebony Book of Black Achievement* (Chicago: Johnson Publishing Company, 1970).
20. Margaret Peters, "In Celebration of Black History Month," *Dayton Daily News*, 1992.
21. James Banks, *Teaching Strategies for Ethnic Studies* (Boston: Allyn and Bacon, 1975), vii–22.
22. Banks, *Teaching Strategies*, 27–49.
23. Banks, *Teaching Strategies*, 8.
24. Geneva Gay, "Beyond Brown: Promoting Equality through Multicultural Education," *Journal of Curriculum and Supervision* 19, no. 3 (Spring 2004): 193–216, Stable URL: http://web.ebscohost.com/ehost/detail?vid=3&hid=111&sis-6e6006f6
25. Gay, "Beyond Brown," 193.

26. Maxine Greene, "The Passions of Pluralism," in *Releasing the Imagination: Essays on Education, the Arts, and Social Change* (San Francisco: Jossey-Bass, 1995), 155–168.
27. Ibid., 157–163.
28. Ibid., 165–167.
29. Christopher M. Span and Raina Dyer-Barr, "Desegregation of Schools," in Craig Kridel, ed. *Encyclopedia of Curriculum Studies* (Los Angeles: SAGE Reference, 2010), 281–283.
30. Catholic Church, Archdiocese of Cincinnati, Dayton Area Catholic Schools. De Facto Segregation Committee, "Racial Segregation in Dayton's Parochial School System: Report of the De Facto Segregation Committee Operating under Commission of the Dayton Parochial Schools" (Dayton, OH: 1968).
31. Catholic Church, Archdiocese of Cincinnati, Dayton Area Catholic Schools. Task Force, Evaluation of the De Facto Segregation Committee Recommendations for Consolidation of the Dayton Area Catholic Schools (Dayton, OH: 1970).
32. Reverend Gail Poynter, "What Position Should Your Parish Community Take toward School Desegregation?" Paper presented to the Ohio Catholic Education Association Convention, Cleveland, OH, March 1, 1977.
33. "Pottinger: Calm Here Helps Others," *Dayton Daily News,* September 15, 1976; Mark Fisher and Scott Elliott, "Poll: Many Black Parents against Busing Program," *Dayton Daily News,* May 20, 2001, 1A.
34. Scott Elliott, "Desegregation Busing Ends: Pact Avoids Court Hearing," *Dayton Daily News,* (April 6, 2002), A1, A6.

CHAPTER TEN

AFRICAN-CENTERED EDUCATION IN THE DETROIT PUBLIC SCHOOLS, 1968–2000

Anne-Lise Halvorsen

In the 1980s and 1990s, several large public school districts in the United States, notably those in New York, Washington, DC, Atlanta, and Detroit, began to introduce an Afrocentric curriculum in grades K–12. The Afrocentric curriculum emerges from the concept of Afrocentrism that Molefi Kete Asante, a professor in the Department of African American Studies at Temple University, defines as "placing African ideals at the center of any analysis that involves African culture and behavior."[1] In general, the Afrocentric curriculum aims to challenge and deconstruct the traditional (Eurocentric) curriculum and to promote positive self-images among African American students. The Afrocentric curriculum focuses on past and present contributions to culture and learning by Africans and African Americans and uses pedagogical approaches adapted to what are considered the unique learning styles of African American students. However, there are mixed opinions on the merit of the curriculum where it has been taught.[2] Some educators object to it on pedagogical and cultural grounds; others claim that school districts lack the funds, administrative support, and incentives to promote such a curriculum. Furthermore, state standardized tests do not emphasize the Afrocentric curriculum. In the era of accountability, what is not tested is generally not taught.

In this chapter, I focus on the Afrocentric curriculum ("African-Centered Education") in the Detroit Public Schools (the DPS) as taught in the years 1968–2000, and I add a few remarks on its current use.[3] Multicultural educators and community activists in Detroit had called for a curriculum and instructional strategies specifically directed towards African American children since the early 1960s. After 30 years, in the 1990s the DPS Board passed a resolution adopting the African-Centered Education curriculum as part of its district-wide philosophy.[4]

In its focus on a large, urban school district, this chapter contributes to our knowledge of an important movement in US education that challenges traditional education curricula and policy. I examine how the DPS conceived of, adopted, and taught African-Centered Education that had (and has) the support of parents, teachers, and community members. I also describe the lack of empirical evidence about the program's effect on student academic achievement, school attendance, dropout rates, and student self-esteem. The program's main goals are improvements in all these areas. The popularity of Afrocentric education, most evident in the years 1988 to 1998, has faded, and most public school districts that experimented with it no longer include it in their curricula.[5] State and national content standards include African American history and multicultural perspectives, but these standards do not reflect an Afrocentric approach. Despite this general decline in Afrocentric education programs, an examination of African-Centered Education in the DPS is of significance. As I explain in the chapter, it is possible for a school district to take an Afrocentric approach to education in ways that the community approves. Moreover, taking a wider perspective, the chapter generalizes about the practical and ideological problems that are common to education change movements.

Afrocentricity and Afrocentric Education

Afrocentric education has its roots in the teachings of Booker T. Washington, W. E. B. Du Bois, Carter G. Woodson, Marcus Garvey, and Malcolm X, among other African American leaders. As Molefi Kete Asante explains, although these leaders advocated different changes in American culture and society, they shared the same goal of "the liberation of African people"—liberation from the dominant Eurocentric worldview (for example, Western cultural ideologies such as Darwinism, Marxism, and Freudism). To counter the perception and reality of repression and racism in Western cultures, African American leaders favored alternative ideologies based in the cultures of Africa, the West Indies, and the Americas.[6] The view of world civilization called Afrocentricity (or Afrocentrism) refers to the centrality of Africans (in terms of their history, mythology, creativity, and spirituality) in postmodern history.[7] Afrocentricity also claims that people of African descent share certain cognitive and cultural characteristics that distinguish them from people of European descent.[8]

Afrocentricity is based in *Njia*, a Kiswahili (Swahili) word defined as "the collective expression of the Afrocentric worldview which is grounded in the historical experience of African people."[9] *Njia* (or "the Way") is a concept that describes a personal belief system based on the experiences of

African Americans and Africans. Those who follow the philosophy and practice of *Njia* often wear African dress and adopt African names as symbolic acts.[10] Furthermore, they argue for an Afrocentric focus in education, so that students can study the cultural and historic heritage of Africans, African Americans, and West Indians. In practice, this means that the Afrocentric curriculum, particularly as taught in social studies classes, is concerned with both content and method.

Afrocentric education is different from Africana Studies (also called Black Studies). Africana Studies deals with the historic, political, and cultural contributions of Africans and the descendants of the African Diaspora in Europe, Asia, and the Americas. Afrocentric education promotes the achievements of African American students and offers an alternative (and often contested) version of the dominant narrative of Western civilization.[11] Nor is the philosophy of Afrocentric education identical to that of multicultural education, despite their similar concerns with strengthening the self-images of children of color and with offering a different perspective from the "mainstream-centric approach."[12] A critical difference is that multiculturalism focuses on many world cultures, whereas Afrocentrism focuses only on those cultures with African origins.[13] According to James A. Banks, a multicultural education specialist, multicultural education often focuses on the contributions of each ethnic and racial group, a curricular approach known as the "contributions" approach. When it is conceived of as a contributions approach, many educators have embraced multicultural education, at least in rhetoric. In contrast, Afrocentric education, with its focus on Africa and African innovations, ideas, and movements, takes a different historical perspective than that of most Western historians.[14] The consensus is that Afrocentric education, in its examination of oppression and resistance, takes a more radical and thus often less accepted pedagogic approach than multiculturalism. In part because of the perceived aggression of its approach, Afrocentric education has been the target of intense criticism.[15]

The Debate over Afrocentric Education

The debate over Afrocentric education—its goals, its premises, its methods, its content, its achievements—has generated much commentary and numerous articles. Since it is beyond the scope of this chapter to examine the entirety of this controversy, I review the Diane Ravitch–Molefi Kete Asante written exchange as a representative example of the arguments presented in the debate.

One of the most vocal opponents of Afrocentric education's fundamental ideology is the education historian Diane Ravitch. In a controversial article published in 1990, following the adoption of Afrocentric education programs by some school districts, Ravitch attacked the broader concept of multiculturalism as an education philosophy, as well as Afrocentric education. She argued that the particularistic approach of multicultural education and, by extension, of Afrocentric education, which aims to build the self-esteem of children with particular racial and ethnic origins, promotes ethnocentrism. She charged that the approach assumes that such children can only succeed in school if they are taught about the influence of their ancestors on the subjects studied.[16]

Ravitch's article sparked a response from Asante that developed into a heated exchange, with each accusing the other of misinterpretation and misrepresentation. In his 1991 response, Asante denied Ravitch's charge that he and other proponents of Afrocentric education wanted to banish the Eurocentric worldview in education. Moreover, he repudiated Ravitch's claim that the primary aim of Afrocentric education is to raise children's self-esteem.[17] He also argued that Ravitch misunderstood the true meaning of multiculturalism and asserted that the word "mainstream" (to describe education content and policy) is a code word for "white." He summarized his argument by pointing to the central distinction between the Eurocentric and Afrocentric approaches: the hegemonic, Eurocentric approach claims to be universal, while the Afrocentric approach makes no such claim. By presenting "the African as subject rather than object," Afrocentric education, Asante wrote, attempts to correct the narrow Eurocentric view of history and culture.[18]

This debate continues, with little ground for compromise.[19] Yet the debate among academics and policy makers rarely refers to empirical evidence from Afrocentric education programs in school districts. Studies by researchers of its implementation are far more useful in explaining the successes and failures of such programs.

Studies of Afrocentric Education

In the 1980s and 1990s, school districts in Atlanta, Columbus, New York, Oakland, Philadelphia, Portland, Sacramento, and Washington, DC, as well as Detroit, adopted Afrocentric education into their curricula, using various approaches. Although Afrocentric education has been institutionalized in schools for more 20 years as of this writing in 2011, there are still few empirical studies, either qualitative or quantitative, that attempt to evaluate such programs. In this section, I review two case studies that have analyzed Afrocentric education.

In his analysis of the adoption of Afrocentric education in schools, Geoffrey Jahwara Giddings focused generally on the school district of Philadelphia and particularly on one of its Afrocentric academies.[20] Giddings argued that two main factors explain the support for Afrocentric education programs: demonstrable, positive effects on students' achievement and strong parental mobilization and interest. Despite the scarcity of evidence on the success of such programs in terms of student achievement, Giddings cited Ollie Manley's review of the objectives of the Afrocentric curriculum, which concluded that student interest in schoolwork increased as a result of studying African and African American culture and history.[21] To gain increased support for this curriculum from education policy makers and administrators, Giddings argued, we need qualitative and quantitative studies that show the effectiveness of Afrocentric education.[22]

Amy Binder studied Afrocentric education programs in Atlanta, New York State, and Washington, DC.[23] Although she found no improvement either in students' learning or in other measures of their success, such as lower dropout rates and increased college enrollment, she observed success in another dimension. For Binder, success was the adoption of such programs. Her research is particularly notable for the identification of various institutional factors that influence schools' adoption of Afrocentric programs. The influences she identified are the following: 1) local (as opposed to state) adoption of the program, 2) racially homogeneous (i.e., primarily African American) settings that are more receptive to the curriculum, 3) the absence of new multicultural education programs (thus leaving space for Afrocentric education), 4) the testing of the curriculum to encourage teachers to teach its content, 5) support from the media, and 6) schools' reputation for offering quality education.[24]

Although there are no empirical studies of the DPS African-Centered Education, parents, school administrators, and the community have judged it "successful" and have continued to support its place in the DPS curriculum. However, there are few formal explanations for this success. For this research, I use curricular documents as well as interviews with three educators who developed the DPS African-Centered Education: Dahia Shabaka, a former DPS high school social studies teacher and DPS Director of Social Studies Education in the 1990s and early 2000s; Marvis Cofield, a key figure in the development of African-Centered Education in the DPS, and a DPS Board member from 1999 to 2009; and an anonymous source (a DPS employee, referred to as Donna Wallace), who helped develop the DPS African-Centered Education Approach. My purpose was to analyze the success of African-Centered Education in the DPS, as well as looking at the challenges it faced and continues to face.

African-Centered Education in the Detroit Public Schools

The DPS officially adopted its version of Afrocentric education in the early 1990s for preschool through twelfth grades.[25] However, unlike school districts in other large cities, the DPS named its program "African-Centered Education" instead of "Afrocentric Education." As Cofield explained, "Afro is a hairstyle." He also stated that the program developers wished to avoid the negative connotations sometimes associated with "Afro" when European Americans use the term.

In this section, I present the following: the roots of the DPS program; the adoption of the program; the responses to the program by teachers, parents, and the community; and the program's curriculum design efforts. In discussing the program's effectiveness, I conclude with an analysis of its success as judged by the community, parents, and the interviewees.

The Roots of African-Centered Education in the Detroit Public Schools

The DPS African-Centered Education has its roots in events dating from the late 1960s. Before its Riot of 1967, Detroit was admired nationally as a "model" city for race relations.[26] Yet beneath the surface of racial harmony, many African Americans in Detroit were increasingly sensitive to and critical of perceived racial injustices in their city. Much of the discontent related to the public schools that served a largely African American student population. In 1968, 59.4 percent of the students in the DPS were African Americans.[27] Annual per-pupil expenditure in the DPS was $193, while in the Detroit suburbs the average was $225; the DPS class sizes often exceeded the maximum of 35 students established by state law; and many White teachers held racist attitudes toward their Black students.[28] Additionally, a study by Detroit's Citizens Advisory Committee on Equal Educational Opportunities reported a systematic pattern of discrimination in the hiring and assignment of African American teachers and principals.[29]

Many Black nationalist groups and Black power groups in Detroit focused on community organizing by showing African Americans how to voice their discontent to city officials. The goal was to achieve racial equity in education, housing, and employment. One such community group, according to Cofield, was the Inner City Sub Center (hereafter, the Center). Founded in 1969 at Wayne State University, the Center offered community programs in youth entrepreneurship, supported after-school and athletic programs (with a focus on the martial arts), and provided emergency food and clothing distribution. The Center's leaders promoted "positive African-American values" in all their activities, a philosophy that developed into the *Nguzo Saba of Kwanzaa*, or the Seven Principles of Blackness, also called the Core Cultural Values. This philosophy was behind the design of African-Centered Education in the DPS.[30]

As a community advocate and a history and social studies teacher at Detroit's Kettering High School in the 1970s and 1980s, Marvis Cofield had long been active in promoting an African-centered approach to education. For example, he began his world history classes by teaching the cultural contributions of Africans instead of those of the Greeks. In 1978, he founded the Alkebu-lan Martial Arts Federation in Detroit, which later became Alkebu-lan Village, a community center devoted to "community involvement and youth character building."[31] In the 1980s, Cofield and other community leaders, parents, and teachers presented the African-centered approach to the DPS administrators at parent-teacher meetings and to the public at block club meetings.

Owing in large part to these grassroots efforts by Cofield and other teachers to promote an African-centered approach in their classes, in the late 1980s the DPS founded several African-Centered Academies, whose purpose was to provide African-Centered Education in all areas of the curriculum. In the 1990s, the DPS passed an African-Centered Resolution that led to the adoption of African-Centered Education in schools district-wide.[32]

The Adoption of African-Centered Education in the DPS

Dahia Shabaka played a key role in introducing the goals and principles of African-Centered Education in the DPS and in shepherding the program through official channels.[33] She played a role in the founding and organization of annual conferences (known as the "African American Child Placed in Crisis Conference") on African-Centered Education, which attracted thousands of attendees from Detroit, from the nation, and from other countries.[34] Among the notable speakers at these conferences were Asa Hilliard (then African American professor of educational psychology at Georgia State University) and Molefi Kete Asante. Shabaka remembers that Asante was "a great part of what we did."[35]

In 1992, the DPS issued "The Framework and Definition for African-Centered Education" (hereafter, the Framework), which explained how African-Centered Education would be incorporated into the district-wide curriculum; presented guidelines for teachers and mentors; described parent and community involvement; and listed essential readings. The Framework also described the curriculum offered by the African-Centered Academies, which were under the supervision of the African-Centered Academies Implementation Task Force.[36]

Educators in Detroit were more receptive to African-Centered Education than educators in other cities were to programs that had similar goals. One reason was the well-thought-out Framework, which defined

African-Centered Education as "multicultural education with an emphasis on African and African American culture." [37] Thus, the Framework was clearly aligned with the multicultural (and accepted) approach in education. In addition, the Framework promoted a universal and inclusive approach. The Framework stated that African-Centered Education in the DPS "is based upon the belief that all humans have their physical, social and intellectual origins in Africa. Therefore, children of all ethnic backgrounds can benefit from this educational experience. Through an inclusionary process, all representative groups are placed, not above or below any group, but alongside the rest of humanity."[38]

The Framework listed ten goals, many of which relate specifically to African-Centered Education. The second goal stated: "Students will improve academically at grade level or above." All the interviewees quoted in this study emphasized the importance of these goals, particularly the second one, in gaining acceptance for African-Centered Education in the DPS. The Framework also specified how African-Centered Education was to be integrated with the existing school curriculum, which was based on the Michigan Core Outcomes of Public Act 25 (the predecessor of the state's 1996 curriculum framework) and the DPS Strands and Objectives. Thus African-Centered Education as proposed by the Framework followed both the Michigan State and the DPS education content standards. Additionally, the Framework aligned with content standards issued by the National Council for the Social Studies and also aligned with national voluntary content standards for civics, economics, geography, and history.[39]

The Framework recommended that teachers take a cooperative and collaborative approach to teaching African American students. According to the Framework, cooperation and collaboration are learning traits that African Americans have historically brought to school. To help teachers and mentors implement this approach, the Framework listed 21 instructional principles. For example, the following principles convey the spirit of the Framework's pedagogic approach: a relatively structured classroom; the use of small groups or the full class (versus individual instruction); an emphasis on twenty-first-century careers and jobs and on African Americans in such work; and relationship of the curriculum to the "whole child as a total person." The ninth principle suggested the ultimate goal of the DPS African-Centered Education: "To develop students who are capable of competing with students from any school in the world."[40]

In addition to reflecting both the state and national content standards for social studies education, the Framework supplemented those standards in several ways. The existing curriculum took a multicultural approach, but the Framework curriculum prioritized African and African American history and culture. Moreover, the Framework curriculum emphasized that teachers should counter myths and stereotypes about Africans and African Americans and should use instructional strategies assumed to be particularly appropriate for African Americans (for example, cooperative group work).

On February 2, 1993, Kwame Kenyatta, vice-president of the Detroit Board of Education, presented the *African-Centered Education Resolution Detroit Public Schools* to the Board.[41] Its preamble stated: "The Detroit Public School district prepares students for self-determination as contributing and participating members in a culturally diverse world." To that end, seven resolutions were proposed, including a resolution that "students must be centered in their own historical and cultural heritage which fosters a positive self-image" and another resolution directing the DPS staff to develop "a comprehensive African-Centered Education program which includes research and curriculum development, staff development, Pre-K–12 curriculum guides, an implementation timeline, and other resources needed for curriculum development and implementation."[42]

On August 30, 1994, the DPS published the *Guiding Principles for an African-Centered Education,* which was the result of a two-year series of study gatherings entitled "The Indaba" (Zulu for "intense discussion"). The 153 participants in the gatherings had been charged with the discussion of "major issues addressing an accurate account of history and a cleansing of unacceptable concepts in the curriculum and purchased textbooks of Detroit Public Schools."[43] A major goal of this new document was to help the DPS teachers understand the purposes of African-Centered Education.

Kenyatta, who played a major role in the adoption of African-Centered Education in the DPS, became a strong advocate of the curriculum and approach.[44] In 2000, CNN interviewed him about African-Centered Education. Several students from Detroit's Aisha Shule Academy, the country's first school to use an African-centered approach, and Bill Johnson, a columnist at the *Detroit News* and an opponent of African-Centered Education, were also interviewed. In the interview, Kenyatta stated: "If [students] come to school and they look in the books and all they see is George Washington...they never see themselves in the process, then there's no room for them to be inspired."[45] The CNN interviewer also asked Kenyatta why students in African-centered schools performed better than students in other schools. Kenyatta attributed their success to the high parental involvement, although he presented no empirical evidence for the claim. He said: "Parents want the best for their children. And when they identify academies like this that's producing the outcome that we're producing here, they want to make sure that they're part of that process."[46]

In 2011, the DPS has three African-Centered Academies; originally there were five.[47] Students at the academies have often done well academically.[48] However, the academies' reputations have been somewhat tarnished by the program's legal problems. The lawsuit that received national attention was brought by the American Civil Liberties Union and the National Organization of Women Legal Defense Fund against the DPS in 1991, just before the three males-only academies (Malcolm X, Marcus Garvey, and Paul Robeson) were to open. The suit claimed the males-only admission policy discriminated against girls, whose problems, such as teenage pregnancy and welfare dependence, were as serious as the drug and crime problems the boys faced. The outcome of the suit was that the academies agreed to admit girls, although their population has remained largely male.[49]

Another controversy related to the academies arose in 1992, when many Warrendale residents objected to the location of the Malcolm X Academy in their mostly White neighborhood. Only one of the 470 students at Malcolm X Academy was White. In this case, the controversy seemed mainly racial, with the usual complaints about lower property values and more crime.[50] However, some residents also opposed the idea of African-Centered Education. One resident stated, "I don't think it is any place for a white kid to go to school.... They teach the kids that blackness is the center of the universe."[51]

Responses to African-Centered Education in the DPS

When I interviewed Shabaka and Cofield in 2010, they stated that the DPS administrators, parents, and the public are supportive of the approach (they did not refer to the Warrendale opposition). They claimed that the positive response is attributable, in large part, to the way the approach has been presented to teachers and the community. According to Cofield, the goals of African-Centered Education are similar to those Molefi Kete Asante advocates. Cofield explained that such a curriculum is intended to increase African American children's "self-respect, [and] self-control" and to give them an understanding of how their African ancestors positively influenced and influence contemporary society. He hoped that children would learn to identify themselves as "heroes or sheroes, not zeroes." Additionally, Cofield explained that African-Centered Education was meant to create unity among diverse peoples. He described the approach as "the thread that ties all people together." For him, African-Centered Education is a pedagogical approach that is "inclusionary, not exclusionary."[52]

However, Shabaka and Wallace (a DPS employee) emphasized that raising students' self-esteem is not a primary goal of African-Centered Education. Its primary goal is intellectual, not affective. Wallace explained,

"It [African-Centered Education] was not designed to be a self-esteem curriculum.... it's really about truth and accuracy."[53] In explaining why the approach works for all students, and not just for African American students, Shabaka concluded that the approach offers teachers the opportunity to correct any historical misconceptions that students have learned. She argued that the approach is for all children "because all children have been taught the same bad history."[54]

Shabaka was also concerned about the mistakes that she perceived other educators have made in promoting the approach. Whereas some educators intended African-Centered Education to be a replacement for traditional (European) history, Shabaka believed the approach is an *additional* approach in the traditional history/social studies curriculum. In promoting the approach, she stated that she often had to dispel the myth that African-Centered Education is only about teaching about Africans and African Americans. She had to refute claims that educators using the approach "just want to take the nursery rhymes and paint them black." Shabaka observed that, of course, the approach focuses on the history of Africans and African Americans: "We wanted to feel a part of history, which we really had not felt before, and for everybody else to know our story." However, she emphasizes that African-Centered Education is not about elevating African history; instead, the approach "has to be respectful of all cultures." She believed that the approach is "for everyone" and is "inclusionary in every sense of the word."[55]

Shabaka believed that the support from DPS Superintendent Deborah McGriff and from the DPS Board of Education have been a major reason for the success of African-Centered Education in the DPS. It also helped that Kenyatta, a DPS Board member, was a key supporter. In addition, parents have been extremely supportive of African-Centered Education. According to Cofield, parents want their children to be educated. They say, "whatever it is that can help my baby, I want that."

There has been some resistance to the DPS African-Centered Education, mostly by a few teachers, although Cofield and Shabaka said these teachers were not opposed to it philosophically. Cofield and Shabaka suggested four reasons for their resistance:

1. a general reluctance to make changes
2. a conviction they were already using the approach
3. opposition to instructional ideas issued top-down
4. embarrassment that they had not previously used the approach

According to Shabaka, conferences and in-service education on the new approach overcame the resistance by these teachers.

Curriculum Design Efforts in the Detroit Public Schools

The DPS produced its own curricular materials for African-Centered Education. The DPS has a long history, dating from the 1920s, of writing as well as disseminating administrative and/or teacher-designed materials.[56] For example, in the 1940s, the DPS teachers created their own activities for teaching Intercultural Education.[57]

After the DPS Board passed the African-Centered Education Resolution, Shabaka realized that some teachers, such as Cofield, were already using an African-centered approach, but many teachers lacked the background and/or resources needed to use this approach in their lessons. Therefore, Shabaka contracted with the Metropolitan Teaching and Learning Company, a New York-based, African American owned publisher of educational materials, for the publication of social studies textbooks with an African-centered focus for its lower elementary (first and second) grades that would meet state content requirements.[58] The textbooks, by authors who were either DPS teachers or administrators, were written for the urban school district market.[59] Of the prodigious effort that the textbook writing required, Shabaka stated, "I don't think anybody realized what you have to do [to write textbooks]. It was a ton of work."[60]

The lower elementary social studies curriculum in the DPS African-Centered Curriculum Program, as in most US schools, focused on families (first grade) and neighborhoods (second grade). The textbook for neighborhoods reflected an African-centered approach in several ways. First, the book celebrated the African American holiday of Kwanzaa (as well as Cinco de Mayo, the Chinese New Year, Hannukah, and Ramadan). Second, photographs of Detroit residents, businesses, landmarks, and streetscapes show ordinary people in settings familiar to a child living in an urban setting. Third, the book presented significant historic events from the African American experience, such as slavery, the Underground Railroad, and the neighborhoods of contemporary Africa. These textbooks, still used today, reflect the commitment of the DPS to supporting African-Centered Education with appropriate resources.

Evidence of the Effectiveness of African-Centered Education in the DPS

The most frequently cited goal of Afrocentric curriculums is raising academic achievement. In her preface to the DPS program, Shabaka wrote, "Full implementation of the Detroit Public Schools' African-Centered Curriculum Program will raise and sustain high academic achievement and thereby close the elusive achievement gap."[61] However, there are no empirical data on the success of the DPS program—for example, in terms of its effect on student achievement, dropout rates, school attendance, or classroom behavior. Nor are there any data on the even more difficult-to-measure increase in student self-esteem. Shabaka wished she had studied the effectiveness of African-Centered Education on student achievement empirically. She stated, "That was the one thing we did not do as well as we should. We knew it made a difference, but we couldn't prove it." Today she does not think new assessments designed to assess students' learning of African-Centered Education specifically are needed. She said, "I don't want a separate test. I want to show improvement on the test that is mandated by the state." Shabaka regretted that she did not conduct a comparative study of students studying African-Centered Education and students not studying African-Centered Education, using the state's standardized tests (Michigan Educational Assessment Profile) or the ACT.[62]

However, there is a good deal of anecdotal evidence that testifies to the positive benefits of the DPS African-Centered Education as far as academic and affective outcomes go. In a promotional video for Cofield's Alkebu-lan Village, Alvin Ward, former DPS principal of Finney High School and Kettering High School, described the positive changes he saw at Finney High School, a school that was, in his words, "African-centerized." He attributed these changes in particular to the daily *Harambe* (Swahili for "working together in unity")—a celebration in which all students, teachers, and staff meet to learn key Swahili words and terms. Ward believed this daily celebration "changed the culture and climate because it created that type of discipline you need and that unity you need in the school." Ward stated that during the 2008–2009 school year at Finney High School, there was "at least a 30% to 40% increase in attendance rates; at least a decrease of 30% to 40% in negative behavior and violations of our student code of conduct."[63] He also remarked, "Even though it wasn't one of the focuses of the curriculum, one of the benefits was the students' self-confidence and ability to feel they could do anything. They could achieve anything they set their mind to."[64] Donna Wallace also attributed an increase in students' self-worth to the use of *Harambe* in schools.[65]

Conclusion

By most accounts, African-Centered Education in the DPS was and is "successful." In recent years, accountability pressures, financial constraints, management problems, and other issues have shifted some of the focus in the DPS away from African-Centered Education to what many consider more pressing problems. Yet the DPS still teaches African-Centered Education, from preschool through grade 12, and operates several African-

Centered Academies. The program and the academies have the support of the community, the parents, the teachers, and the school administrators. It should be noted that in the DPS, "success" has consistently been defined by the program's widespread adoption in the schools and by the strong support it receives from teachers, parents, and the community.

Several factors, such as those identified by Amy J. Binder in her study (see note 2), explain the success of the DPS program. It is locally designed and managed, rather than mandated and supervised by the state; the City of Detroit is, for the most part, racially homogeneous; and the DPS has had considerable experience with multicultural education programs. Three other factors explain its success. First, its supporters have repeatedly emphasized that African-Centered Education is "inclusionary, not exclusionary."[66] Except for the legal challenges to the academies and the Warrendale opposition, there has been very little public opposition to the approach. Second, the DPS made a strong commitment to African-Centered Education by founding the African-Centered Academies, by publishing suitable textbooks, and by providing teachers with relevant in-service education. Third, the DPS has always sought the support of parents and the community for the program.

It may be argued that empirical evidence is needed to support this claim of success for the DPS African-Centered Education if the program is to survive. To date, there are no empirical data to substantiate its success (for example, data on student academic achievement, dropout rates, school attendance, self-esteem, and college enrollment). The affirmative testimonials by DPS educators to the success of the program do not provide such evidence. Nevertheless, because they are the people who taught the students and spoke to the parents, their comments should be taken into account when evaluating the program.

However, this anecdotal evidence, based on individual impressions and experiences, does not seem a sufficient basis for decision making about such programs. Since Afrocentric education, for a variety of reasons, was and is controversial, research is needed that evaluates it as an educational approach that achieves the goals it sets. Just how such empirical evidence can be gathered is not really clear, especially since one commonly cited success factor, the increase in students' self-esteem, relies on educators' anecdotal reports and students' self-assessments. Also, improved self-esteem need not necessarily correlate with improved student academic achievement. Yet, despite the lack of empirical data for the success of African-Centered Education in the DPS, even in an age of ever-increasing accountability and testing in education, its position in the DPS curriculum faces no serious threat. Teachers, parents, and community members alike strongly support the program.

The history of the DPS African-Centered Education is relevant both to Afrocentrism in particular and to education reform in general. The history of the DPS African-Centered Education demonstrates the importance of community involvement in education reform. Parents were and are enthusiastic supporters of the program. This history also demonstrates the necessity of giving teachers the resources to undertake education reform. Teachers in the DPS received training and support in the new program, in addition to the needed instructional materials. The DPS leaders, who effectively promoted their program, avoided much of the controversy and opposition that other school districts faced in establishing Afrocentric education programs. They described African-Centered Education as an inclusive approach that benefits all children, not just African American children. They advertised it as an addition to, rather than a replacement of, the traditional social studies curriculum. These are some lessons for educational leaders who wish to establish Afrocentric education programs in their schools.

Notes

1. Molefi Kete Asante, *The Afrocentric Idea* (Philadelphia: Temple University Press, 1987), 6.
2. See Amy J. Binder, "Why Do Some Curricular Challenges Work While Others Do Not? The Case of Three Afrocentric Challenges," *Sociology of Education* 73, no. 2 (April, 2000): 69–91; Amy Binder, *Contentious Curricula: Afrocentrism and Creationism in American Public Schools* (Princeton, NJ: Princeton University Press, 2002).
3. See Jeffery Del-Shawn Robinson, "The African Centered School Movement and the Detroit Public School System" (PhD dissertation, Michigan State University, 2008) and Kefentse K. Chike, "From Black Power to the New Millennium: The Evolution of African Centered Education in Detroit, Michigan 1970–2000" (PhD dissertation, Michigan State University, 2011) for comprehensive overviews of African-Centered Education in Detroit.
4. Shawn A. Ginwright, *Black in School: Afrocentric Reform, Urban Youth, and the Promise of Hip-Hop Culture* (New York: Teachers College Press, 2004), 3.
5. Algernon Austin, *Achieving Blackness: Race, Black Nationalism, and Afrocentrism in the Twentieth Century* (New York: New York University Press, 2006), 110.
6. Molefi Kete Asante, *Afrocentricity* (Trenton, NJ: Africa World Press, 1988), 8, 16.
7. Ibid., 6.
8. Binder, *Contentious Curricula*, 30–31.
9. Asante, *Afrocentricity*, 21.
10. Ibid., 30.
11. Binder, *Contentious Curricula*, 31.
12. James A. Banks and Cherry A. McGee Banks, eds., *Multicultural Education: Issues and Perspectives*, 7th ed. (Hoboken, NJ: Wiley, 2009).

13. Binder, "Why Do Some Curricular Challenges Work," 75.
14. James A. Banks, "Approaches to Multicultural Curriculum Reform," *Multicultural Leader* 1, no. 2 (Spring, 1988): 1–3.
15. Asante, *The Afrocentric Idea*.
16. Diane Ravitch, "Multiculturalism: E. Pluribus Plures," *The American Scholar* 59 (1990): 339.
17. Molefi Kete Asante and Diane Ravitch, "Multiculturalism: An Exchange," *The American Scholar*, 60 (1991): 267–276.
18. Ibid., 267–276.
19. Clarence E. Walker, a historian at the University of California, Davis, who uses the term Afrocentrism, has been even harsher than Ravitch in his criticism of the philosophy. He agrees with Ravitch that Afrocentrism is not history since its content is historically inaccurate. Like Ravitch, he also criticizes Afrocentrism for its emphasis on raising African Americans' self-esteem. He argues that Afrocentrism is a "vulgar form of identity politics" because of its exclusive focus on race, and he concludes that Afrocentrism is a faith rather than an academic pursuit. See Clarence E. Walker, *We Can't Go Home Again: An Argument about Afrocentrism* (New York: Oxford University Press, 2001).
20. Geoffrey Jahwara Giddings, "Infusion of Afrocentric Content into the School Curriculum: Toward an Effective Movement," *Journal of Black Studies* 31, no. 4 (March 2001): 462–482.
21. Ollie I. Manley, "A Study of Secondary Teachers' Perceptions of an Afrocentric Curriculum," PhD dissertation, Emory University, 1994. Cited in Giddings, "Infusion of Afrocentric Content."
22. Giddings, "Infusion of Afrocentric Content."
23. Binder, "Why Do Some Curricular Challenges Work."
24. Ibid., 78–86.
25. Since the DPS preschool is state-supported, the program was for preschool through twelfth grade.
26. Sidney Fine, *Violence in the Model City: The Cavanaugh Administration, Race Relations, and the Detroit Riot of 1967* (Ann Arbor, MI: The University of Michigan Press, 1989), 17–37.
27. Jeffrey Mirel, *The Rise and Fall of an Urban School System: Detroit, 1907–1981* (Ann Arbor: University of Michigan Press, 1993/1999), Appendix Table 5.
28. Fine, *Violence in the Model* City, 17–37 and 43–44.
29. Ibid.
30. Inner City Sub Center, http://www.slideshare.net/TBArchitect/InnerCitySub Center85x11. The seven principles are: Umoja (Unity); Kujichagulia (Self-determination); Ujima (Collective Work); Ujamaa (Cooperative Economics); Nia (Purpose); Kuumba (Creativity); and Imani (Faith). These principles also guide African-Centered Education.
31. Marvis Cofield and Dahia Shabaka, interview with the author, September 13, 2010.
32. For an analysis of African-Centered Academies, see Todd K. Chow-Hoy, "The Influence of a Powerful Principal and Clear Mission on the Moral Dimensions of Teaching in Two Public Schools," PhD dissertation, University of Michigan, 2000, and Clifford Watson, *Educating African American Males: Detroit's Malcolm X Academy Solution* (Chicago: Third World Press, 1996).

33. See Robinson, "The African Centered School Movement" for an analysis of other key leaders' role in African-Centered Education in the DPS and shepherding the program through official channels.
34. Robinson, "The African Centered School Movement," 101–105.
35. Marvis Cofield and Dahia Shabaka, interview with the author, September 13, 2010.
36. The Framework and Definition for African-Centered Education can be found at http://africancentered.detroitk12.org/ docs/AfricanCenteredFramework.pdf.
37. Ibid.
38. Ibid.
39. Ibid.
40. Ibid., 8.
41. African-Centered Education Resolution, http://africancentered.detroitk12.org/index-3.html.
42. Ibid.
43. Detroit Public Schools, Guiding Principles for an African Centered Education, http://africancentered. detroitk12.org/docs/AfricanCenteredIndaba.pdf, 1.
44. After his tenure on the school board, he became the Wayne County Commissioner for the 7th District and a Detroit City Council Member (from 2005 to the present). City of Detroit, About Kwame Kenyatta, http://www.detroitmi.gov/Default.aspx?tabid=2538.
45. CNN, Transcripts, http://transcripts.cnn.com/TRANSCRIPTS/0002/07/nr.00.html.
46. Ibid.
47. See Robinson, "The African Centered School Movement," for a detailed discussion of the academies.
48. In Michigan's 2009 state assessments Michigan Education Assessment Profile, students at the Marcus Garvey Academy, for example, scored better than the state average in most subjects. Chastity Pratt Dawsey, "How Marcus Garvey Academy Rises Above," *Detroit Free Press*, February 11, 2010.
49. Ronnie Hopkins, *Educating Black Males: Critical Lessons in Schooling, Community, and Power* (Albany: State University of New York Press, 1997), 31.
50. "Hostility Greets Students at Black School in White Area of Detroit," *The New York Times*, December 2, 1992.
51. Ibid.
52. Marvis Cofield and Dahia Shabaka, interview with the author, September 13, 2010.
53. Detroit Public Schools educator, interview with the author, June 11, 2010.
54. Marvis Cofield and Dahia Shabaka, interview with the author, September 13, 2010.
55. Ibid.
56. Anne-Lise Halvorsen, "The Origins and Rise of Elementary Social Studies Education, 1884 to 1941," PhD dissertation, University of Michigan, 2006.
57. Jeffrey E. Mirel, *Patriotic Pluralism: Americanization Education and European Immigrants* (Cambridge, MA: Harvard University Press, 2010), 218–222.
58. Dahia Shabaka, *Living and Working Together: Families* (New York: Metropolitan Teaching and Learning Company, 2000); Dahia Shabaka,

Living and Working Together: Neighborhoods (New York: Metropolitan Teaching and Learning Company, 2000).
59. Detroit Public Schools educator, interview with the author, June 11, 2010.
60. Marvis Cofield and Dahia Shabaka, interview with the author, September 13, 2010.
61. African-Centered Education at the Detroit Public Schools, http://africancentered.detroitk12.org/
62. Marvis Cofield and Dahia Shabaka, interview with the author, September 13, 2010.
63. Alkebu-lan Village, *African-Centered Program Video.*
64. Detroit Public Schools educator, interview with the author, June 11, 2010.
65. Ibid.
66. Marvis Cofield and Dahia Shabaka, interview with the author, September 13, 2010.

Epilogue

Margaret Smith Crocco

> *The function of education is to teach one to think intensively and to think critically.*
> *Intelligence plus character—that is the goal of education.*
> —Reverend Dr. Martin L. King, Jr.

Since Thomas Jefferson promoted the need for education in the fledgling United States in the eighteenth century, citizenship has stood as the core purpose of schooling. Jefferson reasoned that democracies rely for their health and well-being on an engaged and educated electorate, however the body politic was to be defined. Over several centuries, the groups of Americans included among those who could call themselves citizens and vote changed dramatically—from a small slice of the population who were White, male, and landowners to a group that included women, individuals from all races, people as young as 18 years, the rich, and the poor.

Jefferson, James Madison, and most of the other founding fathers were highly educated men who knew the lessons of history well: Democratic republics were fragile and fleeting. Indeed, in "Federalist Paper No. 10," Madison comments, "Democracies have, in general, been as short in their lives as they have been violent in their deaths."[1] One part of the solution to this problem, they wagered, lay in education, although they assumed that schools and colleges would be open only to other "gentlemen."

On at least one issue, however, the founding fathers would have agreed with Dr. Martin Luther King, Jr.: the purpose of education ought to be enhancement of intelligence and character. In eighteenth-century terminology, they saw "civic virtue" as the bedrock of a republic. The ideology of republicanism, so influential in shaping the American experiment in democracy, stood against corruption and tyranny and for liberty, one's moral duty to the common good, and the inalienable rights of free men.

Despite this shared approach to thinking about the aims of education, the founding fathers would not have included Dr. King among those considered free and equal citizens of the United States—he would have been counted only as three-fifths of one person. Nor would they have felt it advisable to educate African Americans, for fear that this would contribute to the possibility of slave insurrections in the South. As eminent historian Edmund Morgan put it, the institution of slavery has, since the birth of this nation, served as the central paradox of American history—that a nation born of freedom could have denied liberty to so many for so long.[2]

It would take centuries for many Americans to consider African Americans and women as full citizens, entitled to the right to vote and to an education that promoted both intelligence and character. The "story of American freedom," according to Eric Foner and numerous other historians, has been one of violent struggles over the scope of freedom, over identity, and over inclusion in citizenship—stuggles that resulted in protracted conflict during the Civil War and Reconstruction over these issues.[3] The civil rights struggle led by Dr. King took up the unresolved aspects of these issues in the twentieth century. Conflict continues, albeit on the streets, in classrooms, and in courtrooms, about the place of race in American society today.

No attribute other than race, not even gender, has been so stubborn in its persistent influence on shaping a citizen's experience of being an American. Even if one concedes that the more virulent forms of White supremacist behavior have receded, few would argue that racism has vanished entirely or that race plays no role in education or in defining one's place in the body politic in the United States.

A certain irony exists in the fact that social studies, born in the early twentieth century as a school subject reacting to the influx of immigrants into American society, should have managed so well to avoid substantial consideration of race and its role in shaping the field. If the central paradox of American history is that a nation born of freedom should have enslaved so many, then the central paradox of the social studies has been its steadfast refusal to engage a topic so thoroughly implicated in its origin and development.

Once the field of social studies began—tentatively and timidly—to take up race and other issues of difference, such as gender, in its curriculum, it did so in ways that were inflected by the historical context.[4] I have posited elsewhere that three phases of "dealing with difference" can be identified in the history of social studies curriculum: the cultural amelioration phase, roughly between 1910 and 1940; the psychological compensation phase, approximately 1941 to 1980; and the knowledge transformation phase, from about 1981 to the present.

The cultural amelioration phase was a period in which educational leaders believed that the motivation for addressing race was akin to the goals that Thomas Jesse Jones brought to Hampton Institute: to pull former slaves up by their bootstraps so they could emulate White society and culture. Schooling in general and social studies in particular served to accomplish these goals at Hampton. And Jones surely believed that nurturing intellect and character were both critical to his enterprise.

The psychological compensation phase produced a variety of sociological and psychological explanations to help explain why African Americans had not made the social and educational progress some felt they should have by mid-century. Bear in mind that it was two African American psychologists, Kenneth and Mamie Clark, who produced the famous "doll studies," so critical to the decision made by the Supreme Court in *Brown v. Board of Education* in 1954. Lead attorney Thurgood Marshall used the social science evidence found in the doll studies to demonstrate the damage done to Black children's psyches by racism. The remedy for this damage, according to the Supreme Court, lay in ending the "separate but equal" system of schooling. Dr. King and other civil rights leaders argued that an end to segregation was not all that was required to undo the social injustice of American society.

In later decades of the twentieth century, scholars such as James Banks pioneered the efforts begun by W. E. B. Du Bois, Carter G. Woodson, and Lorenzo Greene, among others, in bringing Black history and culture into the curriculum. Banks argued for transformation of the social studies curriculum—not from the standpoint of cultural amelioration or psychological compensation, but because he wished to advance knowledge transformation. In other words, ethnic studies scholars, like women's studies scholars, demanded change in the social studies curriculum in order to represent the past more accurately than had been the case when race, class, and gender were ignored.

Invoking the legacy of Dr. King at the start of this epilogue and juxtaposing it with introductory remarks about the founding fathers highlights the distance traveled between the nation's birth and the civil rights movement that he embodied. Continuity and change have characterized the nation's history, with its deeply rooted problem of racism, and the field of social studies, with its deeply rooted ambivalence about discussing race and racism.

Due in large measure to the generous definition of social studies informing this book, we begin to address the silences in our past. We learn here that numerous efforts were underway across the country in bringing race into the social studies throughout the twentieth century. Some, like those initiated by Nannie Helen Burroughs, were developed out of sense of "race pride" and a shared commitment by African Americans to advancing their communities. Others rested on the creativity and determination of little-known educators in Indiana, Louisiana, and Michigan who responded to changing demographic conditions in their schools by revamping their curriculum. The battles over textbooks and curriculum changes in South Carolina, Georgia, and Ohio exemplify the ways in which social studies perennially serves as a battleground for debating who we are as a nation and where we are headed.[5]

No doubt there are many more examples of dealing with difference, especially race, in the social studies that are neither well known nor well documented. One of the major contributions of this book is to bring these stories into the public eye and into the historiography of the field. Perhaps this volume's fascinating episodes in social studies history will stimulate other scholars to uncover other examples around the country throughout the twentieth century of constancy and change in avoiding or expanding the story of freedom in American classrooms.

In conclusion, it is important that such efforts at writing the history of the social studies account fully for multiple levels of historical influences as they impact curriculum change. The factors shaping what and how subject matter gets taught, as scholars such as Larry Cuban have documented, are complex, with some changes that stick and others that do not.[6] In the end, the history of education has often seemed more cyclical than linear, and the same has been said of American history.[7] We have an excellent example of the competing currents of change and the multiple levels of historical influence in the recent situation of social studies.

When the push for standards and accountability gathered steam in the late 1980s and 1990s, the "back to basics" movement, symbolized most prominently by the work of E. D. Hirsch, challenged curriculum reformers who had been promoting multicultural curriculums.[8] As states almost universally moved towards adoption of curriculum standards in the early 1990s, many advocates of multiculturalism faced a backlash that implicated them in the "culture wars." Efforts to provide greater inclusion of topics in women's history and African American history were met with resistance, made ever more potent by the spread of high-stakes testing, especially after signing of the No Child Left Behind Act in 2002. Since that time, the field of social studies has found itself in an increasingly difficult place, having been supplanted in many elementary schools almost totally by literacy and numeracy.

How do historians of the social studies account for these changes? Surely the answer must take into consideration the larger historical context as well as the national, state, and local educational contexts. To the degree that social studies, a small field with few active researchers, was able to control its destiny in light of these factors, it was chiefly a rearguard action focused on mitigating the damages to its inclusion in schools from a weakened position, dictated by forces well beyond its ability to control. Nevertheless, in some places, perhaps, efforts to continue the inclusion of a diverse narrative about the nation's past continued unabated; in other places, assuredly, such efforts got sidetracked by competing agendas.

As the project of reclaiming other stories of social studies and race goes forward, I would encourage scholars to approach its investigation through multiple pathways, taking into consideration, for example, intellectual history,[9] education history,[10] curriculum history,[11] and histories of teaching.[12] The cross-currents are many. Sorting out the most salient factors accounting for continuity and change can be difficult, but is necessary if the analysis is to reflect the complex causes at work.

This final note of admonition should not discourage scholars from making the effort to understand how and why the field has responded—or not—to the central paradox of American life. And, in keeping with the theme enunciated by Dr. King, one would hope that the project of continuing to learn about the field's past, like teachers' daily efforts to bring social studies to their students, might be animated by the understanding that education, as with citizenship, is about both intelligence *and* character. Social studies educators and scholars, with their firm grasp of what is at stake in a democracy when it comes to education, should not be afraid to call out those instances when one or both of these elements are lacking.

Notes

1. James Madison, "Federalist Paper No. 10," in *The Federalist Papers,* by Alexander Hamilton, John Jay, and James Madison, edited by Clinton Rossiter (New York: Mentor, 1999).
2. Edmund Morgan, *American Slavery, American Freedom: The Ordeal of Colonial Virginia* (New York: W. W. Norton, 2003, originally published in 1975).
3. Eric Foner, *The Story of American Freedom* (New York: W. W. Norton, 1999).
4. Margaret Smith Crocco, "Dealing with Difference in the Social Studies: A Historical Perspective," *International Journal of Social Education* 18, no. 2. Fall 2003/Winter 2004: 106–126.
5. Margaret Smith Crocco, *Social Studies and the Press: Keeping the Beast at Bay?* (Greenwich, CT: Information Age, 2005).
6. Larry Cuban, *How Teachers Taught: Constancy and Change in American Classrooms, 1880–1990,* 2nd edition (New York: Teachers College Press, 1993).
7. The classical work is Arthur M. Schlesinger, Jr, *The Cycles of American History* (New York: Mariner Books, 1999), but for a more contemporary work with a related theme, see Rogers M. Smith, *Civic Ideals: Competing Visions of Citizenship in U.S. History* (New Haven: Yale University Press, 1999).

8. E. D. Hirsch, *Cultural Literacy: What Every American Needs to Know* (Boston: Houghton Mifflin, 1987).
9. For example, Nathan Glazer, *We Are All Multiculturalists Now* (Cambridge, MA: Harvard University Press, 1997); David Hollinger, *Post-ethnic America: Beyond Multiculturalism* (New York: Basic Books, 1995).
10. For example, Jeffrey Mirel, "Civic Education and Changing Definitions of American Identity, 1900–1950," *Educational Review* 54, no. 2: 143–52; David Tyack, "Constructing Difference: Historical Reflections on Schooling and Social Diversity," *Teachers College Record* 95 (1993): 8–34.
11. For example, Herbert Kliebard, *The Struggle for the American Curriculum, 1893–1958* (New York: Routledge, 2004); Ivor Goodson, "Aspects of Social History of Curriculum," *Journal of Curriculum Studies* 15, no. 4 (1983): 391–408.
12. Larry Cuban, *How Teachers Taught*.

Contributors

Sarah Bair is associate professor of education at Dickinson College, Carlisle, Pennsylvania.

Chara Haeussler Bohan is an associate professor at the College of Education at Georgia State University. Her areas of expertise include the history of education, social studies education, and educational biography. She is an executive editor of *The Social Studies*. She has published in *Theory and Research in Social Education, Social Studies and the Young Learner, Social Education, Social Studies Research and Practice,* and *Curriculum and Teaching Dialogue.* She has authored and edited several books: *Go to the Sources: Lucy Maynard Salmon and the Teaching of History* (2004); *American Educational Thought: Readings from 1640–1940* (2010); and *Clinical Teacher Education: Reflections from an Urban Professional Development School Network* (2011).

Ronald E. Butchart received his doctorate in United States social history from the State University of New York at Binghamton. He has taught at SUNY College, Cortland, the University of Washington-Tacoma, and, currently is at the University of Georgia, where he is the Aderhold Distinguished Professor. His scholarship has focused primarily on the history of African American education, particularly the efforts of Whites to shape and control Black schooling. His most recent book is *Schooling the Freed People: Teaching, Learning, and the Struggle for Black Freedom, 1861–1876* (University of North Carolina Press, 2010).

J. Spencer Clark is an assistant professor of social studies education at Utah State University in Logan, Utah. He teaches undergraduate courses in social studies methods and graduate courses on the social and historical foundations of education and curriculum. He engages in both empirical and historical research, centered on the concept of agency in civic education, social studies education, and teacher education.

Margaret S. Crocco is professor and dean of the College of Education at the University of Iowa. She spent almost 20 years at Teachers College,

Columbia University, before coming to the University of Iowa in 2011. Her research interests are in the areas of social studies, teacher education, and the history of education, especially regarding issues of race and gender.

Erica DeCuir is former student and teacher at McDonogh #35 High School in New Orleans. As a member of a student-teacher collaborative, she co-created the Students at Center at McDonogh #35 as an innovative pedagogical program to promote social justice through critical discourse and analytical writing. She earned her doctorate in teaching and learning at Georgia State University. Her research focus is on state accountability policy and high-stakes testing programs.

Thomas D. Fallace is an assistant professor of education at William Paterson University of New Jersey, in Wayne, New Jersey. His research interests include history of education, curriculum history, and the works of John Dewey. He has published numerous articles in journals such as *Educational Researcher, Review of Educational Research, Teachers College Record,* and *Curriculum Inquiry.* He is the author of *The Emergence of Holocaust Education in American Schools* (Palgrave Macmillan, 2008) and *Dewey and the Dilemma of Race: An Intellectual History 1894–1922* (Teachers College Press, 2011).

Anne-Lise Halvorsen is assistant professor of teacher education, specializing in social studies education, at Michigan State University in East Lansing, Michigan. Halvorsen's work focuses on elementary social studies education, the history of education, and teacher preparation in the social studies.

Alana D. Murray is an educator-activist who has taught world history and US history in Montgomery County, Maryland, public schools for 14 years. She is coeditor, with Jenice View and Deborah Menkart, of the resource guide *Putting the Movement Back Into Civil Rights Teaching,* which has received recognition from Teaching Tolerance for being an outstanding professional development guide for teachers. She is an advanced doctoral student in minority and urban education at the University of Maryland, in College Park, Maryland. She is also serving as the Senior Fellow for Equity and Excellence at the Montgomery County Education Association (MCEA).

Patricia Randolph received a Bachelors of Science in social science education from the University of Georgia in Athens, Georgia, in 2001. She received a Masters of Education in history from Augusta State University in Augusta, Georgia, in 2006. Patricia is a PhD student in the Middle Secondary Instructional Technology Department–Social Studies of the

College of Education at Georgia State University in Atlanta, Georgia. She began her PhD program in 2007, and she has dedicated her time to researching history and curriculum in Atlanta Public Schools from 1973 to 1988.

Mindy Spearman is an associate professor in the School of Education at Clemson University. She received a PhD in curriculum studies, with an emphasis area in the historical foundations of education, from the University of Texas at Austin. At Clemson, Dr. Spearman teaches undergraduate and graduate classes in elementary social studies education, curriculum theory, the history of American education, and qualitative research methods. Her research interests include artifacts and objects in elementary classrooms, intersections of art and social studies, teaching young learners about sustainability, and American educational history.

Jennifer Ulbrich is a veteran social studies teacher and is currently pursuing her PhD in teaching and learning at Georgia State University in Atlanta.

Joseph Watras has been a professor in the Education and Allied Professions Department at the University of Dayton since 1979. He served in the Peace Corps in Niger, West Africa, and in the Teacher Corps in Honolulu, Hawaii. He received his doctorate from the Ohio State University, and he has published five books and nearly one hundred articles on the history of education.

Christine Woyshner is professor of education at Temple University. She researches the role of voluntary organizations in public education in the twentieth century and conducts research on gender and race in the K-12 school curriculum. Woyshner earned her doctorate at Harvard University's Graduate School of Education. In addition to publishing numerous articles and book chapters, she is the author or coeditor of five books, including *The National PTA, Race, and Civic Engagement, 1897–1970*; *Minding Women: Reshaping the Educational Realm*; *Social Education in the Twentieth Century: Curriculum and Context for Citizenship*; and *The Educational Work of Women's Organizations, 1890–1960*.

Index

Note on Index: As stated in the introduction, chapter authors were given the freedom to define social studies and race as they saw fit. Because of this and the dynamic nature of language over time, indexing a book of this nature is not easy. In crafting this index, every effort has been made to guide readers toward similar phrases without confusion.

Aaron, Hank, 148
abolition movement, 29, 69–70, 148
aboriginal societies, 46, 47
Aborigines, 3, 46, 119, 126, 128, 129, 130
achievement gap, 10, 19–22, 26, 31, 163, 173, 191, 199, 206, 207, 208
Act 146, 164
Adams, Charles Kendall, 100
administrators, 12, 101, 102, 117, 123, 131, 135, 137, 140, 172, 174, 181, 182, 189, 199, 201, 204, 206, 208
Africa, 2, 46, 51, 70, 100, 101, 103, 105, 106, 119, 121, 122, 123, 126, 127, 128, 129, 130, 144, 147, 148, 196, 197, 202, 206
African Diaspora, 102, 104, 197
Africans, 3, 44, 93, 102, 104, 106, 126, 144, 147, 148, 195, 196, 197, 201, 203, 205
African American history, 26, 57–8, 60–1, 67, 68, 72, 73, 74, 101, 103, 196, 202, 216. *See also* Black History
African American History Reconsidered, 58
African American Studies, 6, 7, 195

African American women, 102, 106, 109, 110
African-Centered Education, 11–12, 13, 195–209
African Diaspora, 102, 104, 197
Afro-American History Month, 57. *See also* Black History Month
Afrocentric education, 2, 7, 20, 195–209
  v. Africana Studies, 197
  controversy over, 197
Aisha Shule Academy, 203
Alcott, Louisa May, 69
Allen, William, 26
alternative Black Curriculum, 100–10
American Civil Liberties Union (ACLU), 204
American Historical Association, 5, 100
American History, An, 49, 52
American Indians, 1, 3, 4, 7, 8, 9, 11, 39, 42, 43, 44, 52, 59, 62, 126, 129, 130, 139, 141–5, 147, 152, 154. *See also* Native Americans
Americanization, 83–4, 89, 116
American Social Problems, 50, 51
American Tract Society, 27
Anderson, James D., 29, 162
Appleton, Daniel, 118–19, 122, 124

Anti-White, 183
Arabs, 124, 127
Armstrong, Samuel Chapman, 28–31
Asante, Molefi Kete, 195, 196, 197, 198, 201, 204
Assessment, 160, 164–5, 173, 207
Asia, 100, 121, 126, 127, 130, 197
Asians, 83, 86–7, 89, 142, 153
assimilation. *See* Americanization
Association for the Study of Negro Life and History (ASNLH), 57–74
Athens, Georgia, 136
Atlanta, Georgia, 60, 135–55, 195, 198, 199
Atlanta Journal, The, 140
Atlanta Public Schools (APS), 135, 138, 140–1, 145
Australia, 46, 126, 129

Baldwin, James Mark, 39, 42
Banks, James, 187–8, 189, 197, 215
Baptists, 103, 137
barbarians, 3, 11, 39, 40, 44, 45, 47, 49, 51, 52, 106. *See also* civilization, savage
Beard, Charles and Mary, 59
Before the Mayflower, 184
Bernier, François, 4
Berry, Martha, 152
Bethune, Mary McLeod, 61, 102
Billings, Gloria Ladson, 110, 139
Black High Schools, 161, 173
Black History, 6, 7, 9, 11, 12, 57–74, 99, 109, 136, 139, 150, 169, 179–91, 215
Black History class, 136
Black History Month, 57, 66, 186. *See also* Afro-American History Month
Black History and the Historical Profession, 58
Black labor, 102, 109, 145–9

Black Studies, 166, 167, 172, 179, 183, 184, 197
Black newspapers, 60, 71
Boas, Franz, 40, 42, 44, 52
Bourne, Randolph, 40
Booker T. Washington High School, 136
Bridges, Ruby, 165
Brigham, Albert, 126–8, 130–1
Brown, Charlotte Hawkins, 102
Brown, John, 109
Brown v. Board, 4, 30, 188, 215
Browne, James F., 162
Bruner, Jerome S., 137
Burch, Henry Reed, 50, 51
Burkeholder, Zoe, 85, 93
Burroughs, Nannie Helen, 11, 99–111, 215
busing, 180, 186, 190–1
Bussler, Ron, 141, 144, 148
Butler School, 26

Carl, Wayne, 180, 182, 184
Carlyle, Sonia El Janis, 3
Carnegie, Andrew, 68
Carnegie, Institute of Technology, 138
Carnegie Corporation, 66
Carter, Jimmy, 152
Caucasian, 39, 106, 119, 124, 142
Catholic Schools, 189–90
Central America, 121, 123, 130–1
Charleston, South Carolina, 23, 24, 146
Charlottesville, Virginia, 23
Chase, Lucy, 25
Cherokees, 141–5
Chicago Defender, 60
Chicago, Illinois, 58, 63
Chief Vann, 145
Chinese, 84, 86, 88, 124, 125
Chinese Exclusion Act of 1882, 86
citizenship, 1, 6, 38, 40, 41, 48, 50, 79–94, 108, 111, 213, 214, 217

civics, 2, 7, 8, 50, 80, 84, 100, 165, 166, 167, 202
civic virtue, 213
civilization, 39, 40, 42, 43, 44, 45, 46, 47, 49, 50, 51, 52, 61, 101, 105, 106, 123, 129, 142, 196, 197
Civil War, The, 19, 24, 27, 41, 91, 107, 135, 146, 149, 151, 214
Clark, Kenneth and Mamie, 4, 215
Cleveland, Ohio, 181
clubs, 61, 67, 68, 162, 163, 164. *See also* extracurricular activities
Cobb, Howell, 151
Cobb, Thomas R.R., 151
Cofield, Marvis, 99–201, 204–5, 206–7
colonization, 2, 129–31, 142–3
Color Purple, The, 189
Columbia University, 7, 41
Columbus, Christopher, 59, 65
Cooper, Anna Julie, 101, 102, 103
Commission on Interracial Cooperation, 107
Community and the Citizen, The, 45, 46
Community Civics, 50, 84
Community Life and Civic Problems, 50
community service, 159, 163, 169, 170, 171
conditions of society, 118
Confederacy, The, 135, 141, 150–1, 154
Counterculture, 22, 161
Craft, William and Ellen, 68
Creole, 161
Crim, Dr. Alonzo, 135
Crocco, Margaret Smith, 1, 2, 6, 12
Cuba, 88
Cuban, Larry, 216
cultural development, 46, 47, 48, 49, 52, 116, 121, 124, 126, 129, 130
culturally responsive curriculum, 20–1, 22, 28
culture wars, 216

Dagbovie, Peter Gaglo, 58, 59, 109
Dallas, Texas, 180
Darwin, Charles, 39, 118–19
Davis, Jefferson, 136, 151
Dayton Classroom Teachers Association, 183
Dayton, Ohio, 2, 11, 179–91
Descent of Man, 118–19
desegration, 6, 11, 135, 140, 154, 159, 164, 165, 174, 179–91
democracy, 1, 2, 8, 38, 48, 52, 80, 83, 85, 100, 163, 213, 217
Democracy and Education, 44
De Priest, Oscar, 72
de Soto, Hernando, 143
Detroit, Michigan, 2, 7, 12, 195–209
Detroit News, 203
Detroit Public Schools, 7, 12, 195–209
DeVorsey, Louis Jr., 141, 143, 148
Dewey, Evelyn, 48
Dewey, John, 3, 10, 38, 39, 43–5, 46, 47, 48, 51, 52, 100
Donnan, Laura, 11, 79, 80, 81–2, 84, 85, 93, 94
Dorantes, Stephen, 109
Douglass, Frederick, 102, 109, 167, 168
Du Bois, W.E.B., 4, 9, 37, 40, 44, 52, 58, 101, 104, 108, 109, 150, 185, 196, 215
Dunn, Arthur, 10, 38, 45–8, 51, 52
Dunning, William, 41
Dyer-Barr, Rana, 189

Early Black History Movement, Carter G. Woodson, and Lorenzo Greene, The, 58
Ebony Book of Black Achievement, The, 185
Education Commission of the States (ECS), 164
Egyptians, 105–6
Elementary and Secondary Education Act of 1965, 136

Elementary Geography, 118, 119, 121, 123
Eliot, Charles, 100
Ellison, Ralph, 3
Ellwood, Charles, 39, 50, 51, 52
Elson, Ruth Miller, 129
Essentials of Geography, 126–8, 130–1
Erickson, Leif, 59
Ethical Principles Underlying Education, 45, 46
Ethics (by John Dewey and James Tufts), 43, 44
Ethnic Heritage Act of 1972, 136
Eurocentric, 29, 137, 152, 195, 196, 198
Evans, Frank, 120, 126
Evans, Ron, 137
Excelsior School, 29
extracurricular activities, 79, 80, 81, 82, 160, 162, 163, 166, 169–70, 174

Fenton, Edwin, 138
Fifteenth Amendment, 107
Filipinos, 84, 86, 87, 88
Finn, Chester, 164
Fourteenth Amendment, 107
Franklin, John Hope, 60, 65, 136
Freedmen, 27
Frye, Alexis Everett, 121–3

Garrison, William Lloyd, 70
Garvey, Marcus, 196, 204
Gay, Geneva, 139, 188, 189
Geographies, 121–3
Geography, 26, 115–31
Georgia, 2, 4, 11, 135–55, 216
Georgia flag, 150–1
Georgia History and Government, Georgia History Book, The, 141, 142, 146, 147, 149, 150, 151
Georgia History Teacher Guides, 138–40
Georgia Parent Teacher Association, 139
Georgia State Board of Education, 138
Gerstle, Gary, 83, 92

Giddings, Franklin, 7, 37, 38, 39, 41, 42, 43
Glatt, Charles, 180
Good Citizens Project, 163
Gone With The Wind, 151
Grant, D.S., 140
Grant, Madison, 51
Grant, S.G., 173
Great Society, 160
Green, Lorenzo J., 72, 215
Greene, Maxine, 188, 191
Greenleaf's Arithmetic, 23
Grey, Richard, 168
Guyot, Arnold, 23, 129

Haeckel, Erne, 118
Hampton Institute, 1, 7, 28, 37, 41, 43, 51, 72, 215
Hand, William H., 131
Harris, Herbert W., 3
Harris, Joe Frank, 152
Harris, William Torrey, 115
Harvey, James, 100
Hepburn, Lawrence, 141, 142, 143, 146, 147, 149
Hertzberg, Hazel, 5
Hiawatha, 47
high stakes testing, 159, 160, 165, 172, 173, 174, 216
Hill, Howard Copeland, 50
Hinman, Russell, 121–3
Hirsch, E.D., 216
Historically Black Colleges and Universities (HBCUS), 64, 163, 182
historical pageants, 104
historiography, 1, 5–7, 13, 99, 216
Hoffman, Lionel, 161, 166
"home geography," 115–17
Hope, John, 60, 65
Hughes, Ray Oswald, 50
Hundley, Mary Gibson, 174
Hunt, Avril, 168

Hunt, Dr. Herald, 163
Hunter, Charlayne, 152

Illinois, 49, 71, 181
imperialism, 3, 29, 128, 131
   American Imperialism, 86–8, 100
immigrants, 9, 11, 37, 40, 44, 49, 82, 84, 86–90, 93, 146, 152, 214. *See also specific groups*
In Celebration of Black History Month, 186
Indiana Negro History Society, 67
Indian Removal, 4, 141–5
Indianapolis, Indiana, 10, 45. *See also* Shortridge High School Senate
Indianapolis High School, 79. *See also* Shortridge High School Senate
Invisible Man, 3
International Council of Women of Darker Races, 102, 103

Jackson, Andrew, 147
Japanese, 87, 88, 119
Jefferson, Thomas, 213
Jim Crow laws, 29–30, 41, 73, 101, 170. *See also* segregation
Johnson, Bill, 203
Johnson, Karen, 103
Jones, Thomas Jesse, 1, 7–9, 10, 28, 31, 37, 39, 40–3, 51, 160, 215
Journal of Negro History, 58, 60, 62, 64

Kallen, Horace, 40
Kenyatta, Kwame, 203–5
Keyes v. Denver School District, 181
King, Rev. Dr. Martin Luther, 141, 148, 149–50, 151, 154, 213
Kipling, Rudyard, 3
Kiswahili, 196
Kliebard, Herbert, 8, 9, 37, 41
Klu Klux Klan, 151
Kozol, Jonathan, 138–9
Kwanzaa, 169, 206

Land of the Free, 136
Latin America, 88. *See also individual countries*
Laws of Imitation, The, 42
Lee, Robert E., 151
Liberator, The, 70
Lincoln, Abraham, 136, 151
Locke, Alain, 40
London, Bonnie, 141, 148
Louisiana Educational Assessment Program, 160, 165
L'Ouverture, Toussaint François, 109
Lybarger, Michael, 8, 37, 40
lynching, 90, 105, 107

Madison, James, 213
Malays, 121
Malcolm X, 196, 204
Malcolm X Academy, 204
Manley, Ollie, 199
Mansa Musa, 109
Marshall, Thurgood, 215
Massachusetts, 25
Man: A Course of Study (MACOS), 137, 138, 140, 154
McDonogh #35 Senior High, 11, 159–74
McFarlane, Charles, 126–9, 131
McGriff, Deborah, 205
McGuffey's Reader, 23
McMurry, Charles, 117, 126
Mead, George Herbert, 42
media. *See individual newspapers*
Medieval and Modern Times, 47, 52
Meier, August, 58, 62
melting pot, 50
Metropolitan Teaching and Learning Company, 206
Mexican Americans, 188
Mexicans, 84, 88
Middle Passage, the, 104
"mint julep," 136
Mirel, Jeffery, 49, 83
Mis-Education of the Negro, The, 62

Missouri, 49
Mitchell, Clara, 44
Mitchell, Margaret, 152
Moreau, Joseph, 136
Morehouse College, 60
Morgan, Edmund, 214
multicultural education, 11, 179, 187–90, 197, 199, 202, 208
Musgrove, Mary, 145
Muzzey, David Saville, 49, 52, 58

National Assessment of Education Programs (NAEP), 160
National Association for Colored Women, 101, 103
National Association for the Advancement of Colored People (NAACP), 59, 139, 191
National Baptist Convention (NBC), 103
National Commission on Excellence, 164
National Council for Social Studies, 5, 99, 202
National Education Association (NEA), 5, 8, 84
    Committee on Social Studies (1912), 8
    Committee on Social Studies (1916), 1, 10, 37–9, 41, 45, 47, 48, 105
    The Committee of Ten, 115, 100
Nation At Risk, A, 164
Native Americans, 4, 37, 38, 41, 42, 48, 49, 50, 51, 52, 84, 130, 141, 142, 143, 152, 153. *See also* American Indians
Native Son, 189
National Training School for Women and Girls, 99, 103, 107, 108, 110
Natural Elementary Geography, 121–3
Negro History Bulletin, 58, 64, 67, 68, 69, 70, 72
    "Book of the Month," 70

Negro History Week, 10, 57–74
Negro in Our History, The, 67
"Negro Problem, The," 50
Negro Womanhood, 108–10
neo-Lemarckianism, 3, 43
New Elements of Geography, 123–6
New History, The, 47
"New History" movement, 59
New York Times, The, 11, 60, 65, 71, 80
New Orleans, Louisiana, 11, 26, 72, 159–74
New Orleans School District, 72
New Social Studies, 136–8, 154, 168
No Child Left Behind (NCLB), 216
Norfolk Journal and Guide, 60, 71

Ohio, 2, 7, 11, 25, 92, 179–91, 216
Ohio State Department of Education, 184, 191
Ohio State University, 180
Oklahoma, 50
Oliver, Donald, 1
oral traditions, 144
Orleans Parish School Board, 161
Organization of Women Legal Defense Fund, 204

pageants. *See* historical pageants
Panorama of Georgia, A, 141, 143, 144, 148, 149, 150, 151, 153
Passing of the Great Race, 51
Patterson, S. Howard, 50, 51
pedagogy, 6, 7, 9, 10, 19, 20, 21, 22, 23, 25, 26, 27, 28, 29, 30, 31, 45, 52, 81, 129, 160, 165, 170, 171
Pemberton, Joseph S., 152
Perry, Theresa, 104
Peters, Margaret, 184–7, 191
Petersburg, Virginia, 24, 26, 149
phases of dealing with difference, 214
Philadelphia Tribune, 65
Philippines, 59, 86, 87, 88, 93
Pittsburgh Courier, 60, 65, 71

Plessy v. Ferguson, 165
Problems of Democracy Course (POD), 8, 48–51, 52
Progressive Era, 5, 20, 50–2, 81, 82–5, 93, 101, 161
Progressivism, 102
primitive, 3, 39, 40, 41, 44, 45, 46, 47, 49, 51, 52, 141, 142, 144, 145. *See also* barbarians, savage
Puerto Rico, 130
Pulsipher, Lydia Mihelic, 116, 120, 129
Puritan, 25
Putnam, Caroline F., 29

Queen of Sheba, 109

race, definitions of, 3, 38–9
race-as-nation, 85, 86, 89, 92, 93, 94
Randels, Jim, 169–71
Ravitch, Diane, 37, 40, 41, 164, 197–8
Reagan, Ronald, 164
Reconstruction, 10, 41, 50, 51, 104, 151, 214
"Red Man," 47, 50, 120, 124, 127
Red Summer of 1919, 107
Redway, Jacques, 121–3
reform, 2, 10, 11, 41, 46, 84, 100, 101, 180, 182, 190, 209, 216. *See also* Standards Based Reform (SBR)
Reif, Michelle, 103
Report on Social Studies (1916), 1, 10. *See also* National Education Association (NEA), Committee on Social Studies
Rice, Marion, 141, 148
Rising Tide of Color, The, 51
Robinson Crusoe, 46, 47
Robinson, James Harvey, 1, 10, 38, 45–8, 49, 51, 52
Roderick, Juanita, 146
Roth High School, 184
Roosevelt, Franklin D., 152
Roosevelt, Theodore, 83, 87

Root, Maria P.P., 3
Royce, Josiah, 42
Rudwick, Elliot, 58, 62
Rugg, Harold, 1
Russians, 88, 89
Rutherford, Mildred Lewis, 136

Sabbath schools, 22
Salaam, Kalamu ya, 170
Sausalito, California, 183
savage, 3, 11, 28, 39, 40, 42, 43, 45, 46, 47, 49, 52, 118, 121, 123, 124, 125, 126, 128, 129, 130. *See also* barbarians, primitive
Saye, Albert B., 141, 142, 143, 146, 149
School and Society, 44, 45
Schools of To-morrow, 48
self-esteem, 7, 12, 103, 196, 198, 204, 205, 207, 208
segregation, 4, 9, 38, 81, 161, 181, 190, 215. *See also* Jim Crow laws
"Separate but equal," 215
Serress, Etienne, 118
Shabaka, Dahia, 199, 201, 204–7
Shortridge High School Senate, 9, 10, 79–94
Sission, Tack, 185
slavery, 24, 25, 27, 51, 67, 69, 91, 104, 139, 141, 145, 147, 148, 154, 185, 186, 206, 214
Small, Albion, 39
Smith, Jane Briggs, 25
Smith, Neil, 129
Smith, Rogers, 83, 86
Sociology and Modern Social Problems, 50, 52
Social Darwinism, 123, 129, 131
social justice, 7, 9, 11, 12, 21, 22, 26, 30, 159–74, 189
social studies
    curriculum, 165–70
    definition of, 2

social studies education, 1, 2, 3, 4, 6, 7, 8, 9, 10, 11, 12, 22, 136, 138, 153, 159, 164, 174, 202
Souls of Black Folk, The, 4, 40
South, The, 19, 22, 24, 41–2, 127, 135–6, 146, 151, 161, 214
South Carolina, 2, 9, 23, 24, 26, 91, 115–31, 146, 216
Span, Christopher M., 189
Special Method in Geography: From the Third through the Eighth Grade, 116
Spencer, Herbert, 39–40
spiral curriculum, 137
Spriggins, Belfield, 162
Sputnik, 136
Standards Based Reform (SBR), 159–74
standards movement, 2, 10, 11, 140, 196, 202, 216. *See also* Standards Based Reform (SBR)
Star of Ethiopia, The, 104, 108, 109
Stephens, Alexander H., 135, 151
stereotypes, 11, 59, 116, 162, 170, 189, 203
Stoddard, Lothrop, 51
Stokes, Anson Phelps, 28
Striving to Overcome, Negro Achievers, 184–5
Student government, 2, 10. *See also* Shortridge High School Senate
Students at the Center, 166, 170–1
suffrage, 81, 90, 91, 92
Sumner, Arthur, 24
Swahili, 196, 197, 207

Tarde, Gabriel, 42, 43
Taylor, Traki L., 103
Teacher Preparation Program, 161
testing, 139, 140, 159, 160, 165, 172, 173, 174, 199, 206, 216
Temple University, 195
Terry, S.M., 141, 148

textbooks, 2, 4, 9, 10, 11, 12, 23, 26, 27, 28, 47, 49, 50, 51, 52, 59, 60, 61, 67, 74, 115–31, 135–55, 165, 167, 173, 185, 203, 206, 208, 216. *See also individual book*, Georgia History, Geography
Tilford-Weathers, Thelma Cayne, 174
Times-Picayune, 163
Thirteenth Amendment, 107
Thomas, Norman, 139
Thomas, William I., 39–40, 42
Tomochichi, 145
Trail of Tears, 141–5, 154
Towne, Laura, 23–4
Tubman, Harriet, 102
Tufts, James, 43, 44
Tuskegee Institute, 69, 150

US Bureau of Education, 8, 45, 84
US Civil Rights Commission, 180
US Constitution, 1, 71, 91, 167. *See also individual amendments*
US Department of Health, Education, and Welfare, 182, 183
United Daughters of the Confederacy (UDC), 136
University of Chicago, 44, 59
University of Georgia, 152
Urban, W.J., 136
urban, 8, 25, 29, 37, 82, 138, 162, 196, 206

Valenzuela, Angela, 21
Virginia, 3, 23, 24, 26, 103
vocational training, 51, 107, 161, 163

Wagoner, J.L., 136
Walker, Alice, 167, 189
Ward, Alvin, 207–8
Ward, Lester F., 39
Washington, Booker T., 9, 51, 58, 91, 106–7, 146, 150, 196, 198

Washington, DC, 27, 60, 71, 99, 103, 104, 195, 198, 199
Washington, George, 65, 203
Watkins, William H., 7, 8, 9, 37, 40, 41
Webster's Speller, 23
Wells, Ida, 185
Wesley, Charles, 63
West, Cornel, 3–4
West Indies, 121, 196
Western Journal of Black Studies, 58
West Virginia, 59
Wheatley, Phyllis, 68
When Truth Gets a Hearing, 11, 99, 100, 102, 104, 105, 107, 108, 109, 110, 111
Whig, 25
White Culture, 29, 38, 105, 141, 143, 145, 151–5

White Flight, 160, 172
"Whiteman's Burden," 3
Williams, Elmer, 141, 148
Wilson, Woodrow, 65, 100
World War I, 103, 104, 105, 107, 126
World War II, 163
Woodson, Carter G., 10, 57–74, 99, 101, 108, 136, 196, 215
Women's History, 216
Women's History Month, 57, 66

Yamacraw, 145
"Yellow Man," 50, 127
Young, Andrew, 149, 150, 153

Zack, Naomi, 3
Zagummy, Lisa, 116, 120, 129
Zimmerman, Jonathan, 59

GPSR Compliance
The European Union's (EU) General Product Safety Regulation (GPSR) is a set of rules that requires consumer products to be safe and our obligations to ensure this.

If you have any concerns about our products, you can contact us on

ProductSafety@springernature.com

In case Publisher is established outside the EU, the EU authorized representative is:

Springer Nature Customer Service Center GmbH
Europaplatz 3
69115 Heidelberg, Germany

www.ingramcontent.com/pod-product-compliance
Lightning Source LLC
LaVergne TN
LVHW051913060526
838200LV00004B/124